ROUTLEDGE LIBRARY EDITIONS:
WORK & SOCIETY

Volume 20

IN PLACE OF WORK

IN PLACE OF WORK

Policy and Provision
for the Young Unemployed

Edited by
ROB FIDDY

Routledge
Taylor & Francis Group

LONDON AND NEW YORK

First published in 1983 by Falmer Press.

This edition first published in 2024
by Routledge
4 Park Square, Milton Park, Abingdon, Oxon OX14 4RN

and by Routledge
605 Third Avenue, New York, NY 10158

Routledge is an imprint of the Taylor & Francis Group, an informa business

British Library Cataloguing in Publication Data
A catalogue record for this book is available from the British Library

ISBN: 978-1-032-80236-7 (Set)
ISBN: 978-1-032-82012-5 (Volume 20) (hbk)
ISBN: 978-1-032-82024-8 (Volume 20) (pbk)
ISBN: 978-1-003-50258-6 (Volume 20) (ebk)

DOI: 10.4324/9781003502586

Publisher's Note
The publisher has gone to great lengths to ensure the quality of this reprint but points out that some imperfections in the original copies may be apparent.

Disclaimer
The publisher has made every effort to trace copyright holders and would welcome correspondence from those they have been unable to trace.

IN PLACE
OF WORK

*Policy and Provision
for The Young Unemployed*

Edited by Rob Fiddy

 **The Falmer Press**

A member of the Taylor & Francis Group

ISBN 0 905273 45 1 (paper)

ISBN 0 905273 46 X (cased)

First published 1983

Jacket design by Leonard Williams

Phototypeset in Linotron 202 by
Graphicraft Typesetters Hong Kong
The Falmer Press
Falmer House
Barcombe
Lewes, Sussex
BN8 5DL

Contents

A visiting Jamaican poet, reciting Wordsworth's ode *On Westminster Bridge* for a TV documentary, caught sight of the illuminated total of London unemployed: 'How come', he asked with a smile, 'this guy Wordsworth didn't notice that?' They turned to look . . . but the number was too familiar for them to see.

Introduction: In Place of Work

Rob Fiddy

Pick up almost any newspaper or journal, or tune into almost every current affairs production and the chances are that you will be confronted with the latest unemployment figures. As total numbers of unemployed climb inexorably towards their next million, so too increases the slice of these under the age of eighteen. Accordingly, the concern of those involved with the transition from school to work focusses more and more sharply on the transition from school to unemployment.

Government reaction to the problem of the growing number of young unemployed has evolved in the main via an *ad hoc* agency, the Manpower Services Commission (MSC). Although not originally conceived as being primarily concerned with unemployment amongst school-leavers, this became an issue of such growing importance that by 1976 the MSC regarded '. . . young people's unemployment as a major problem for manpower policy' (MSC 1976:4).

The early 1970s saw the germination of extra-educational agencies with a role to play in the area of transition, culminating in the birth of the MSC following the Employment and Training Act of Summer 1973. The late 1970s witnessed the introduction of the Youth Opportunities Programme (YOP) which has in the 1980s taken on the guise of the staple diet for school-leavers – if not in that all taste it, then at least in that it, or a version of it, has become expected. This is a situation which has been formalized by the present Employment Minister Norman Tebbit's proposals for the Youth Training Scheme (YTS), contained in the Government White Paper *A New Training Initiative*, to provide a year's training for all school-leavers 'who are unemployed during their first year after leaving school' (DofE 1981:8). The YTS is to begin in September 1983 and will draw on the experience of Unified Vocational Preparation (UVP)[1] but, most importantly, on that of the YOP. Just before the release of *A New Training Initiative*, this foreshadowing epitaph on YOP was offered by a careers officer with special responsibility for the unemployed:

"I don't think YOP can last very much longer because it's becoming much more the norm for youngsters to do. It's no longer successful in getting youngsters into work, and we know that a lot of firms are using YOP to fill their vacancies. Firms are being very selective, they seem to have forgotten the idea of giving youngsters a helping start...''[2]

This careers officer was one of a number recruited by the MSC and paid and trained by them to help deal with the ever increasing flow of YOP applicants. She has high-lighted here a widely held suspicion of the ineffectiveness of the YOP and one which has since been increasingly expressed. Not only has the YOP been attacked for failing to place its youngsters into employment, it has also been criticized for making that very aspiration its major thrust. This is a criticism which has also been regularly levelled at the new government proposals. Harry Salmon, for example, declares that 'the White Paper is written on the basis of values which place competition above compassion, the needs of the labour market above the needs of people' (1982:25). These are aspects of courses for unemployed school-leavers which we shall meet again in the following pages.

In Place of Work seeks to go beyond merely assessing that which exists, however. It is an exercise in promoting understanding of the provision for the young unemployed, both in policy and practice, through a series of research-based papers. Its aspiration is a constructive one, to inform the future rather than denigrate the efforts of the present or past. Among the contributors are protagonists as well as critics of the current provision. Our common goal is to learn from what has happened so far.

In 1974, the MSC was designed to 'rationalize and restructure all training and employment services provided by the Department of Employment' (CCCS 1981:229) and was established with a staff of twelve. By 1978, it had mushroomed to a staff of 22,000 and a national annual budget of £630 million. In the 1980s it continues to expand and remains, as Martin Loney says in this book, 'Britain's fastest growing Quango'. The MSC is split into three Divisions (originally designated Agencies). The Employment Services Division (ESD), the Special Programmes Division (SPD), and the Training Services Division (TSD).[3] The ESD is mainly responsible for administering Job Centres. The area of the transition from school to work, or indeed unemployment, is under the aegis, in the main, of the SPD – with the TSD's responsibility in the YOP being the administration of Work Introduction Courses (WIC). More of WICs later. However, if you think that this marks the end of the acronyms, read on. In August 1976, £19 million of government funds were allocated to the MSC for the establishment of a Work Experience Programme (WEP) as part of a '... more coherent and long term approach ... to alleviate unemployment's worst effects, especially for the young' (MSC 1977(a):2). The WEP was aimed at the unemployed school-leaver. The scheme would last for six months for each individual, who would be paid £16 per week. Its broad aims were:

1 To provide opportunities to learn about different types of work.

2 Further education and training off the job

3 Counselling on the progress and problems of young people.

The YOP, the MSC's present dominant provision, was drawn up in 1977 by

Mr Geoffrey Holland, the Commission's Director of Special Programmes, to provide what the then Employment Secretary called 'a better deal for Britain's youth' (CCCS 1981:229). In what came to be known as The Holland Report it was suggested that a variety of schemes should be integrated under the title of 'The Youth Opportunities Programme'. The report highlighted increasing youth unemployment and recommended that the schemes should have '. . . the aim of improving their employability and helping them find suitable employment' (MSC 1977(b):7). Besides the WEP, which in 1978 became Work Experience on Employer's Premises (WEEP), the YOP contained WICs, also referred to as Work Preparation or Remedial courses; Project Based Work Experience and Community Service Schemes, which have been amalgamated into Community Projects; and Training Workshops. Again, more of these later.

In the first section, Martin Loney provides an overview of the YOP from its inception in 1978, when it was as he says 'dealing with one in eight young people', to the projection of the YTS which will face an estimated 68 per cent of unemployed eighteen year olds. In the words of Mr Holland, 'an unprecedented situation fraught with both social and economic consequences which demands an unprecedented response' (TES 17 July 1981;9). A response which Martin Loney refers to as representing 'not so much an acknowledgement of YOP's findings, as a tightening of control over school-leavers'. The second section of this book examines in detail specific experience of the various components of the YOP.

First, let us briefly look at David Raffe's contribution in the first section, which analyzes the strategies available to policy makers in this area. Raffe describes four strategies by which governments might approach youth unemployment, given that total levels of unemployed cannot be reduced – as far as policy-makers are concerned – 'without prejudice to other policy objectives' and that consequently the young have a prior claim. Although, as Raffe says, the strategies do not represent distinct alternatives, they do allow an insight into policy directions. One of the most widely discussed aspects of the YOP is its attempts to increase its clients employability. This is a criterion which allies it to Raffe's third strategy – 'Giving Young People a Competitive Edge'. This is an area which also largely contains the major thrust of the YOP's proposed successors – the YTS and the considerations of the MSC's Task Group discussions of 1982. Training Workshops are the smallest and most capital intensive provision under the YOP, and provide three per cent of places[4]. Encompassing release to further education on a part-time basis, Training Workshops aim to give 'at least six months of basic training in a productive environment' (FEU 1979:47). Training Workshops contain relatively few placements, but they account for 'the largest ever amounts of capital and revenue ever expended by the state on a traditionally neglected group of unqualified school-leavers' (Allinson 1980:11). These Workshops claim to provide a mix of work experience and basic training, but, additionally, to include personal support and development. The second section of this book begins with an account by Tom Logan of a visit to a Training Workshop in the North West of England and a comparison by him between that and an alternative scheme in the same area. The supporters of Training Workshops promote them as 'arguably the most important new service since the beginnings of the education system' (Allinson 1980:11). Logan's visit led him to pose the question 'Is this the acceptable face of state capitalism?'

Project Based Work Experience was designed to 'give young people the opportunity to sample a range of activities and to acquire skills and knowledge through involvement in projects of benefit to the local community' (FEU 1979:48). Community Service Schemes 'supplement services provided by voluntary organizations and involve young people in face-to-face contact with the clients for whom the services are provided' (FEU 1979:48). Both Projects and Community Service have provision for day release to further education and after amalgamation make up 14 per cent of YOP placements. Tom Logan's second visit was to a Project Based Work Experience Scheme.

The second section continues with Mary Hopkins' experience as a worker in Interskills, a Community Project in Coventry. Both Logan and Hopkins see benefits in the community side of the YOP provision. Logan argues that the scheme he visited 'represents a firm rejection of the conventional work ethic youth opportunity. It offers an alternative model – that training can be primarily in social and community skills'. Hopkins suggests that her experiences in Coventry contained '. . . some of the elements that could provide signposts towards radical youth training policy and practice'.

The second largest single element of provision under the YOP is the Work Introduction Course, constituting 15 per cent of places. The third paper of this section examines one such course in the east of England from the point of view of its teachers and administrators, but most importantly its trainees. WICs, being the remedial end of the YOP, are not necessarily designed to place their 'graduates' into jobs. As the careers officer says of her area:

"For the WIC I'm looking for somebody . . . who just lacks a worldly feel about them . . . WICs have been fairly successful with students moving onto something else, generally a WEEP course. I can't remember any young people leaving the WIC to go into a job. . . ."

Those youngsters who move from a WIC to a WEEP course have then taken up places on the largest scheme under the YOP, making up the remaining 67 per cent of provision. The intention of a WEEP (Work Experience on Employer's Premises) course is to give young people 'a realistic introduction to the requirements, disciplines and satisfactions of working life' (FEU 1979:47). WEEP schemes last for six months, with the possibility of a half or a full day-release into further education and the rest of the week 'on Employer's Premises'. Howard Williamson, in the last part of the section, examines the advantages and disadvantages of the WEEP experience in Oxfordshire.

Section Three moves beyond the experience of specific schemes under the YOP. Derek Kirton looks at an important aspect of the transition from school to unemployment – the impact on careers guidance, in this case with special reference to the Durham coalfield. Kirton explores 'the threat which mass unemployment poses to the teaching paradigm' and how careers staff in schools meet this threat. He goes on to assess the effects of government provision for unemployed school-leavers on the careers service, 'the degree to which unemployment and counter measures create new and distinct problems and how far they merely aggravate existing ones'. Another set of problems associated with the lack of work which regularly feature in discussion are the reverberations on the social behaviour of adolescents. Sue Bloxham considers 'the socio-psychological consequences of unemployment or precarious or substitute employment for the young people concerned'. The further education provision within courses for unemployed school-leavers has featured Social and Life Skills as an acknowledgement that '... the possession of technical skills is not sufficient for young people to be successful at work' (FEU 1979:21). Sue Bloxham continues by investigating the strength of the arguments for including this element of the courses, and its effect on social behaviour and the young unemployed.

The third contribution to this section of the book deals with the place of black youth amongst the unemployed, and the connections between unemployment and street violence. John Schostak traces the recent history of the incidence of riots in this country and relates this to growing discontent amongst adolescents who are faced with increasing repression and dwindling opportunities. Schostak argues that Government responses to youth unemployment avoid addressing the causes and blame the unemployed for 'purposes of social control' which 'continues the tension which leads to social unrest'.

In Place of Work is primarily concerned with British provision for unemployed school-leavers. The problem and the response are nationwide, as the broad geographical base of the research reported here reflects. But high levels of youth unemployment are to be found all over the Western world, of course, and many governments have explored problem-solving strategies which pose alternative courses of action to those considered in the first three parts of this book. Take, for example, the French proposals contained in Professor Bertrand Schwartz's *L'Insertion Professionelle et Sociale des Jeunes* (1981). Produced two months before *A New Training Initiative*, Professor Schwartz's report contains a different emphasis to the British White Paper which describes itself as 'first and last a training scheme' (DofE 1981:9). Chris Pilley (1982:6), writing about the French proposals, says they are 'based on a dialogue with young people and a recognition that a successful entry into working life is, in large, dependent on a satisfactory social environment'. To be able to provide a complete range of alternatives, albeit a fascinating exercise, would require an additional volume however.[5] There is, nevertheless, a need to apply some degree of perspective to the mainland British experience, and to that end the final part of this book contains two comparatives. First, Robert Nelson and James Leach present the case for entrepreneurship education in the USA which, they claim, '... can help people discover work on their own and thus create employment opportunities for themselves and for others'. Teresa Rees' comparative from Northern Ireland is much closer to home, both in miles and experience, but is still significantly separate. Northern Ireland not only has the highest level of unemployed youth in Europe but also, as Rees says 'the long years of economic collapse, poverty, hardship, civil and political unrest and the imposition of Direct Rule combine to create a society qualitatively different to live in'. Teresa Rees analyses the sex-stereotyping contained in the special measures for unemployed youngsters and discusses the reasons why 'there is no pressure from any quarter to give a fair deal for girls'.

Any overview of activity in the area of provision for the young unemployed could not fail to note both a breadth of practice and a state of rapidly changing policy. As to the former, for logistic reasons there is no attempt within these pages to cover every available course. Similarly, the book does not deal with some interesting innovations which are attempting to disseminate different models of training. One such example is the Information Technology Centres (ITECs) at present being set up around the country. These are funded jointly by the MSC and The Department of Industry and are based on the experience of Notting Dale Technology Centre in equiping trainees with skills related to computing and electronics. It remains to be seen how innovative or effective the ITECs will become however. In any case, high cost and low numbers must raise questions about ITECs as a response to the scale of the problem.

As to rapidly changing policy, *A New Training Initiative* was released by the government in December 1981. The Youth Training Scheme is to begin in September 1983. There is therefore a lot in the YTS which could change before it becomes established. The strength and quality of these and subsequent potential changes will in part depend on the quality of the continuing debate which *In Place of Work* seeks to inform and augment.

Sometimes, looking at articles and papers on the problems addressed by this book, one is reminded of Kurt Vonnegut's (1981:48) Presidential Special Advisor on Youth Affairs – Walter F Starbuck – who:

> ... knowing full well that everything he wrote would be shredded and baled with all the rest of the White House waste paper, unread, still turned out some two hundred or more weekly reports on the sayings and doings of youth, with footnotes, bibliographies, appendices and all.

In Place of Work is produced in the hope of a better fate.

Notes

1 UVP is not dealt with in this book. Interested readers should turn to JAMIESON WRAY M. *et. al.* (1980) '*Unified Vocational Preparation: An Evaluation of The Pilot Programme*' NFER.
2 Taken from the authors research archive.
3 At the time of writing the SPD and the TSD are separate divisions, however plans are afoot for their merger.
4 Figures for percentage breakdown of components within the YOP are from 1981.
5 One similar volume already in existance is REUBENS B.G. (1977) '*Bridges to Work*' Martin Robertson.

Bibliography

ALLINSON, C. (1980) 'Training workshops in YOP' pp. 10–12 in '*Basic Education*' Cambridge, January.

CENTRE FOR CONTEMPORARY CULTURAL STUDIES (1981) '*Unpopular Education*' London, Hutchinson.

DEPARTMENT OF EMPLOYMENT (1981) *A New Training Initiative: A Programme for Action* London, HMSO.

FURTHER EDUCATION CURRICULUM REVIEW AND DEVELOPMENT UNIT (1979) '*Supporting YOP*' London.

MANPOWER SERVICES COMMISSION (1976), '*Annual Report 1975/76*' London, HMSO.
MANPOWER SERVICES COMMISSION (1977a) '*Annual Report 1976/77*' London, HMSO.
MANPOWER SERVICES COMMISSION (1977b) '*Young People and Work*' London, HMSO.
PILLEY, C. (1982) 'French lessons' pp. 6–7 in '*Youth in Society*' Leicester, March no 64.
SALMON, H. (1982) 'Unhealthy competition' pp. 24–25 in '*Youth in Society*' Leicester, June no 67.
SCHWARTZ, B. (1981) *L'Insertion Professionelle et Sociale des Jeunes – Rapport au Premiere Ministre* Available from La Documentation Francais, 29–31 quai Voltaire 75340 Paris CEDEX 07.
Times Educational Supplement, London 17 July 1981.
VONNEGUT, K. (1981) *Jailbird* London, Granada.

1
Overview

Can There Be An Effective Youth Unemployment Policy?

David Raffe

The central limiting assumption underlying recent state policy for youth unemployment is that government cannot substantially reduce aggregate levels of unemployment, at least in the short term, without prejudice to other policy objectives. This assumption has been made by governments of both parties. It was evident in James Callaghan's 1976 assertion that the country no longer had the option of spending its way out of a recession and it continues in Margaret Thatcher's repeated claims that 'there is no alternative' to her government's deflationary policies.

A second assumption is that young people should have prior claim on the consequently limited resources for dealing with unemployment. Although increasingly questioned in recent years (Bell *et al*. 1981; Showler and Sinfield 1981:227–228) this assumption has also been accepted by governments of both parties. The major part of the Callaghan administration's spending on unemployment policy was directed towards young people through the Youth Opportunities Programme (YOP) and its predecessors. The Thatcher administration substantially increased the scale of YOP while cutting expenditure on programmes (such as STEP, subsequently CEP) designed for the adult unemployed.

In this paper I discuss the policy options open to a government which accepts these two assumptions: its policy priorities require it to act to ease the burden of youth unemployment; yet its refusal to contemplate a large scale attack on the aggregate level of unemployment requires it to devise a policy whose effects can be accurately focussed on unemployed young people, rather than dissipated across the unemployed of all ages. I describe four of the main strategies by which governments might attempt to do this. I call them strategies rather than policy options because they are not all alternatives; indeed, at least three of them are implicit in recent policies for youth unemployment. In part they reflect different priorities; but the choice of strategy or mix of strategies (and especially the choice between stragegy 1 and strategies 2 or 3) also rests on empirical assumptions about the labour market and about the effectiveness of different policy measures.

The first strategy would provide schemes or other measures with the effect of reducing supply within the youth labour market. The second strategy would also withdraw young people from the labour market, but it would do so selectively, taking only those young people who were, and would in any case have been, unemployed. The third strategy would reduce youth unemployment by giving young people a 'competitive edge' over adults in the labour market. The fourth strategy would try to alleviate the consequences, rather than remove the causes, of youth unemployment.

The purpose of this paper is not to argue the merits of any particular strategy, although it does suggest reasons for doubting whether any of them is likely to be fully effective. The main purpose is to elucidate the possibilities for, and constraints on, government policy. The need for such elucidation is illustrated in the final section, which briefly refers to recent policy proposals and argues that the discussion of policy has been hindered by the shifting terms of the debate and by a lack of clarity both about the ends of actual or proposed policies and about the relation of ends to means.

Strategy 1: Non-Selective Reduction in Youth Labour Supply

Within the self-imposed constraints of the two assumptions described above, a government must design a policy for youth unemployment whose effects would not be dissipated across other age groups. How it does this depends on its view of the relation between the youth and adult labour markets. Strategy 1 assumes that these are substantially segregated: that young people work only in 'young peoples' jobs', that they rarely compete with adults for jobs, that the age break between youth and adult labour markets is clearly defined and that supply and demand within the youth labour market are substantially independent of supply and demand within the adult labour market. The strategy would act directly to reduce supply within the youth labour market. It would do so by keeping a number of young people off the labour market, placing them either in extended full-time education or on schemes of training, vocational preparation or community or military service. The schemes would be non-selective; that is, they would not be restricted to the unemployed. The effect of withdrawing or withholding some young people from the labour market would be to reduce the competition of jobs among the young people who remained there. Because of the assumed segregation of youth and adult labour markets, this knock-on effect would largely be confined to the youth labour market; the resulting fall in unemployment would be concentrated among young people.

However, were the youth and adult labour markets not segregated, the effects of any reduction in supply in the youth labour market would be dissipated across other age groups. The benefits of the reduced competition for jobs would be felt by adults as well as by young workers. The proportionate reduction in unemployment might be little or no greater among the young people who remained in the labour market than among adult workers. Strategy 1 therefore rests on the empirical assumption of substantial segregation between youth and adult labour markets. This assumption also affects the prognosis for youth unemployment, regardless of policy. If the youth labour market is segregated, the problem of youth unemployment will be substantially eased by the reduction in the size of the age group, by about one third, by the mid 1990s. If the youth labour market is not segregated, however, the benefits of the reduced competition for jobs will be spread across all age groups and the effect on young people will be relatively small.

The extent to which young and adult workers compete in the labour market is a matter of degree. Age, along with many other personal characteristics, is certainly an important 'factor in employment' (Jolly *et al.* 1980:10). But age can be an important factor within a labour market that nevertheless allows extensive competition, direct or indirect, between age groups. On balance the evidence suggests that there is substantially more competition than segregation between young and adult workers.

The MSC's employers survey found that 'young people compete alongside people of all ages for the majority of jobs for which they are eligible. Only apprenticeships are the preserve of young people alone' (MSC 1978:38). It is true that young people are disproportionately represented in certain sectors of the labour market; however, this is not evidence for a separate youth labour market, for young people form only a small minority of workers in each of the industries and occupational categories in which they are employed (Jolly *et al.* 1980:83–84, 94–95). Most teenagers apply for jobs for which adults are also eligible, even if they only have access to a limited range of the jobs that are available to adults. Even when employers do specify age limits for job vacancies, or form prior preferences for the age group they wish to recruit, this is often the result of indirect competition between age groups rather than evidence that competition does not exist. In such cases, where young people do not compete directly with adults for vacant jobs, the employer must decide in advance on the age group he wishes to recruit. His decision will be influenced by the relative competitive advantages, in his eyes, of the different age groups (Hunt and Small 1981: 9–11, Tyrrell 1981: 55). This indirect competition differs from direct competition mainly in that the choice depends on the employer's generalized perceptions of different age groups rather than on the observed characteristics of the individuals of different ages who apply.

If young people and adults were members of the same labour market one would expect youth and adult unemployment to respond to the same economic conditions. Probably the most important evidence that the youth and adult labour markets are not segregated therefore comes from the econometric studies which show that the rise in youth unemployment during the 1970s can be explained almost entirely as the result of the state of the economy as a whole (Layard 1979a, Makeham 1980; see also Hutchinson *et al.* 1979). These studies leave little or nothing to be explained by trends in supply and demand that are specific to the youth labour market. They suggest that the recent disproportionate rise in youth unemployment results from the disproportionate sensitivity of youth unemployment to both the ups and the downs of the employment cycle. Youth unemployment always rises faster than adult unemployment in a recession. This is mainly because young workers include a large number of job-seekers (both school-leavers and job-leavers) who are affected by the suspension of recruitment that accompanies a recession. Young people are also affected disproportionately by last-in-first-out redundancy policies, by the tendency to shed less skilled workers first in a recession and by cutbacks in training. The corollary is that youth unemployment falls faster than adult unemployment when the economy recovers. If adult unemployment were ever to fall to the levels of the 1950s and 1960s, so too would youth unemployment.

The problem of youth unemployment is therefore part of the more general problem of unemployment among all age groups; both respond to the same economic trends, even if the response of youth unemployment is proportionately larger. The econometric studies also reveal a small or negligible effect of demographic trends (the size of the age group) on the rate of youth unemployment and comparisons of youth unemployment across towns find no significant effect on youth unemployment of the local industrial structure (Makeham 1980:51–63); if the youth labour market were segregated these effects would be large.

The British evidence is therefore consistent with the conclusions of the report of an international conference on youth unemployment; while acknowledging the 'many shared experiences' of young people in the labour market, this also argued:

> It is questionable whether, in fact, there is any such thing as a 'youth labour market' which operates separately and distinctly from other areas of the economy. It is certainly true that current increases in youth unemployment can only be understood in the general context of the slowdown in aggregate economic performance. Very few jobs, in fact, are held by only young people. Youth themselves . . . are not a homogeneous group. (OECD 1978:38).

Resting as it does on an inadequate view of the labour market, strategy 1 would indiscriminately reduce adult as well as youth unemployment. Its specific effect on youth unemployment would be relatively modest.

Strategy 2: Selective Reduction in Youth Labour Supply – or Re-defining Youth Unemployment

Both strategy 2 and strategy 3 accept that the youth labour market is not segregated. Strategy 2 would attempt to reduce youth unemployment, not by reducing the supply of youth labour non-selectively, but by schemes (such as YOP) which selectively removed only unemployed young people from the labour market. Unlike strategy 1 it would not attempt to reduce youth unemployment through a knock-on effect by reducing the competition for jobs among the young people who remained in the labour market. Strategy 2 recognizes that the youth labour market is not segregated and that much of this knock-on effect would benefit adults rather than the young people. The main effect of strategy 2 on youth unemployment would be the direct effect of removing a number of unemployed young people from the register.

For this effect to be maximized the schemes would need to be organized in specific ways. They would need to avoid substituting for, or displacing, permanent jobs. They would need to be restricted to the unemployed and, more specifically, to those who would in any case have been unemployed. They would need to be discontinuous with full-time education; school leavers would have to have entered the labour market first and have tried, but failed, to find a permanent job before becoming eligible for the schemes. Once on the schemes they should continue to look for permanent jobs as actively as if they were unemployed; otherwise the net effect of the schemes would be to delay entrance into employment for many young people; many of the jobs they would have found would be taken by adults and the schemes would have to cater for many more young people than would otherwise have been unemployed.

An effective policy pursuing strategy 2 would, therefore, have to provide schemes which did not displace ordinary jobs, which only recruited young people who had already entered the labour market but failed to find work, and which encouraged them to continue their search for employment. In most senses of the term these young people would not have left the labour market; strategy 2 could therefore be accused of proposing to solve the problem of youth unemployment by re-defining it as something else. This does not invalidate the strategy, for youth unemployment thus re-defined might still be far preferable to unemployment without such schemes. The design (if not always the practice) of YOP has largely satisfied these conditions. However, YOP has been targeted mainly on sixteen and seventeen year olds and it has had few knock-on effects on young workers outside this age range. Unemployment among eighteen and nineteen year olds rose from 128,300 to 303,700 between October 1979 and October 1981, despite the massive expansion of YOP over the same period. A further condition for effective schemes under strategy 2 is that they should be available to unemployed people of all ages within the target age group.

A number of proposed schemes for young people are discussed in the last section of this paper. Most of them are either claimed, or implicitly assumed, to have a direct effect on youth unemployment; yet most of them pursue additional objectives, typically to provide the young people who go on the schemes with good quality education, training or experience (thus to pursue strategy 3, described below). However, a scheme which is discontinuous with full-time education, which restricts recruitment to the unemployed and which risks losing its students at any time if they can find a job, is unlikely to be fully effective as an educational or training scheme. There is therefore a conflict between these objectives and the requirements of strategy 2, and the majority of proposals tend to place their education and training objectives foremost, for example by including the employed (or those who would have been employed) in their schemes and by making no provision for participants to leave before the end of their schemes if they find permanent employment. As a result, most proposed schemes for dealing with youth unemployment are less selective than strategy 2 would require. In part, they would pursue strategy 1 and thus invite the objection, raised above, that their effects would not be focussed on the young. However, those proposing such schemes tend to place most emphasis on the value of the education or training that is provided on the schemes, which is claimed to facilitate entry into permanent employment. This is the third strategy for responding to youth unemployment.

Strategy 3: Giving Young People a 'Competitive Edge'

Strategy 3 is also premised on the assumption of substantial competition, direct or indirect, between adults and young people in the labour market; it would seek to tilt the competitive balance between young and adult workers, making young workers more attractive to employers.

One way to do this is to reduce the relative wages of young workers. The demand for youth labour responds to the relative wage rate; this is evident both from surveys of employers (Hunt and Small 1981:9–11; Tyrrell 1981:55) and from econometric studies predicting youth unemployment or the demand for youth labour (Layard 1979a: 17–22; Merrilees and Wilson 1979: 22–32). However, relative wages are only a minor influence on youth unemployment, compared for example with the effects of the recession; and they are not at all responsible for the rise in youth unemployment during the late 1970s because the earnings of young people relative to adults actually fell, if very slightly, between 1975 and 1980 (Unemployment Unit 1981:4). Nevertheless it is likely that a further fall in the relative cost of employing young people would generate at least a marginal increase in youth employment. In the past, subsidies for young workers appear to have had some effect; however, since a majority of workers for whom the subsidies are paid would have been employed anyhow, employment subsidies, and especially recruitment subsidies, tend to be a relatively costly way to reduce youth unemployment (Layard 1979b:195; Lindley 1980:344). The Young Workers Scheme, introduced in 1982, aims to reduce relative employment costs in two ways: directly, through a subsidy for employers of young workers, and indirectly by restricting the subsidy to those paying low wages and thereby encouraging youth wage rates in general to fall. The scheme should be seen as part of a general strategy to make labour markets more competitive and wages more flexible, and to encourage greater disparity between the earnings of different types of workers. The ultimate success of the scheme may depend on its ability to increase the quantity of youth employment without loss of quality. There is a danger that the scheme, as currently devised, may merely encourage the employment of young workers in dead-end jobs of limited duration and that when their subsidies expire they will once more be at the mercy of a depressed labour market, without training and without prospects.

YOP has also aimed to give young people a 'competitive edge' in the labour market (MSC 1977:43), but it has tried to do this by enhancing the quality of their labour rather than by reducing the price. It has not, for the most part, attempted to increase young peoples' job-specific skills, for few such skills are currently scarce and in demand in the labour market (Lindley 1980:335). Instead, it has attempted to augment young peoples' general work skills (Holland 1979) and, in particular, to enhance their 'social skills', experience and personal qualities such as adaptability and motivation (MSC 1977:34). This approach was strongly influenced by the employers survey which was commissioned for the Holland working party and conducted at the time of the Great Debate; employers rated 'willingness/attitude to work' as the most important quality desired in new recruits and they tended to regard young people as inferior to adults on this and other criteria (MSC 1978:38–40). Moreover, young workers were perceived to face competition from increasing numbers of adult workers, particularly married women (MSC 1977:20). Relatively few married women have high-level, job-specific skills and they tend to be attractive to employers on account of their perceived stability, flexibility and controllability, and their tolerance of monotonous work (Ashton and Maguire 1980). Competition (direct or indirect) with married women in the labour force has encouraged the salience of personal qualities, attitudes to work and social skills as criteria for choosing between young and adult workers. (However, whereas there is certainly competition in the labour market between adult and young females, there is conflicting evidence on whether adult females compete with young males (Abowd *et al.* 1980:6–11; Hutchinson *et al.* 1979:29).) YOP has therefore attempted to give young people a 'competitive edge' in the labour market by enhancing their general work skills, personal qualities and attitudes and their 'social skills'. Can such a strategy succeed?

The experience of YOP itself has been mixed. Rates of subsequent employment of YOP trainees fell sharply over the first three years of the programme (MSC 1981c:7) but this reflected the deteriorating employment situation for all young people. It is difficult to determine whether YOP has made any difference to the employment chances of its trainees, largely because of the difficulty of identifying an appropriate control group, but studies using different bases for comparison suggest that YOP may have given its trainees a slight advantage (Raffe 1981; Stafford 1982). However, this effect may have come about, not through YOP's effects on the skills and personal qualities of its trainees, but through its more direct effects on selection procedures in the labour market (Raffe 1983). YOP has performed a screening rather than a training function by providing employers with a more convenient and reliable source of recruitment of young workers; although to the extent that it has made young people easier to recruit relative to adults it may thereby have enhanced the competitive advantage of young people albeit in a largely unintended way.

The potential effectiveness of the strategy cannot, of course, be finally judged on the success of failure of a single programme. YOP has, in any case, faced the same problems as all innovatory programmes; in the words of its chief architect 'we were having to invent and discover as we go along' (Holland 1981:14). These problems were aggravated by the rapid growth of YOP and the inevitable displacement of quality by quantity as its immediate target. More recently, the main drive of policy has been towards improving the quality of training provided by YOP and by the programme that replaces it (MSC 1981a, 1981b). The proposed Youth Training Scheme, to come into effect from September 1983, is intended to replace YOP with a longer and higher-quality programme of training and experience (DE 1981); this, it could be argued, might achieve greater success in making young people more competitive.

Nevertheless, there are at least three reasons for doubting whether this strategy, however competently implemented, can have more than a modest impact on the level of youth unemployment. The first is based on a historical comparison. In the 1950s and 1960s education was widely regarded as a panacea for a range of social and economic problems. In the colder light of the 1970s this faith came to be regarded as excessively optimistic and as founded on a simplistic and inaccurate view of the social functions of education. The contemporary parallels are ominous; it is difficult to resist the conclusion that training, or maybe 'vocational preparation', has become the universal panacea of the 1980s, supported only by a superficial analysis of its likely impact on social and economic conditions. These fears are heightened by the use of the term 'training' to describe the acquisition of attitudes, motivation and personality traits and the use of the term 'skill' to describe these attributes. Such 'skills' are more usually regarded as the preconditions, rather than the outcomes, of the learning process. (In practice the perceived abuses of YOP have made at least some of its trainees less positive and more cynical in their attitudes towards the world of work.) Any programme which aims to improve the attitudes and motivation of unemployed young people must neutralize the demoralizing effects of their declining employment prospects. There is a further vicious circle whereby any attempt to raise young peoples' skills (however defined) might raise their job aspirations more than it increases their ability to meet those aspirations. Conversely, any scheme which does not arouse such aspirations may lack the necessary (vocational) basis for motivating its participants.

Second, there is little evidence that the standards of young people, at least as defined in conventional educational terms, have declined (Choppin 1981). Employers have complained for decades about the calibre of school leavers (see, for example, BACIE 1936:37); those who claim to perceive a *decline* in standards tend to be the employers of apprentices (MSC 1978:40) who have moved 'down market' and have increasingly recruited from the lower levels, in relative terms, of the attainment range. The task of YOP and its successors is therefore not to reverse a decline but to raise standards well above their level of the past few decades (House of Commons 1977:xiv–xv). It must, therefore, succeed where formal education has failed, a difficult task even for an innovatory agency such as the MSC.

The third and most important reason for doubting the effectiveness of strategy 3 lies in the scale of the task. In times of recession youth unemployment rises above adult unemployment for reasons that have nothing to do with the relative quality of adults and young workers (see the discussion of strategy 1 above). To offset this and, thereby to reduce youth unemployment even to the level of adult unemployment, young people would have to be made considerably more attractive than adults to potential employers. Even the best designed of training schemes would have to work miracles to achieve this.

Strategy 4: Palliatives

The three strategies described above aim to achieve a substantial reduction in the level of youth unemployment. All, it has been suggested, are likely to be only partially effective. If this analysis is correct, there is a strong case for giving policy a stronger and more explicit emphasis on alleviating the consequences of youth unemployment even if its causes cannot be removed. The consequences of youth unemployment are widely feared, if inadequately understood. First, unemployment is often a demoralizing and depressing experience for young people (Gow and McPherson 1980:87–97). It has been associated with poor mental health (Stafford *et al.* 1980) although it does not necessarily follow that it causes it. Second, youth unemployment may be linked to social 'disorders' such as juvenile crime (Ridley 1981:24–27), riots and political extremism (Sinfield 1981:22). Once again, cause and effect are less certain. As Carroll (1979:24–25) points out:

> several studies . . . give figures on the number of young people in their samples who had been in trouble with the law. Unfortunately such figures throw no light on whether, for example, law-breaking results in unemployment or *vice versa*. . . . In any case an apparent causal link between crime and unemployment may be merely a spurious reflection of policing methods.

The problem of finding a causal connection is further compounded if the link between youth unemployment and social problems is indirect, operating via the 'social malaise' of an area (Ridley 1981:25) and not just through the behaviour of unemployed individuals. Third, youth unemployment is believed to retard the social, psychological and occupational development of young people. There is some evidence that it retards psychological development (Gurney 1980, Poole 1981). The Holland Report (MSC 1977:34) made explicit its fears that youth unemployment would retard occupational development, creating a generation of unmotivated, inexperienced and unemployable workers. However, we do not know for certain what the long term effects of present day youth unemployment will be; it may be misleading to generalize from past experience, because the the youth unemployment of today is qualitatively different from that of a few years ago.

Our inability to demonstrate clear and certain consequences of present day youth unemployment reflects basic methodological problems together with the lack of suitable evidence. It does not necessarily mean that such consequences do not exist, or that government policies should not attempt to alleviate or avert them; although it does mean that the design of such policies is handicapped by considerable ignorance.

YOP and similar schemes appear to have been reasonably successful in averting the immediate consequences of unemployment; they have offered something preferable to unemployment (Jackson and Hanby 1979) and they have had a favourable, but short-lived, effect on mental health (Stafford 1982). Their effect on social disorders is harder to identify, although casual observation suggests that this cannot have been great. Their effect on young peoples' development is equally difficult to determine, although most young people on YOP felt that it had boosted their self-confidence (Bedeman and Harvey 1981:364); and a study of Community Industry (CI) tentatively concluded that it may have had a 'holding effect', that 'the CI experience may offset the development of "unfavourable" work-related attitudes' (Murray 1978:196–197).

Although evidence on the palliative effects of YOP and similar measures is scanty, it would appear that their main effects are short term and based on the provision of a substitute for employment; and that their emphasis is on helping unemployed young people to find employment, rather than on helping those who will remain unemployed for a substantial period to make the most of their situation. It has been suggested that young people might be prepared for unemployment in other ways than merely by helping them find paid employment as soon as possible (Watts 1978). Such proposals have rarely been tried and they might in practice be difficult to implement; we have yet to see whether young people can be effectively inoculated against the effects of unemployment.

Youth Unemployment Policy: The State of the Debate

The strategies described in this paper do not exhaust the logical possibilities of government action on youth unemployment. For example, they tend to presuppose conventional definitions of employers and employment and do not take account of the possible relation of young people to the 'informal economies' (Watts 1981) or of proposals to make a programme such as YOP help 'young people create work for themselves, not work experience, but work' (Ball 1979:18). Nor is it suggested that most policies or policy proposals for dealing with youth unemployment slot neatly into one of the four strategies. Not only do many of the proposed schemes also have educational, economic or community service objectives that are not directly related to the problem of youth unemployment, but their responses to youth unemployment itself usually combine two or more of the strategies listed above. Yet many of the proposals, and much of the related discussion, remain confused and unclear concerning the combination of strategies they wish to pursue, the priorities among them, and the assumed relation of means to ends; and the discussion of policy is further confused by the tendency for the terms of the debate to shift over time.

Space does not permit a detailed description of the various proposals referred to. They include: proposals to enchance the quality of training and increase the length of YOP and its successors (Youthaid 1981), including the government's Youth Training Scheme proposals (DE 1981) and the more ambitious MSC (1981b) plans on which they were based; proposals to extend an (improved) YOP-type programme to all or most young people (Williams 1981); proposals to delay entry to paid employment through extended education, vocational preparation or training (Rees and Gregory 1981); and proposals for compulsory social service (Colombatto 1980) or for combined social service, vocational preparation and training (Tyrrell 1981). These are, of course, only a selection of the large number of plans that have been put forward. Various proposals on these lines, and also plans for wage-sharing and for subsidizing traineeships, were considered by the MSC's task group in 1982. Despite extensive public discussion, the exact balance of objectives pursued by the these various proposals remains obscure. Most of them would apparently tackle youth unemployment mainly by reducing the supply of young people to the labour market, either non-selectively (strategy 1) or focussing on the unemployed (strategy 2). Sometimes it is implied that the proposals would also have a palliative effect (strategy 4). Yet, nearly all the public discussion has been about the tactics (not even the strategy) of strategy 3: about how to provide training or experience for young people to give them a 'competitive edge' in the labour market.

There are several reasons for the lack of clarity about means and ends in the public discussion of policy for youth unemployment. Such confusion has been a feature of manpower policy in general and especially of training policy, discussion of which 'has been affected by a number of factors tending to make communication difficult and consensus all but impossible' (Lindley 1981:17). It has been aggravated by the *ad hoc* and incremental nature of the development of policy. Each stage in the development of policy is justified by an explicit account of its objectives, but it is implicitly assumed to continue to pursue the objectives of the programmes from which the current policy has developed. This may explain the vagueness and apparent ambiguity of the strategy of the Holland Report; it certainly accounts for some confusion concerning the Tebbit proposal for a Youth Training Scheme (YTS) (DE 1981). YTS is to develop out of the existing policies for youth unemployment and has probably gained much political support from the belief that it is a policy for youth unemployment; yet the White Paper which proposed it described it solely as a training scheme and made no claim that it would reduce youth unemployment.

A second reason for the confusion of ends and means has been a failure to base proposals on rigorous analyses of the labour market, or at least a failure to make such analyses explicit. Proposals that would remove or withhold young people from the labour market rarely made clear whether they assumed a segregated youth labour market (in which case the non-selective approach of strategy one would be sufficient) or substantial competition between adults and young workers (in which case the selectivity and other stringent conditions of strategy 2 would need to be met).

Third, policy proposers are reluctant to dwell on those aspects of their plans which are politically unappealing. Proposals to remove or withhold young people from the labour market (strategies 1 and 2) are vulnerable in this respect, for they lead to accusations of concealing unemployment or 'massaging' the statistics. This is specially true of strategy 2, which would remove only the unemployed and which (as argued above) could be accused of merely re-defining youth unemployment as something else. Strategy 4 is also unpopular; to propose explicitly palliative policies is to acknowledge one's inability to tackle the problem at its source and to plan palliatives for the longer term involves admitting that the problem will be around for a long time. It is not surprising therefore that the public discussion of most proposals tends to focus, not on how well they might pursue strategies 1,2 or 4, but on how they might give young workers a 'competitive edge' (strategy 3): on the content of the training or whatever is being offered and on its alleged benefits for the future employability of the trainees.

This in turn reinforces a fourth reason for the lack of clarity in policy debate: the widespread and rarely questioned assumption that training is a good thing, however unconventional the content of the training and however slight the demand for its products. This assumption has gone hand in hand with the tendency for manpower policy to focus on the supply side, and ignore the demand side, of the labour market. I do not question either that training is important or that it may play an important part in eventual economic regeneration. What is questionable, however, is the belief that because training is 'a good thing' it is therefore an answer to youth unemployment. I have suggested several reasons for doubting this, in the discussion of strategy 3. Yet not only is this belief widespread, it is usually regarded as axiomatic, and rarely made explicit let alone defended. For example, a House of Commons

David Raffe

Committee report, significantly entitled *Youth Unemployment and Training*, described the deterioration of youth unemployment and proposed extensions and improvements of YOP. Its key assumption, underlying the whole report but never justified, was that 'a new positive orientation towards training is needed' in order to tackle the problem of youth unemployment (House of Commons 1981: xviii). The same assumption is implicit in many of the other proposals (Williams 1981:89; Youthaid 1981:17–18; Tyrrell 1981:39–40).

One consequence of the confused and lop-sided nature of the policy debate is that proposals fail to allow for the conflicting demands of different strategies. Supporters of the various policy options direct most of their energies to discussing the content of schemes and thus to strategy 3 (giving young workers a competitive edge). They, nevertheless, imply that their schemes will also have a direct effect on youth unemployment equivalent to the number of young people on the schemes at any one time; in other words, they assume that their proposals would successfully pursue strategy 1 (non-selective reduction in youth labour supply). This is almost never based on an explicit analysis of the labour market, although such an analysis would indicate that strategy 2 (selective reduction in youth labour supply) might be more effective. Strategy 2 however would require schemes to be discontinuous with formal education, to be restricted to the unemployed and to encourage trainees to continue seeking work; such restrictive conditions would conflict with the educational, training and social service objectives of the schemes and thus with strategy 3. Similar conflicts are likely to arise between strategy 3, which aims to prepare young people for employment, and strategy 4, which aims to prepare young people for unemployment, although these too are overlooked because of the reluctance to accept strategy 4 as an explicit part of the policy.

By 1981, a number of commentators appeared to acknowledge that training and work experience schemes, and strategy 3 generally, were unequal to the scale of the youth unemployment problem. However, their response to this perception of failure was not to place more emphasis on strategies 1, 2 or 4; it was rather to take the existing policy framework as a starting point and look for new reasons for its existence, modifying and improving it accordingly. The Youthaid report on YOP argued that the programme 'must find a new justification and set of objectives'; rather than concentrate on unemployment as a target it should 'make a virtue of the necessity of high youth unemployment and ... embrace this opportunity to invest in the continuing education and training of young people who would in the past have ... lived the rest of their lives with no further education and training' (Youthaid 1981:14, 16). This change of emphasis was taken further in the Tebbit proposals for a Youth Training Scheme, which was presented as '*first and last a training scheme*' (DE 1981:9; original emphasis) and not at all as a policy for youth unemployment; and in April 1982 the MSC's youth task group introduced its report by saying that it was 'not about youth unemployment' (MSC 1982:1).

The 'shifting rationalization' of training policy (Lindley 1980:359) has shifted a step further. On the one hand, the Tebbit proposals could be seen as an opportunist exploitation of youth unemployment in order to pursue (training) objectives not directly related to the problem of youth unemployment. Alternatively, the Tebbit proposals could be seen as a continuation of youth unemployment policy, and the White Paper's emphasis on training could be seen as an attempt to change the criteria for evaluating the policy and thus to pre-empt criticisms of the policy should youth unemployment remain high. Either way, the abandonment of youth unemployment as an explicit target of policy (except for the Young Workers Scheme) suggests a recognition by government that the problems of youth unemployment is intractable, at least within the constraints of its macro-economic policy.

When proposals for a Youth Training Scheme were announced in December 1981, critical comment focussed on the low allowance for participants, the withdrawal of benefit entitlements for sixteen year olds and the likelihood that unions would not co-operate with the scheme as proposed. In the longer term, possibly the greatest danger facing the proposed scheme *as a training scheme* is that it will continue to be regarded as a policy for youth unemployment. If unemployment remains high among young people leaving the scheme, then both the motivation of trainees and the public credibility of the scheme will suffer.

And what of future policy for youth unemployment? At least three points arise from the argument of this paper First, *the state of the debate*: policy proposals must be more explicit about ends and means. In that way we might recognize the conflicts between different strategies and objectives and we might avoid over-simplified solutions based on implicit but false assumptions about the labour market. Second, *the prospects for success*: none of the strategies described in this paper appears to offer an adequate solution to youth unemployment on its present scale. Taking young people off the labour market would not eliminate youth unemployment, unless this were done on such a scale and in such restrictive conditions as to be politically unacceptable. Nor can improved training, or other measures to make young people more competitive, provide an answer to the present problem of youth unemployment. Perhaps more should be done to provide palliatives for youth unemployment, whether by educational or other means – but here we are hampered more by ignorance than by the inherent impracticalities of policy. Third, *the assumptions underlying policy*, described at the beginning of this paper: are they compatible? The analysis of this paper suggests that government cannot expect to have a strong influence on youth unemployment while the problem of high aggregate unemployment remains unsolved. Perhaps the next change in government policy will respond to this by relaxing the priority currently given to the problem of youth rather than adult unemployment. This paper has not sought either to defend or attack the case for this priority, for the priority itself may be a dead letter. The relevant question may be, not whether a policy for youth unemployment should be given high political priority, but whether such a policy can be effective without a similar attack on unemployment among all age groups.

Acknowledgements

Rob Fiddy, Neil Fraser, Andrew McPherson, Brian Main and Adrian Sinfield made helpful comments on an earlier draft of this paper. The Centre for Educational Sociology receives financial support from the Social Science Research Council, the Scottish Education Department and the Manpower

David Raffe

Services Commission. The author alone is responsible for the views expressed in the paper.

References

ABOWD, J., LAYARD, R. and NICKELL, S. (1980) 'The demand for labour by age and sex,' Working paper no. 110, *Centre for Labour Economics* London School of Economics.

ASHTON, D. and MAGUIRE, M. (1980) 'Young women in the labour market: stability and change', in DEEM, R. (Ed) *Schooling for Women's Work* London, Routledge and Kegan Paul.

BALL, C. (1981) 'The Youth Opportunities Programme – facts, figures, issues', in YOUTHAID *Briefing Conference for MPs on the Youth Unemployment, Education and Training* London, Youthaid.

BEDEMAN, T. and HARVEY, J. (1981) 'Young people on YOP', *Employment Gazette*, August, 362–364.

BELL, D., FRASER, N., KIRWAN, F. and TAIT, E. (1981) *Youth Unemployment: Some Key Questions?* Edinburgh, Scottish Centre of Political Economy.

BRITISH ASSOCIATION for COMMERCIAL and INDUSTRIAL EDUCATION (BACIE) (1936) *Report of and Inquiry into Vocational Education after General Education up to the Age of Sixteen* London, BACIE.

CARROLL, P. (1979) *Social and Psychological Consequences of Unemployment for Young People: A Literature Review* (Unpublished) London, Department of Employment.

CHOPPIN, B. (1981) 'Is education getting better?' *British Educational Research Journal*, 7, 3–16.

COLOMBATTO, E. (1980) 'Nation-wide social service: a proposal for the 1980's, Discussion Paper No. 84 *Centre for Labour Economics*, London School of Economics.

DEPARTMENT of EMPLOYMENT (DE) (1981) *A New Training Initiative: A Programme for Action* Cmnd. 8455. London; HMSO.

GOW, L. and MCPHERSON, A. (1980) *Tell Them From Me: Scottish School Leavers Write About School and Life Afterwards* Aberdeen, Aberdeen University Press.

GURNEY, R. (1980) 'The effects of unemployment on the psycho-social development of school-leavers', *Journal of Occupational Psychology*, 53, 205–213.

HOLLAND, G. (1979) 'More than half our future: 16- to 19-year olds in employment, *Oxford Review of Education*, 5, 147–156.

HOLLAND, G. (1981) 'The lessons of YOP', in YOUTHAID *YOP and UVP: The new FE or a Tertiary Modern System?* London, Youthaid.

HOUSE of COMMONS (1978) *People and Work: Prospects for Jobs and Training* Thirteenth Report from the Expenditure Committee, Session 1977–78. Volume 1. London, HMSO.

HOUSE of COMMONS (1981) *Youth Unemployment and Training* First Report from the Committee on Scottish Affairs, Session 1981–82. Volume 1. London, HMSO.

HUNT, J. and SMALL, P. (1981) *Employing Young People: A Study of Employers' Attitudes, Policies and Practices* Edinburgh, Scottish Council for Research in Education.

HUTCHINSON, G., BARR, N.A. and DROBNY, A. (1979) 'A sequential approach to the dynamic specification of the demand for young male labour in Great Britain', Department of Economics, Queen Mary Collge, London.

JACKSON, M. and HANBY, V. (1979) 'Work creation programmes: participants' responses', *Industrial Relations Journal*, 10, 23–30.

JOLLY, J., CREIGH, S. and MINGAY, A. (1980) 'Age as a factor in employment', *Research Paper No. 11*. London, Department of Employment.

LAYARD, R. (1979a) 'Youth unemployment in Britain and the US compared' Discussion Paper No. 52, *Centre for Labour Economics*, London School of Economics.

LAYARD, R. (1979b) 'The costs and benefits of selective employment policies: the British case', *British Journal of Industrial Relations*, 17, 187–204.

LINDLEY, R. (1980) 'Employment Policy in transition', in LINDLEY, R. (Ed) *Economic Change and Employment Policy*, London, Macmillan.

LINDLEY, R. (1981) 'Education, training and the labour market in Britain', *European Journal of Education*, 16, 7–27.

MAKEHAM, P. 1980, 'Youth unemployment: an examination of evidence on youth unemployment using national statistics', *Research Paper no. 10*. London, Department of Employment.

MANPOWER SERVICES COMMISSION (MSC) 1977, *Young People and Work* London, MSC. (The Holland Report).

MANPOWER SERVICES COMMISSION (1978) *Young People and Work: Manpower Studies No. 19781* London, HMSO.

MANPOWER SERVICES COMMISSION (1981a) *A New Training Initiative: A Consultative Document* London, Manpower Services Commission.

MANPOWER SERVICES COMMISSION (1981b) *A New Training Initiative: An Agenda for Action* London, Manpower Services Commission.

MANPOWER SERVICES COMMISSION (1981c) *Review of the Third Year of Special Programmes* London, Manpower Services Commission.

MANPOWER SERVICES COMMISSION (1982) *Youth Task Group Report* London, Manpower Services Commission.

MERRILEES, W. and WILSON, R. (1979) 'Disequilibrium in the labour market for young people in Great Britain', *Disscusion Paper No. 10*, Manpower Research Group, University of Warwick.

MURRAY, C. (1978) *Youth Unemployment: a Social-Psychological Study of Disadvantaged 16–19 year olds*, Slough, NFER Publishing Company.

ORGANIZATION for ECONOMIC COOPERATION and DEVELOPMENT (OECD) (1978) *Youth Unemployment: a report on the High Level Conference Volume 1* Paris, OECD.

POOLE, H. (1981) 'Psychological effects of unemployment on school leavers', Paper presented to British Association for the Advancement of Science, Section L, York.

RAFFE, D. (1981) 'Special programmes in Scotland: the first year of YOP', *Policy and Politics* 9, 471–487.

RAFFE, D. (1983) 'Education and unemployment: does YOP make a difference (and will YTS)?', in GLEESON, D. (Ed.) *Youth Training and the Search for Work* London, Routledge and Kegan Paul.

REES, T. and GREGORY, D. (1981) 'Youth employment and unemployment: a decade of decline', *Educational Analysis*. 3.3, 7–24.

RIDLEY, F. (1981) 'Unemployed youth in Merseyside' in CRICK, B. (Ed) *Unemployment* London, Methuen.

SHOWLER, B. and SINFIELD, A. (1981) 'A most unequal tax' in SHOWLER, B. and SINFIELD, A. *The Workless State* Oxford, Martin Robertson.

SINFIELD, A. (1981) *What Unemployment Means* Oxford, Martin Robertson.

STAFFORD, E. (1982) 'The impact of the Youth Opportunities Programme on young peoples' employment prospects and psychological well-being', *British Journal of Guidance and Counselling*, 10, 12–21.

STAFFORD, E., JACKSON, P. and BANKS, M. (1980) 'Employment, work involvement and mental health in less qualified young people', *Journal of Occupational Psychology*, 53, 291–304.

TYRRELL, R. (1981) *Youth Unemployment: The Appropriate Response* London, Jobs in the 80s.

UNEMPLOYMENT UNIT (1981) 'Near myth?', *Unemployment Unit Bulletin*, 1, 4.

David Raffe

WATTS, A.G. (1978) 'The implications of school-leavers unemployment for careers education in schools', *Journal of Curriculum Studies*, 10, 233–250.
WATTS, A.G. (1981) 'Careers education and the informal economies', *British Journal of Guidance and Counselling*, 9, 24–35.
WILLIAMS, S. (1981) *Politics is for People* London, Allen Lane.
YOUTHAID (1981) *Quality or Collapse? Report of the Youthaid Review of the Youth Opportunities Programme* London, Youthaid.

The Youth Opportunities Programme: Requiem and Rebirth

Martin Loney

It should be pointed out that the Youth Opportunities Programme aims to break the vicious circle which yearly traps many thousands of unemployed young people ... they cannot get jobs unless they have work experience and some basic skills. But they cannot get that experience and those skills without a job.

(Richard O'Brien, former Chairman
Manpower Services Commission, March 1978)

Cheap labour at the cost of permanent jobs is the most usual description.

(*Guardian* report, 25 May 1981)

The Youth Opportunities Programme was launched in 1978 by the then Labour Government as a response to rising youth unemployment. The programme promised the young work and provided clear evidence of government concern, albeit at relatively modest cost. For a government which was pursuing cuts in public spending and a generally deflationary economic policy, the new programme appeared to provide a welcome public affirmation of continuing concern for the unemployed.

The growth in youth unemployment has been dramatic. In July 1974, there were 80,000 under-twenties unemployed. By July 1976, the number of young people under twenty who were unemployed had risen to 390,000. By July 1978 the figure had risen to 441,000 and by July 1980 to 532,000. If current trends continue the MSC estimate that 68 per cent of under eighteens will be unemployed in 1983.

The increase in youth unemployment has been triggered by both the economic recession and technological changes which have reduced the demand for young unskilled labour. The increase in the youth wage, relative to adult workers, has also made youth a less attractive proposition to employers. The fact that Britain has a higher number of sixteen year old school leavers than many other advanced industrial countries exacerbates the problem: nearly 50 per cent of Britain's sixteen year olds leave school to look for work.

When YOP started, in 1978–79, it was dealing with one in eight young people. In 1979–80 it was assisting one in six, in 1980–81 it was assisting one in four and in 1981–82 there was a further increase in provision. As the number of young people using YOP has risen so the relative advantage, previously gained by programme graduates over other members of the young unemployed, has disappeared. At the same time there has been evidence of increasing dissatisfaction amongst young people on the programme and of a growing refusal to accept YOP placements.

There are four different YOP programmes: community service and environmental projects, various work preparation courses, training workshops, and Work Experience on Employers Premises (WEEP). The last two have been the most contentious but all the programmes have run into difficulties. Training workshops frequently lack capital investment and an adequate number of skilled supervisors. This means that trainees can only be familiarized with simple tasks and are unable to gain experience using the sort of equipment involved in the expanding, highly technological industries, the very industries the trainees might hope to enter. The amount of employment for those using woodwork machinery – a great favourite – is severely limited. The market for dolls' houses, cat cradles and the like is already being met by other branches of the burgeoning community industry.

WEEP has been widely criticized as a straightforward subsidy to employers, a point to which we will return. The community service schemes and the environmental projects, though free of some of the abuses of WEEP, have often been badly organized and succeeded, not in introducing young people to the world of work, but rather to a world of constant confusion. The continual increase in the target for YOP places has resulted in lax controls over funded projects, many programmes are so badly organized that the trainees are not obliged to clock in and can absent themselves with little difficulty.

When the programme was launched the MSC's then Director of Special Programmes, Geoffrey Holland, claimed that only ten per cent of programme graduates would find themselves 'reunemployed' (*Observer*, 2 April 1978). Employers who sought to abuse the scheme to obtain cheap labour would, he said, be excluded. The MSC has now conceded that one in three of the positions created has cost a permanent worker a job. It is characteristic of the MSC's performance that it took three years to discover that employers have been taking advantage of the scheme to reduce permanent staff and replace them with YOP-funded trainees. Those in the field saw this happen in 1978. The MSC has also conceded that instead of finding regular employment for 90 per cent of programme graduates, less than 40 per cent find work, with some local projects finding work for scarcely any of their trainees. In fact, it is arguable that the programme provides little direct help in the labour market. In a recent national survey of 51 programme graduates only two said that YOP had helped them to find jobs (McKie, 1981). Some young people now proceed through an MSC sponsored Employment Induction Course, into a YOP community service scheme and then, after a six month wait, they are eligible for a six month placement on WEEP. When they reach the age of 18 they are no longer the responsibility of the career's office and they graduate from WEEP to the dole queue at the local Job Centre.

The lax supervision and the use of trainees as non-unionized cheap labour are reflected in the admission that in the year ending June 1981 there were 3,000 accidents involving trainees. These included five fatalities and twenty-three amputations (*Guardian*, 20 November 1981). In spite of these figures, the growing pressure to find places on the scheme, coupled with civil service cutbacks, means even less rigorous monitoring of employers. In August 1981, the MSC acknowledged that it had already accumulated a backlog of 36,000 visits to supervise placement arrangements (*Guardian*, 25 November 1981).

Marsland *et al.* (1980), in an MSC commissioned evaluation, summarized YOP's recruitment policy thus:

> The basic recruitment policy for YOP is that it should be available to and suitable for *all* unemployed young people. Concern was expressed that it should provide for those who normally miss out, *'the less able, less self confident and the less motivated'*, and that is should reach out to the non-registered unemployed, reportedly as high as 40 per cent among black youth. The MSC was concerned that programmes might be subject to 'slippage' – the tendency to recruit more able trainees to make the scheme look more successful.
>
> Marsland, Brelsford and Terpstra,
> 1980:5 (emphasis in original)

In fact, it is precisely the socially disadvantaged and those who might be deemed to be in particular need of assistance in finding work, even in a more promising labour market, who have lost out. The scheme has been most successful in providing social skills and work experience to those in least need. Dawes *et al.* (1982), summarizing the findings from three MSC surveys, noted that in terms of employment prospects WEEP participants did comparatively well:

> This is probably because WEEP participants tend to be better qualified than the participants on other types of YOP scheme . . . some groups identified by their personal characteristics appear to do worse than other groups. In particular, blacks and those with no qualifications did worse than average, as did those with a long period of unemployment prior to their YOP scheme.
>
> Dawes, Bedeman and Harvey, 1982:12.

In the face of the continuing recession YOP's failures are hardly remarkable, though they must have come as some surprise to the MSC. The MSC has persistently portrayed youth employment as a problem rooted, not in the operation of the economy, but in the characteristics of young people. The focus on the supply side of the labour market suggests that employment is a function of a shortage of suitably skilled and motivated workers. Young people, the MSC told the nation in full page advertisements, were trapped in a vicious circle: 'I can't get a job without work experience, but I can't get work experience without a job'. The MSC claimed, in the same advertisements, that YOP was based on the best elements of existing schemes that have succeeded in helping as many as eight out of ten participants into jobs.' Not quite the 90 per cent of Mr. Holland's prophecies, but still a clear promise that YOP would make a major impact on youth unemployment.

The MSC's claims were politically attractive and no doubt helped to bolster the reputation of Britain's fastest growing quango. There was, however, already evidence that the Commission were unlikely to meet these ambitious targets. A 1978 survey revealed that half the people taking courses provided by the MSC's Training Opportunities Programme (TOPS) did not make any subsequent use of their skills and that a third remained unemployed. In short, providing the unskilled with skills and providing the skilled with new skills did not necessarily produce work. The MSC has yet to produce evidence to suggest that the YOP programme has made any difference to the amount of regular employment available to school leavers. All that has happened is that a disproportionate number of those jobs, already available for young people, have been filled by YOP trainees. Employers hiring school leavers could rely on the state providing the first six months wages for the new 'trainee'.

The American War on Poverty had provided ample evidence of the failure of supply side programmes to combat high levels of unemployment amongst young people. Expensive and elaborate training schemes had been launched with the intention of opening up fruitful careers for young people from the slums. The description of those programmes which Marris and Rein (1974) offer in their classic account, *Dilemmas of Social Reform*, could be applied word for word to YOP's impact on the disadvantaged:

> These young people suffered, not because they would not grasp at opportunities, but because they could not keep hold of them. They lack the skills, the resilience, the tolerance of authority to meet the expectation of teachers and employers. The opportunities, for them, were too few and too often spurious – designed for someone else with a different background, skin and more amenable talent. The projects did what they could to overcome prejudice, and teach young people how to disarm it. But as each door they opened led nowhere, they were continually adding ante-rooms in which an appearance of hopeful activity disguised the ultimate frustration. The economy did not really want what these young people could offer.... *However resourceful the project's employment programmes, they could do little to influence the economy which determined how many usable skills were in demand.*
>
> Marris and Rein, 1974: 125–126
> (emphasis added)

Governments who are reluctant to change the way in which the economy is run, and who lack policies for economic growth, naturally welcome the idea that what is at fault is not the socio-economic system but the individuals who are its victims. If we can tackle youth unemployment by retraining youth, and giving them that illusive work experience, then why tamper with the existing mechanisms for distributing wealth and opportunities? In that sense YOP falls firmly within the social pathology tradition of social problems. It is a tradition aptly summarized by William Ryan (1976) as 'Blaming the Victim'.

Faced with evidence of acute deprivation in many inner urban areas in the late 1960s the government responded with the Urban Programme and the Community Development Projects. These programmes saw urban poverty not as a reflection of wider inequalities or of the failure of successive governments to improve Britain's economic performance, rather poverty was a function of the peculiar life styles, values, family and community patterns of low income inner city residents. Defined in this way urban problems were amenable to government policies which were low in resource implications and which, unlike proposals for redistribution of wealth or control over the activities of multi-national corporations, did not threaten powerful interests. Similarly, faced with spiralling youth unemployment, government found it attractive to define the problem as being a function of the maladaptive characteristics of young labour market entrants, rather than a function of the increasing failure of the economic system as a whole.

YOP had two other clear political attractions: it promised an immediate reduction in the unemployment statistics and it catered to the growing concern over the social order implications of rising youth unemployment. Government work creation programmes, of which YOP is by far and away the largest, are keeping more than 300,000 people off the unemployment register. The social order implications of YOP have been visible from the start. An earlier work creation scheme, directed at young people, was the Canadian Opportunities for Youth Programme. This contributed to some of the early thinking about YOP though the scale of the latter is now far more extensive. The Canadian programme was confined to the summer months and primarily directed at students and marginal youth. It was created in response to growing youth unrest. A confidential government evaluation of the programme explicitly reviewed it in terms of its success in absorbing potentially dissident young people. Referring to the establishment and orientation of the programme, the evaluators wrote:

> The decision to focus the Summer '71 effort primarily on students, and also to some small extent on the marginal youth subculture – as opposed to dealing with youth and other disadvantaged groups generally – must be examined in terms of the perceived relationship between unemployment, inactivity, and social unrest. For it was not unemployment *per se* which was seen as creating social unrest but rather inactivity and non-participation in general.

The evaluators further reported that: 'It may be thought slightly ironic to describe these individuals as "inactive" since it was precisely their activity, rather than their idleness, which was of concern' (Loney, 1977).

The British programme has been directed at a rather different youth group, but the concern with social order has been equally explicit. The MSC warned in YOP advertisements of the dangers of 'a growing number of young people who feel discarded by the "system"'. Elsewhere they expressed the fear that growing unemployment would result in 'an ever-increasing number of young people who feel alienated and embittered'. Politicians were equally forthright. Labour Education Minister, Gordon Oakes, told a 1978 conference on education:

> With all the training and work experience in the world, some youngsters may never find a job. That is a horrifying prospect ... a growing number of youngsters are bound to develop the feeling that society has betrayed them. Such feelings can very easily lead to crime

and, even more sinister, can provide a fertile ground for the breeding of various kinds of political extremism. I do not think it is exaggerating to suggest that these factors pose a threat to the fabric of society potentially as serious as that of armed conflict between nations.

Adams, 1974:14

These fears were expressed by a number of speakers in a House of Commons debate on youth unemployment in April 1981. The chairman of the National Youth Bureau, Conservative MP John Lee, recalled his comments in the debate a year earlier: 'The social and political dangers of substantial numbers of unemployed young people cannot be overestimated. Extremists of the Left or of the Right are gathering like vultures', and he went on to warn MPs: 'Nine months later it is apparent that the schemes that were in operation were inadequate to deal with the size of the problem ... A disinterested generation will pose a threat to the cohesiveness of our society, (Hansard, 7 April, 1981, Col. 843–844).

The objective of curbing the growth of racism and vandalism amongst young people is a worthwhile one and it is hardly surprising that governments should find left wing activism worrying, but again it seems the MSC has overstated its case. The programmes have not been notably successful in attracting the most disadvantaged and alienated youngsters, particularly those from ethnic minorities. The £25.00 which is provided, significantly as an 'allowance' may be insufficiently attractive, and those who are offered sixty-five pence an hour to stack supermarket shelves may rightly see this as another rip-off. More importantly, the continuing reduction in the number of real jobs can only add to the frustration of those who complete six months YOP only to rejoin the dole queue. On the rare occasions when trainees have an opportunity to express their views accusations of 'slave labour' are commonplace. There is also growing evidence of resistance to YOP. In December 1981 Youthaid estimated that seven per cent of young people were now refusing places (Short, 1981). This may well be an underestimate particularly for ethnic minority youth. In Sheffield, in October 1981, 2,200 young people were on temporary programmes but 628 were listed, by the careers service, as not interested. In Liverpool ten per cent of the city's YOP places were unfilled (*Guardian*, 24 October 1981). The failure to raise the allowance in line with inflation means that after paying travel and other work related expenses trainees are little better off than those drawing benefit.

A genuine concern to deal with youth unemployment should suggest measures to combat the general level of unemployment. There are, however, particular attractions to work creation programmes in that they absorb a high number of the unemployed at a relatively low cost. YOP trainees are not usually eligible for union membership and receive pay well below the going rate. YOP will create 550,000 openings in 1982, at an approximate cost of £340 million, most of which is in fact recouped from savings on social security. Since EEC social funds cover 60 per cent of the cost, the government's contribution must, in reality, be negligible (*Voluntary Action*, 1982:15). In contrast, the same amount of money spent in public sector construction would provide an estimated 50,000 jobs, attract no subsidy and make a much smaller saving on benefits. There are good reasons for arguing that this expenditure would provide other tangible social benefits but for governments opposed to redistributive policies, this kind of public spending may have undesirable consequences. In addition, the beneficiaries of government work-creation programmes do not have the status of workers or the power that that implies, they are rather state dependents with no real bargaining strength. The existence of such programmes serves to depress wage levels not to raise them.

The Proposed Youth Training Scheme

The announcement of a new training scheme for sixteen year old school-leavers, to be launched in September 1983, represented not so much an acknowledgement of YOP's failings as a tightening of control over school-leavers. In the new scheme the government proposed to simultaneously remove school leavers entitlement to supplementary benefit and to reduce the allowance paid from the £25 per week received by YOP trainees in January 1982 to £15 per week[1], to be paid to those on the new scheme in September 1983, by which time the allowance would have been worth rather less than half the existing figure. This low allowance was defended, in the White Paper, on the grounds that the trainees would be engaged in a process which increased their chances of future employment and, hence, that they must be prepared to make a financial sacrifice:

> The young people catered for by the scheme will benefit from having a wider range of skills and experience. As trainees, it seems right that they should receive allowances that reflect their learning role. That is how they will make their contribution to the cost of a foundation training which improves their prospects of employment.
> Department of Employment, 1981:9.

There is no more reason to suppose that the provision of the kind of 'training' envisaged will increase the number of real jobs for young people than there is to suppose that YOP should have had a similar effect. The number of jobs for young people will after all be determined by demand in the economy as a whole not by the supply of young people pouring out of the Youth Training Scheme. In April 1982, the MSC's Youth Task Group recommended that the present allowance of £25 should be maintained and not decreased to the £15 suggested in the White Paper. The Task Group also called for a retention of entitlement to supplementary benefit for those school-leavers who declined a place on the YTS. In a statement to the House of Commons on 21 June 1982 the Minister of Employment, Mr. Tebbit, announced acceptance of these two amendments, thereby helping to smooth one major problem that the scheme will face, the transitional one. It was quite possible either that trainees on the new scheme would co-exist with remaining YOP trainees, who would have been receiving twice the allowance, or that the government might have attempted to shift the whole basis of the scheme overnight and reduced all allowances simultaneously to £15. It is typical of the way in which the scheme was cobbled together that attention appears to only have been given to this issue, or to the uproar that the actual transition would provoke, as an afterthought.

The new scheme has been presented as a more sophisticated training programme offering sixteen year olds a twelve month experience rather than the less than six months averaged on YOP. The training element has been emphasised but in fact the 'trainees' will spend three quarters of their time on work experience, leading one critic to comment:

> This makes the actual mix of work and training very similar to YOP, it calls into question the arguments for a training allowance rather than a wage and throws doubts on the proposition that the new training scheme will do away with the problem of job 'substitution'.
>
> Edginton, 1982:10

Even the Director General of the CBI, Sir Terrence Beckett, was moved to express doubts about the viability of the new scheme in the context of the industrial recession, which made it difficult, he argued, for employers to provide new training opportunities. Beckett also drew attention to the dubious prospects faced by trainees: 'Nothing could be worse for young people who have received additional training if there is no prospect of a job at the end of it' (*Guardian*, 5 March 1982).

It is not clear that the new training emphasis, even if the government were actually capable of delivering a programme which reflected it, is what is required. Existing schemes with a strong training focus were in fact experiencing some short fall in recruitment. Ford's training workshops at Dagenham and Halewood both reported difficulties in filling places (*Guardian*, 2 March 1982).

The proposal to reduce the allowance was consistent with government measures to reduce the wages of young people. The young workers' scheme offered employers a £15 per week subsidy for every young person under the age of eighteen who was taken on at a wage below £40. Those taken on at a wage below £45 were eligible for a £7.50 subsidy. The new chairman of the MSC, right winger David Young, a former real estate financier and advisor to Industry Secretary Patrick Jenkin, is on record as believing that 'the young should be a source of cheap labour because they can be trained on the job' (Walker, 1982). Soon after his appointment was announced it became clear that the MSC were working on their own scheme to withdraw *all* sixteen year olds from the labour market and impose traineeship on them, whether currently employed or not. Those currently earning more than the allowance, which in the MSC scheme would be no more than £25, would have their pay reduced to the allowance level.

The announcement of the Youth Training Scheme followed the government's decision to cut back university expenditure and consequently the level of student enrolment. This may not, at first sight, appear to directly impact on sixteen year old school-leavers, however, the reduction in post-secondary opportunities for more able or more privileged school-leavers serves to increase competition lower down the labour market. Local authority cutbacks, caused by central government policies and sometimes aggravated by the excessive zeal of local Thatcherite councils, have further reduced post-secondary educational openings in the polytechnic and further education fields. One of the ironies of the new scheme is that it proposes the equivalent of perhaps 80,000 full-time places funded by the Manpower Services Commission, in local education authority institutions (Department of Employment, 1982:8). In some further education institutions it may be that one group of staff will be leaving by one door as a new group, perhaps recently redundant school teachers, will be being recruited through another door. MSC control over the funding will give it the ability to influence the content of further education courses. Traditional academic and applied educational offerings will be reduced and replaced with lower level social and practical 'skills'-based training. The fact that a quango, the MSC, should increasingly usurp the traditional role of elected local education authorities is entirely consistent with the Thatcher government's desire to strengthen central government control and weaken local democracy. Local democracy is after all susceptible to control by alliances interested in increasing social provision to meet social need, rather than seeking to use government power to redistribute wealth to upper income groups.

The Youth Training Scheme was announced one month after the government's decision to end financial support for Industrial Training Boards and after a further fall in the number of apprenticeships. Fewer young people entered engineering apprenticeships in 1981 than in any year since records were first kept (Williams, 1981). The apparent absurdity of closing down or reducing established training and educational places for young people whilst simultaneously announcing a new £1 billion training programme only makes sense as a political manoeuvre. The new scheme will not in fact cost anything like £1 billion since much of this will be recovered from savings on supplementary benefits and through contributions from the EEC Social Fund. The scheme appears to indicate a significant government measure to combat youth unemployment, an issue which has aroused a particular concern both amongst its own backbenchers and the general public. It provides a certain window dressing for government policies, at very low cost, whilst reinforcing the dependent status of young people and removing a significant number from the unemployment totals.

The finally specious nature of the proposal becomes clear when we ask what happens at seventeen? The YOP offered seventeen year olds a central role, but under the new programme seventeen year olds will only be eligible for any places which are surplus to the demands of local sixteen year old school-leavers. At the end of the new scheme the 'graduates' will face the same future as most YOP graduates – the dole. The main difference will be that unlike their predecessors they will arrive one year sooner – seventeen year old ex-YOP trainees could, after all, always hope for another YOP scheme.

The record of job creation programmes to date is one of grand promises and paltry achievements. There is no evidence that they have had any positive effect on the availability of real work, rather they would appear to have destroyed a sizeable number of permanent jobs and provided a subsidy to employers who are not too fastidious about who pays their wages bill. The disillusionment of those who find it their fate to be shuffled from one make-work scheme to another is apparent. It remains to be seen how long the MSC can continue to win trade union support for such programmes.

Afterword

In this paper I have concentrated my criticisms on the assumptions and practices which characterize the government's response to youth unemployment. There is, of course, another story, that of the irretrievable damage which present policies have inflicted on a whole generation of young people. The damage is visible to the naked eye in the increasingly nihilistic and destructive behaviour of young people, condemned to a life without work. A MORI poll conducted among the young unemployed, to establish their views on the riots, found that two-thirds blamed unemployment for the riots, three-quarters blamed the government for unemployment and 28 per cent thought the riots were justified (Youthaid, 1981:2). Much of the violence and anti-social behaviour which is triggered by unemployment is of a less spectacular variety, its victims are other young people and the residents of decaying inner city areas.

Unemployment may contribute to anti-social behaviour and, contrary to the official wisdom, it may help to explain it, even if it does not excuse it. Not all of those denied work will respond by inflicting their anger on their neighbours. Other young people respond to the stress of unemployment through alcohol or drug abuse, mental breakdown or suicide. The magnitude of the present situation is difficult to overstate. To provide young people with a future must be a central social priority for any government concerned about the quality of life in Britain in the decades ahead. Relevant policies must be based on the recognition of the centrality of employment for the transition from adolescence to adult life. Policies directed to improving social services and refurbishing decaying urban areas would simultaneously ensure expenditure on labour intensive activities and direct resources to those most in need. The fact that solutions will not be easy is no excuse for continuing with policies whose impact is to increase unemployment and redistribute wealth in favour of the rich.

Bibliography

ADAMS, R.V. (1978) *The Unemployment Business* York Community Council, York.

DAWES, I., BEDEMAN, T. and HARVEY, J., (1982) What Happens after YOP – a longer term view, *Employment Gazette*, January.

DEPARTMENT OF EMPLOYMENT (1981) *A New Training Initiative: A Programme for Action* Cmnd. 8455, London, HMSO.

EDGINTON, J. (1982) Never mind the numbers feel the quality, *Voluntary Action*, Spring.

LONEY, M. (1977) A political economy of citizen participation, in PANITCH, L., (Ed) *The Canadian State: Political Economy and Political Power* Toronto, University of Toronto Press.

MARRIS, P. and REIN, M. (1974) *Dilemmas of Social Reform*, Harmondsworth Penguin.

MARSLAND, D., BRELSFORD, P. and TERPSTRA, E. (1980) *Community Service for Unemployed Young People* National Youth Bureau.

McKIE, D. (1981) Public wants action on new jobs for the young, *Guardian*, 30 November.

RYAN, W. (1976) *Blaming the Victim*, New York, Vintage.

SHORT, C. (1981) Letters, *Guardian*, 16 December.

VOLUNTARY ACTION (1982) *Reading Between the Lines*, Spring
WALKER, D. (1982) Young blood, *New Society*, 11 February.
WILLIAMS, S. (1981) A cheap and cosmetic exercise, *Guardian*, 15 February.
YOUTHAID (1981) *Annual Report*, London, Youthaid.

2
Experience

Factory Training or Community Scheming? A Comparative Analysis of two aspects of the MSC Youth Opportunities Programme

Tom Logan

This paper examines the assumptions made by MSC operatives about the young people to whom they are offering opportunity. Within the thetoric of the MSC it may be assumed that any form of conventional work training is seen as more desirable than other forms of preparation for life. This may be as true about the attitudes inculcated as the experience offered. Through the statements made about and from within two schemes[1] which represent conventional and alternative approaches to youth employment, I will compare the explicit and implicit models of youth opportunity that each operates.

The Training Workshop, which I visited first, exists to produce in young people a realistic approach to future work: a denial of self characterized by passivity, punctuality and depersonalized job mobility. The Community Scheme (PBWE) that I went to later accepts the possibility of long-term unemployment and seeks to develop self-awareness and self-confidence amongst its trainees, and to instil the ability to see worth in their personal territory. The question the reader is left with is not so much which scheme is relevant, fair and valid but which hybrid scheme could contain the best aspects of both (particularly bearing in mind the proposals of the New Training Initiative). The question is given greater sharpness by consideration of the fact that, whilst economically backward, the area of the North-West within which both schemes operate is attitudinally advanced in terms of the expectations, understandings and coping strategies of the young people that the schemes exist to serve.

It is by now well documented that there are many instances where practice on schemes under the Youth Opportunity Programme falls far short of what is desirable and that many trainees gain little from their experiences. The two situations herein described are both idiosyncratic and personality dependent – but they are not untypical. The point here is not to catalogue deficiencies by generalization and anecdote, but to construct a context and from there analyze the implicit models of opportunity and their implication for a future in which previous levels of employment will never be re-attained.

That the organization, management and thetoric of the training workshop and the PBWE community-linked scheme contrast is by chance[2]. They were selected by the MSC Co-ordinator of the Local Authority as representative of two types of initiative he was developing in order to meet present demands and future needs. His perception – as someone who rose from the ranks of twelve months unemployment and STEP to his current position – is acute and balances the apparently polarized initiatives to the detriment of neither. It must be stressed that whilst this interpretation of the 'data' is entirely that of the author, as much verbatim quotation and direct observation as editorial constraints would allow has been included.

The local authority which sponsors both schemes was created in 1974 and as George Martin, the MSC Co-ordinator who showed me round, puts it:

> "Every social problem you can possibly think of, including unem-
> ployment we (this Authority) inherited. Because we were the back-
> end of the City, the City threw us out and said, 'No. Now we no
> longer want it after reorganization'. That's not what they actually said
> but its virtually what they said. 'That can go and look after itself'.
> Since 1974, we've been trying to grapple with those problems, you
> know? The population explosion was worse here than anywhere else,
> and we've had the resulting problems. *And* getting them three years
> before anyone else. People will be into Schemes in two years time like
> crazy. We've been into them like crazy for the past two years already.
> We've had the problems, and we've been through the fire if you like.
> We've still got a lot to come."

So the area has had, and continues to bear, more than its share of social problems – including youth unemployment. There isn't room here to document young peoples' attitudes but my research evidence suggests that whilst economically backward, this area is attitudinally advanced in terms of the expectations and understandings of many of the young people the YOP exists to serve. The youngsters here speak sarcastically of YOP as job creation. They have grown up amongst trading estates and 'advance' factories which were already deserted by the mid-70s. Even those who might share the still high expectation of their peers in the south-east have the January 1982 school leavers figures to make them confront reality – 10 per cent in 'real' jobs, 40 per cent on Government schemes, 40 per cent officially unemployed and 10 per cent staying on in education – and this from a number of established, custom-built 1960s comprehensive schools.

Those who work for the MSC to help the young cope with such obvious lack of opportunity are also aware of the look of the place to an outsider. I comment on the presence of the new facilities. The new Sports Centre, the new Information Centre, the Law Courts and the Police Station. George replies:

> "Its cosmeticization, isn't it. See that? (pointing to a superstore). Well
> they built the library for us on the basis that they would get a
> reasonable lease on that building. That's the kind of trade off we've
> got. But the council is responsible for buildings and allocation. You
> see we inherited a lot of the housing and tried to build up. It's not the
> best way to do things. Normally you get things together – communi-
> ties if you can get them. We didn't get communities. We got a lot of

old ex-city corporation housing, plus some new housing which we put up ourselves which wasn't particularly successful. And then tried to turn that into a coherent grid pattern. We're still trying to get (the Authority) to be itself."

It is within this environment that the two approaches to youth opportunity we are to consider exist. The Training Workshop, only recently acquired and staffed, is not yet fully operational. It has only fifty six[3] of a future 100+ trainees:

"The idea is to operate from suitable premises. This is the industrial estate I've always aimed to operate from. It's not a necessarily impressive building but suitable. We tried to get one of the DOI factories here but they said they didn't want a voluntary scheme, they wanted real business. It was very disappointing – but they would rather attract 'real' work to the area. What we think we're offering *is* real work.... This place had closed down, hence the 'For Sale' notice. It's one of the ones who are leaving like lemmings. What can you do?"

(Int) "I don't know."

"Well, what you can do is try to replace it with something else."

... "Normally the scheme lasts for 12 months for the youngsters. The supervisory jobs can be extended through application to MSC so we can keep a continuity of supervisors. But we can't keep a continuity of shop floor labour. Young people have to get a job – hopefully – within the 12 months. So it's not a cushy number and they're told that when they first come in. The idea of the scheme is to give them some kind of experience and some kind of, I don't know, 'push' or backing to get a job within the time of the scheme. If they are employed within six months I'm delighted. That's the point of the scheme. It's not to employ them for twelve months then throw them back on the dole. We'll get a couple of careers supervisors, who will actively go out and canvass for places on this estate to find a place for these lads. To say, 'Look, we've got a factory down there – it's not just Work Experience, it's a mini-apprenticeship if you like – why wouldn't you take them on from here?' And that's going to be a useful function. And we've got a good selling point there. We can ask employers to come in and see if they can do anything."

So his description is about complete. The package is austere, utilitarian, functional. Are the trainees merely units to be shaped and placed? Let's see how the delegation has worked. This is the Manager, Ron McCartney, offering us a walk-and-talk guided tour:

"This is the admin area. Let's look at it this way. While there's a council there I look on it as Head Office. Of a factory complex – more and more factories. As far as I'm concerned they are just Head Office. Here there is a full administration in to give WE for all the people doing exercises on everything. We only feed back figures that we would do in a Head Office situation. So, if you can get it in your mind, this is a factory. The names they give it don't mean a thing. It's a real live factory. The thinking is real life. We'll have the same rules as a factory. There will be punishments for disobedience, there will be a formal procedure of getting rid of people if things go wrong. We'll have clocking-in clocks."

Here the LEA and MSC are delineated as a Head Office situation. Ron very forcefully mans the controls – clocking-in, rules, punishments, formal dismissal procedures – it very clearly isn't a cushy number. He reminds us regularly that it exists to offer genuine experience to the young people, but to what ends?

"We commercialize the product. I'm doing an exercise, of advertising ourself, costing measures which give experience to young people in the offices of how you do marketing. Only on a small scale, but we're live – you have certain budgets and targets to aim for. Just think of a real-life factory."

It seems impertinent to think of the dozens of real-life factories surrounding the TW which are lying empty or laying off skilled and experienced workers. But back to the tour – and with the unasked question of trainee needs still in mind.

"... This is the canteen. I also use it as a lecture room. Again a real-life situation. Young people who have to produce their own budget, who have to sell – not at a profit – but who have to balance the books, as a canteen. Also we hope to make things – cakes and what have you – to sell ... so again a commercial proposition even though the figures are downgraded 'cos it's government aided."

Is this the acceptable face of state capitalism? Are the young people commercialized marketable products too? Or trained for skills other than those of producer/consumer?:

"... This is where we do the fibreglass work ... it's an ideal situation 'cos its away. We've got a lot of regulations to worry about. Breathing and fire-risks and God knows what ... we can isolate it here. Bearing in mind what I said before, it's a real factory not a back-street place. So every regulation in the book has to be adhered to. And people know about this. So when they go from work experience they know they'll have to have certain extensions in this sort of situation. They'll know you have to have the machines guarded in such a way. A lot of schemes have too much of the back street method so although they're getting work experience, knocking nails in, they're not getting a real-life situation. Here we're trying to get it as near as we can."

More regulations. Some indication of offering the trainees knowledge which could be to do with their *rights* to safety at work, but here more to do with correct behaviour. (And a reminder that what is on offer here is vastly superior to many YOP schemes).

"This is just the general workshop. Here we do joinery ... either one-offs or mass production. It just depends on how the marketing exercise goes on and what work we can get. Initially it's a series of one-offs. We'll test the market. I'm hoping to get some brilliant ideas."

(Int) "Are the young people involved from the design stage upwards?"

"You don't know exactly what will happen. It will be just like a normal works. You'll have a suggestion box. Involve them in a Works Council, with a representative from the floor, to have a meeting each month, discuss production, safety first. Again, going back to the original thing, a real-live factory. I don't want them to think of it as training or anything like that, I want them to think of it as work, and real work and honest work."

So the trainees are involved. They do get a feel of the system as a whole. But there is no mention of delegation at the bottom of the pyramid – or trade unions, or wage negotiation – or the reality of closing if the product doesn't sell. What of the trainee-products? They are blue-overalled and uniformly intent on their variety of jobs as the boss brings around suited visitors. None are interrupted or introduced. What has the TW offered them? George replies:

"Traditionally the emphasis on Training Work-shops has been placed on training rather than work. I see it personally, as the policy-maker, that the emphasis should be on the work. Although the wages are training wages, I feel the kids need emphasis on the end product, pride in it. The end product is very important. We've all been in industry. We don't see 'training' as being the end of the line. What we see is giving work experience, proper work experience in a factory environment and from there on getting jobs. That's what we see as the end of the line, 'cos at the end of the day the end-product situation, the goods accumulated can be a spin-off into real jobs. That's what we're looking for for all of these kids."

Echoes of job creation resound from the last comments. 'Real' experience, but realistic expectations? As with all YOP, placement figures have declined with rising unemployment. The problem of maintaining motivation rises too as the rhetoric/reality gap widens. The trainees live in the *real*, real world outside the workshop. There are problems with Training Workshops as schemes generally (apart from being the most expensive opportunity per capita) attracting qualified staff when wages are low: motivating adult labour who also only have twelve months maximum; selling the social and lifeskills concept to a product-oriented, industry trained management – and allowing 'time off' the process/product conveyor to allow re-training for such skills, if bought! That training workshops have great potential has been demonstrated by some of the more cooperative experimental initiatives, but the majority are LEA funded, staffed from the unemployed industrial workforce and pragmatic in character. A better context for analysis can be given if juxtaposed against the data from the other scheme. For that we need to leave the industrial estate and enter the residential area.

The PBWE site is located in the exact centre of a high-density council estate. Here the area's problems and the young peoples' environment are revealed through the visible dereliction of the community, for example in the provision of shops which was poor at the planning stage and has been exacerbated by lack of money and the closure of many. Those shops which remain are all shut by whatever time it goes dark and all have metal grilles and shutters. Housing too is visibly vandalized, as much by ill-repair and poor maintenance as child stone-throwing and youth arson. Along this same parade of shops is sited 'the project'. George again, in his initial description, chooses to set the project and its leader within a political scenario:

"This is a community scheme – this is a project work-experience scheme, not a training-workshop, it's not funded in the same way. It started off at a Youth Centre ... but they had to find alternative accommodation in what really ... what really is a shithouse, you know. I mean it's only a flight of shops. And they've still made it successful. What they're trying to do is expand the situation. They're doing craft-work at the moment. Woodwork, some community work – fitting deadlocks on old peoples doors, some refurbishment for OAP's. And various other activities. It's a very successful scheme ... 70 per cent of the people leaving that place leave for jobs – he reckons that high ... I think he's got 40 down there at the moment ... it fluctuates. He's had an uphill battle. Not all ... how can I put it more nicely than that ... not many officers on the Council are happy with the kinds of schemes we're running at the moment. For various reasons. They see it as threats to their own jobs. They see MSC taking over the local council function. They see various things. As you probably are aware, with many bureaucrats the status quo is all ..."

Here we see the initiative coming from a youth and community base. Apparently a precarious one in terms of recognition and status:

"He originally ran a youth workshop, using local lads who were unemployed – like the rest of them – before it became a formalized scheme ... He then turned it into a scheme and he was operating very well. He then got turned out – by the council – and has now had to find accommodation up here ... It's all political ... basically the Council won't get off their backsides to do anything about the youth unemployment problem ... yet this particular person – Jim Lennon – had, right? It all became very political."

To an observer the shop-front scheme looks like a cross between an Oxfam Shop and a school craft area display case: hand-made baby/toddler clothes and toys, old newspaper pictures 'aged' and mounted on varnished wood, rustic style benches and stools, bird tables, wooden table decorations, found objects re-presented artistically. Inside the place is buzzing, literally from the sawing, planing and hammering next door (in the wood-working shop), and around us from the noise of young people on coffee break[5]. In the midst of this organized chaos, Jim Lennon, Project Leader, is less than pleased at the intrusion. As George persuades him that my interest is in understanding rather than judging, some trainees enquire about my motivation too. In between giving young people keys, instructions, tool-kits, advice (and asking them to answer the 'phone whilst we speak), Jim begins with the number one issue on his agenda – how to get the MSC to extend trainee staying time:

> "Everybody has something to offer, obviously, right across from you know, er ... people with difficulties reading and writing.... These are reasons why we want to keep people on (for more than the 12 months) ... Because, you know, we take a high proportion of people on here who are ... educationally backward, if you like, or come from bad homes or whatever. Anyway they've got some hang-ups or other.... Something's been worrying them that's held them back in getting jobs or anything like that. What we believe in is that the obvious way to cure these 'wrinkles' if you like is to mix them with people who are from different backgrounds anyway, so eventually they'll all be re-socialized together."

The vocabulary this time is socially derived, coming perhaps from client-centred therapy more than industrial work-experience. It is underpinned conceptually by a belief in creative expression, but becoming hybridized along the way:

> "Because I went to Art College and all that and we all got ourselves together ... I've always believed that art is a load of crap ... as far as people like Picasso and what's in museums and galleries go – people can't relate to it. Art is ... is what *you* actually like. If you like an old table or old desk – if you like old pieces of wood then why can't that be art? We believe that art belongs to everybody, you know. So if a young person makes something that to an 'expert' it's a load of garbage, it can be fulfilling to them." (Interruption)

> "So we started the scheme up with that idea in mind. That what we would do, we'd have young people coming in making useful objects – artistically useful objects that people could buy, really cheap, put in their homes. So – we started off, and what we found out – because we're in the area we're in, which is really depressed – these young people just had no confidence in themselves. They had no kind of ... beauty to them was just an unknown word. If you said, 'that's beautiful', you were just a little bit funny – anyway, you were looking for a belt in the nose of whatever. So we realized that the problem lay in the backgrounds of these young people, in their environment if you like. They've come from an environment where beauty or richness or love – anything good – has never taken any part or place in the home."

This experimental and rather unconventional approach did not only lack status when viewed from above – at the top of the pyramid – but below too, mis-matching the trainees socialization and expectations:

> "So what we found ourselves doing ... the Art and Craft thing sort of slowly sank into the background and the social problems were coming to the front. It took us a lot longer to convince these young people that working in an environment with their own fellows, their own friends like, was a much better way to start work – than suddenly

being thrown in at the deep end. Out of school and into a factory or whatever. This is what we thought."

Here we have the relationship first, the concept second – but what of the training and work experience? But this is a potted history amidst constant interruption, not a carefully guided tour:

"So – we started off a garden scheme, a fence-erection scheme, removal scheme, a deadlock scheme ... we've got a whole spectrum of schemes, but they're all linked with this community involvement, and with what our idea of art is. And what friendship is, and what companionship is and ... social intercourse if you like. So what we've done is built up a group of young people here who identify with each other and feel responsible for each other. So they all know that the scheme is as good as they or the next guy or girl make it. And all that means – lads wearing aprons or whatever – it doesn't matter here."

"George Martin here provided, he went to the local authority, we had loads of points in our favour ... They are still convinced that their way is the better – the conventional way, the uniform way of work if you like. But we're convinced that it's not better ... so ..."

This represents a firm rejection of the conventional work-ethic youth opportunity – it offers an alternative model – that training can be primarily in social and community 'skills'. It can be responsive to need and it can develop working experiences suited to identified wants – internal (trainee) and external (community).

"So what we take here is ... a large proportion of the 'back-end' of the educational lot, if you like. We take lads and girls who can't read or write a word. We also take a lot from the middle who want work but can't find jobs through no fault of their own. What we find out is that by mixing the two groups together it brings the lower end through. That there's no shame 'cos you think you're of low ability. And it's usually that lower end who end up being our best, you know, our success".

The problem of nine to four support ending when the group is thrown back into the deep end (of a community perhaps less than sensitized yet into the PBWE alternative way of thinking) is allowed for:

"... What it is ... is ... once you've laid down all these barriers ... – you know, 'I've been educated to this standard' or 'I'm good at football' – you've made the most important thing, this work unit. Establish that you're all pulling away for *this* works."

"We go out for an evening for other events. You'll find us out together, mining, for a drink or whatever. We're going to run a dance for them in a few weeks ... and if we can, give them some sort of identity with this area. Instead of moving away from the area, saying it's bad, there's nothing going on ... we're getting them to say 'it's a great area ... (Interruption – 'phone rings – 'Answer that one of you, find out who it is') ... this is our place, we're going to make it better''. We're having people involved, see. Instead of having people sitting down and saying 'You're doing this, you're doing that', we're trying to get these young people to stand up and say 'No, why the 'ell should we? Why isn't there a theatre, a cinema, a restaurant. Why isn't there any pubs, why isn't there any cafes, or . . .' There's absolutely nothing in (this area). Yet the young people of (this area) are known all over Europe as hooligans and vandals and all that. What does it prove? There's nothing to do.''

"On Friday for instance, we just stopped work at about four, and sat here until seven, just sitting, talking. No-one went home. It's just that it belongs to them, their own, somewhere to do. We couldn't say, 'Oh well, see you at a dance later'. There's no restaurant we can go to for a meal. . . . It's a cultural desert. I am writing forever to people trying to make them realize it's not a bad place – it's not the people's fault, it's the authority.''

This type of commitment – admirable, rare, but open to criticism of personality dependency – reveals something of the need for trainee-time extension. Time to promote trainees as active and evaluative participants in developing community awareness and support.

Here endeth the lesson. We are now ordered out by Jim beseiged as he is by a dozen youths and needing to start winding down formal operations. We are told to talk to adult labour and trainees to get the 'real' picture. What emerges from the following informal disorganized tour as we take his advice is a version of the after-care aspects of some of the scheme. Young people fit dead-locks for OAPs and go back and test them and end up visiting regularly, shopping and minding the old people and the single parent families, generally acting as a community support group. As to the training and work experience aspect, it is stressed that involvement is from initial idea to product. They, for example, collect lumber, negotiate for factory waste or 'shut-down' materials, dissemble them and re-assemble them according to their ideas. Tolerance of failure is high, as is motivation. Our guide, a supervisor, contrasts this scheme with others he has had experience of.

"It's basically what it is – job creation. But what we find is not many schemes succeed in being creative, that's the problem. (They) just end up standing at a bench all day. The way we look at it is – let him (the trainee) work at the scheme and use his imagination and his creativeness which he automatically has. We try to draw it out instead of putting the kid down and saying 'You're a nonentity'. Instead, we say, 'You're important'. But having said that we then have to say let's draw it out.''

"The satisfaction that they get also is – a lot of the youngsters come from round this area – a lot of people see what they've made, come in and put orders in. They get satisfaction out of making something which is useful. In most of these schemes you're producing and producing and producing and it's all going on the shelf – you know? What have you achieved? Nothing really. We believe in it''.

(Int) "George said you got good results at the end, when they come out?"

We did have but placements with high unemployment now (shakes head) we've had good figures but now it's difficult. Our figures do show good ... we're pretty happy with it. We'd like it to be better ... we just keep trying and trying."

The two schemes can be seen to be in juxtaposition. However, both would claim, rightly, to be operating a realistic opportunity given their knowledge, understanding and pre-existing skills. The question is not so much 'which scheme is the more relevant, fair or valid' as, 'which hybrid scheme could incorporate the best aspects of both? Assuming the New Training Initiative to not be employing redundancy in it's title then consideration of such 'live' accounts as the two presented here – representing a range of YOP in one sense – must have led to *new* initiatives being developed. A table such as the one following might serve to demonstrate the complexity and danger of operating judgement based on pre-existing models. In using the two accounts here I am not attempting to judge, although the retreat to apportioning blame is often the course taken by those whom understanding would overwhelm.

The following table is one interpretation of the data. Based on interview, observation, linguistic and semiotic preliminary analysis, and my second record of impression, it is edited and guilty of bias through processing. The accounts are negotiated with participants however who are confident of what they, as local experts, are trying to attain. The structural elements, central themes to any programme opportunity are 'listed' down the middle of the page. They are intended to help organize the beginnings of analysis.

If the New Training Initiative succeeds in best serving the needs of trainees, then by definition it is succeeding in serving the needs of society. One of the major problems in obtaining research data from young people is that of communication, negative or positive. An outsider may pick up all the bad feeling and desire to 'sound off' about what schemes offer. An insider can be fooled or fobbed off by answers designed to please someone whom the trainee might see as instrumental in improving his/her future opportunities. Certainly, as the table would suggest, those involved in the workshop appeared passive, punctual, obedient, industrious and willing to move to find work – a conventionally well-balanced correctly motivated nascent work force. And the PBWE?

One of the problems which has to be faced is the dichotomy between policy-makers and clients, with MSC operatives caught in the middle. For example a recently published MSC survey (Bedeman 1981) in which 3,000 young people on YOP schemes were interviewed in March 1980 and again a year later, reports that only about half the participants felt that they had access to someone who could help them, if they needed guidance and support. One reviewer (Kingsland 1982:23) went further in reporting on the survey describing the social and life skills components as 'awful' and: 'Totally lacking in the broader type of personality development that youth workers would hope to encourage.' This fits Jim and the trainee-centred experience. But the stated aim of the proposed Youth Training Scheme fits the TW approach.

Table 1: *Comparative Profile of the Two Schemes*

Training Workshop	STRUCTURAL ELEMENTS	PBWE/Community Scheme
Institutionally CLOSED	CONCEPTUAL CHARACTERISTIC	Institutionally OPEN
Industrial relations Market responsive	DERIVATION OF MODEL	Social Community responsive
Hierarchic Inflexible	ORGANISATION	Anarchic Flexible
Autocratic	DECISION-MAKING PROCESS	Democratic
Pre-structured	DEVELOPMENT	Organic
Conformist	ATTITUDE TO HIGHER AUTHORITY	Non-conformist
Product-centred Market responsive	OPPORTUNITY ORIENTATION	Person-centred Community responsive
Set: to be learned and ahered to Sanctioning	RULES	Negotiable: according to agreed social conventions Rewarding
Participant modular	PROCESS INVOLVEMENT	Participant wholistic
Established skill training	PEDAGOGIC MODEL	Experiential learning
Assembly Work-confidence Obedience Product-awareness Self-marketability	TRAINEE EXPERIENCE/ CHARACTERISTICS EMPHASIZED	Creativity Self-confidence Autonomy Human-awareness Self-motivation
Role specific Utilitarian Instrumental	COUNSELLING & GUIDANCE	Shared Individualized Non-directive
Alienation	ATTITUDE TO WORKPLACE	Indentification
Trainees must learn to effectively adapt to systems needs	ULTIMATE AIMS	System must learn to respond effectively to trainee needs

To equip unemployed young people to adapt successfully to the
demands of employment to have a fuller appreciation of the world of
industry, business and technology in which they will be working and
to develop basic and recognized skills which employers will require in
the future. (D of E 1981:7).

And the PBWE? Just what is on offer to those young people involved in
their community? They are also learning craft skills, but learning also how to
apply them. The emphasis seems to be on learning *first* what skills are needed
through contact with self and community. Here I will stray from interpretation into opinion. Doubtless, many of the young people in the Training
Workshop did learn a good deal, most of which was valuable. The problem is
that they, as well as 'management', are working with dangerously outmoded
models of what constitutes value in work experience. Currently, and especially after the Youth Training Scheme, an increasing percentage of our young
people will be 18 before they have left institutional learning or training. The
danger is of extending childhood without aiding the transition to adulthood.
If, during that newly extended period, we emphasize an increasingly redundant passivity and conformity to anachronistic work-patterns, then the future
work-force will be incapable of taking the reins of the industrial work-horse –
if and when it get back on its feet. If, however, we accept that the future
pattern of work has been irrevocably changed, in ways we can currently only
guess at, then self-confidence, adaptability and an ability to evaluate will be
essential skills in order to make communities work.

Notes

1 All quotes are verbatim – transcribed from tape-recordings made at the time.
Fictitious names for people involved have been employed.
2 Shortly after my visits, PBWE was amalgamated with Community Service to
become Community Projects. In principle this PBWE had already made the change.
3 So far only a very few of the trainees are girls – another aspect of the conventionalized
approach which cannot be fully explored here.
4 In referring to the selection of STEP workers the co-ordinator spoke of 'someone
who had more claim, was more qualified through unemployment'.
5 There was apparently a roughly equal gender mix here, and an apparent mixture of
social background. I noticed gender differentiation in task however, e.g. boys –
woodwork, girls – clothes.

Bibliography

BEDEMAN, T. and HARVEY, J. (1981) *Young People on YOP: A National Survey of
Entrants to the Youth Opportunities Programme* London, Manpower Services Com-
mission.
DEPARTMENT OF EMPLOYMENT (1981) *A New Training Initiative: A Programme For Action*
London, HMSO.
KINGSLAND, M. (1982) 'Reviews' in *Youth in Society*, April, No. 65, p. 23.

Community Projects: Signposts to More Radical Practice?

Mary Hopkins

YOP and its successors may be little more than a political holding operation, a new method of social control to keep young people out of the unemployment figures, and possibly off the street; an attempt to 'quell vocal political forces,... by trying to reduce young people's alienation from the economy and to instil the discipline of work' (Craig *et al* 1977:9). But these and many similar criticisms levelled at YOP have often related to Work Experience on Employers Premises (WEEP!) which involved an appalling high level of job substitution and minimum training for the young people concerned. Community Projects, which form one of the smaller sections of YOP (14 per cent of places in 1980–1, as opposed to WEEP's 67 per cent) have tended to set themselves apart from such criticism, and with some justification. They have not usually been organized through the private business sector but have been run by a variety of sponsors, roughly half of them voluntary agencies, and half local education authorities. Thus their ideology (though not always their practice) tends to have been closer to the liberal, person-centred values of teaching and youth work than the purely 'social control and work discipline' stereotype. They have also had a better record for off-the-job training, further education and counselling opportunities than WEEP (Community Schemes Resource Unit 1981:15). At their best Community Projects have provided examples of what good social education should be about.

Unless they go beyond this, however, those involved in Community Projects are in danger of colluding with the whole myth of YOP and the subsequent New Training Initiative – that 'training' will somehow 'solve' unemployment when clearly it will not. Unless Community Projects openly acknowledge this fundamental contradiction and attempt to develop a practice that arises from a clear political analysis of mass unemployment, then they are being dishonest and are condemning young people to yet another year of dependency and traineeship for the dole, however palatable and full of 'good practice' that year might be.

Youth workers who are aware of the political dilemmas of working with the young unemployed often feel they have little choice but to retreat defensively; individualizing their work and hoping that 'social education' with individuals *may* change societies, without being too clear about the links in between (Hopson and Scally 1981:78–80). This statement is not intended to be a put-down of youth work or social education ideals, but to high-light the problems faced by any politically aware practitioner. Although daily practice is often experienced as confused and limited it is through the analysis of our practice that we may begin to find answers:

> to contract out of the messy business of day-to-day problems is to deny the active, and contested nature of social and cultural reproduction: to condemn real people to the status of passive zombies, and actually cancel the future by default.
>
> Willis 1977:186

If we are not to cancel the future then we must be involved and experimenting, not just standing critically in the sidelines. I believe that there was considerable scope for experiment in Community Projects. In the rush to set up YOP schemes in response to rocketing youth unemployment from 1978 onwards, some of them were able to develop practice which, if examined more closely, could provide some of the guidelines that are needed to back up the demands made by critics of YOP for more meaningful training and job creation.

With the introduction of the New Training Initiative and major vocational preparation schemes the scope for radical or experimental practice could be drastically reduced as the whole programme becomes institutionalized and more tightly controlled. The radical Left and the Labour movement are ill-prepared to fight the regressive aspects of these proposals, because, while they have always demanded the 'Right to Work' they have developed little prescription for the type of work or training that should be aimed for. In the face of massive job losses, government attacks on union power, and punitive income policies for the unemployed, it has been difficult to progress beyond a purely defensive stance. As a result creative responses to the very real prospects of technological unemployment, de-industrialization and the 'collapse of work' (Jenkins and Sherman 1979) have been few and far between. If the call for full employment is to be followed up with specific proposals then we must develop in far more detail concepts of socially useful work and must rethink the whole relationship of education, work and training that is needed for a more equal and humane post-industrial society. What follows is an attempt to salvage from my own experience of working at Interskills, a small, independently-sponsored Community Project in Coventry, some of the elements that could provide signposts towards radical youth training policy and practice.

Process – Choice and Self-determination

Central to the philosophy of Interskills were the principles of choice and self determination by the young people for whom the scheme existed. While it was true that they had not chosen to be unemployed it was crucial to the way we worked that young people's decision to join the scheme was made out of choice. If choice is to be meaningful then it should be more than the absence of coercion or financial threats; it implies that there is a real variety of training schemes and it requires that young people have adequate information about them.

To a certain extent these conditions were met in Coventry. There was a variety of schemes, and information about them was circulated by means of a free weekly newspaper produced by the Careers Service and sent to all registered unemployed young people, including those on YOP schemes. This allowed them to make a more independent decision than if they had been totally reliant on information channelled through a Careers Officer. The closing of this newspaper late in 1981 signified a considerable reduction in young people's degree of choice and an increase in the bureaucratic power of sections of the education authority. Of course young people were not in any case dependent only on official information. They had their own networks and as a result often 'referred themselves' directly to us on the advice of friends.

Not only must the *context* within which training schemes operate be that of informed and real choice, these elements are crucial *within the scheme* as well. This can be argued first on educational grounds: that learning and understanding will never take place on a more than superficial level in a situation of coercion, or where the content of the 'education' is not seen by the student to be relevant to her own needs and life experience (Community Schemes Resource Unit 1981:42). Secondly, in the short-term at least, the majority of young people on training schemes will be unemployed at the end of their course. They will thus find themselves in a vacuum in which they have to make choices, albeit restrained by lack of income. To run a training scheme which is geared to adapting young people to forms of external authority – the supervisor/boss/timekeeping syndrome – rather than developing a sense of self directiveness and inner discipline – is completely failing to acknowledge the realities of unemployment, whatever one's views about the nature and aims of education.

The element of choice was therefore built in at all stages of a young person's progress through the scheme. Within their first week new trainees were helped to plan their own timetables. These were centred on the training section to which they had applied, but could include other training and work experience which they felt would be useful in the light of their own aims for the future. There were 'resource' sections within the scheme offering crafts and clothes making, cookery, English and maths, which trainees could choose to attend on a regular weekly basis. In a few cases use was made of courses run at local FE colleges or community schools, as well as practical work-experience sessions in business or community-care settings. The following extract from an assessment recording illustrates the way in which trainees were encouraged to participate in planning their own learning:

– November 198 –

Tracey has been in the office section for six weeks now, doing basic typing, filing and reception tasks. She has also been attending craft sessions on Wednesday and Thursday afternoons and English on Monday mornings, as agreed during her first week.

We discussed Tracey's progress over the last six weeks, her ideas about her future, and what kind of work she likes doing best. She agreed that she has not got very far with the typing as she finds it difficult to concentrate and doesn't like it much. She has an extrovert personality and it seems that the kind of office work she sees herself doing is reception work – the talking part of office work, not the writing, typing or filing part! Tracey mentioned that she had thought about working in a shop, or doing social work – so we discussed the possibility of her transferring to the community care section. She agreed to discuss this with the Community Care Supervisor. If she does transfer, we agreed that she would continue to spend one day per week on reception, and continue her English on Monday mornings. She will be finishing her craft sessions next week as she has nearly finished the jacket she wanted to make.

– June 198 –

Tracey has now completed six months in the Community Care section. After her initial training period working with under at the Family Centre, she started her external placement at Laurel House old people's home in January. During the four months she has spent there Tracey has worked hard and her attendance has been excellent. She is enjoying the work and is appreciated by the residents for her lively personality . . .

In addition to the ongoing options special courses were run within the scheme, either by scheme staff or by specialists brought in for the purpose, on topics such as welfare and legal rights, health and First Aid, job-hunting skills, rights at work and trade unions, social and community work and alternatives to unemployment. The style of these courses differed depending on the content but the emphasis continued to be on self-determination by the trainee. To a great extent the curriculum was also something over which the trainees could exercise choice – and was developed in response to their needs – rather than being run along the lines of a fixed syllabus. The content of the English and maths sessions for example does not appear exceptional – spelling, letter-writing, basic maths covering the four rules of number, and 'practical problem solving'. It was the context and style in which these were taught that enabled real learning to take place, even for those trainees who had started with a deep-seated lack of confidence and dislike of 'school, pens, and paper etc.' The appreciation by trainees of this approach was perhaps indicated by the fact that for most of the time about half of them were attending English or maths sessions regularly and only a minority never attended sessions during their time on the scheme.

Ironically, the timetables that resulted from individually negotiated learning led to difficulties when trying to encourage collective action and decision-making by trainees. They were never with the same group of people for a whole week and rarely had the opportunity to get to know and identify with all seventy five trainees who made up the scheme as a whole. This created problems in the utilization of the formal channel for collective decision-making, the Trainee's Council. The Council was successful on a number of occasions in organizing social events including a scheme holiday. It also effected some changes within the day-to-day running of the scheme, particularly over timetabling. However, it was often experienced as irrelevant by the majority of trainees, and section representatives tended to face the usual problems of an apathetic 'constituency', having to lobby hard to obtain views or backing for their plans. While this may have been a salutary experience in the problems of representative democracy it also indicated the need to search for different forms for collective decision-making.

In practice, trainees identified most strongly with their own section (community care, arts and crafts, office skills etc.) and it was on a section basis that there was most scope for group decision-making. This varied from section to section depending on the constraints of the work undertaken. Within Community Care for example, the needs of 'clients' limited flexibility to some extent, and necessitated longer term planning; whereas the Arts and Crafts section were able to decide on and plan an excursion at a few hours or days notice. The Arts and Crafts section also illustrated ways in which a group of trainees could make important choices about the direction of the work being undertaken. They were responsible for stocking and running a small craft shop and were involved, together with the supervisor, in deciding on the kind of products that should be made and sold.

Decision-making is not a 'technique' that can be isolated and practised only within a 'life and social skills' curriculum. It is a recognition of the right of any individual to determine his or her own life, and this principle should underly the structures and processes of any youth training programme. Fortunately, ideas of 'learning contracts' and 'negotiated curriculum' are now beginning to gain some ground in the discussion of 16–19 education and training: 'Vocational preparation needs to be matched to the perceived needs of the young person as much as to those of any employer, potential or otherwise' (Further Education Unit *Vocational Preparation*, quoted in Labour Party draft discussion document p. 70a). It is only on such a basis that youth training schemes can proceed if they are to avoid becoming a barely disguised attempt to raise the school leaving age' – with its compulsory attendance and fixed curriculum. A situation of which young people have had more than enough experience at school.

Our experience of operating a Community Project on the basis of negotiated learning showed it to be appreciated by the youngsters themselves, in that it gave them value and status as people capable of making decisions. Experience also showed that it is possible, and probably preferable, to operate such a system within a small scheme. Small schemes enable young people to create the close personal relationships with staff that give them the confidence and self-awareness to negotiate and discuss their learning:

> . . . a trainee is not a parcel that can be passively processed but a person who will need to make relationships with scheme staff as an important part of the experience of being a trainee. The staff – trainee relationship should form a coherent experience on the scheme rather than remain discrete and disjointed'.
>
> Brelson *et al* 1981:14

Self determination is not a question of sitting back (or being 'laid back'!) and waiting for it all to happen in an aimless atmosphere characteristic of some youth clubs and drop-in-centres. It involves flexibility of timetabling and resources combined with small group units that allow young people to develop co-operative and collective decision-making skills. It necessitates a staffing structure that allows considerable autonomy in the context of a close knit and well co-ordinated team. This is crucial if young people are to be able to make use of the resource offered by the different sections. It also requires timetabling which, while being structured enough to enable planning, also has sufficient space to allow for innovation and the take up of ideas developed by trainees. At the broader policy level it necessitates a willingness to experiment and the encouragement of a wide variety of sponsoring agencies, particularly in the voluntary sector.

This section has referred to a style of operating a training scheme, a process. There is still the question of content – 'training for what?' Do we capitulate and talk about training for unemployment? – If we decide to train young people in 'employable skills', what are they?

Content – Transferable Skills

Much of the discussion of youth training and vocational preparation is based on a theory of 'mismatch' between the skills acquired by young people in school and the skills demanded by the modern labour market. Yet what these skills are is rarely spelt out in specific terms. They are referred to vaguely as 'basic skills' such as 'calculating, practical problem solving and use of tools' (MSC/SPD 1981a:8). Some of the training literature talks of 'learning trans-ferability' and 'experiential learning' backs up proposed strategies for action with a mass of learning theory which is in danger of mystifying the real issues. The fact is that the future facing the young unemployed is uncertain, both in the long and the short term, and neither the government, the MSC, nor the radical youth workers have a sufficiently accurate crystal ball to be able to come up with *the* answer. The acknowledgement of uncertainty is not a popular pastime of politicians or professional educators. Youth workers and others with a genuine concern for the interests of young people have a responsibility to face this uncertainty honestly and not collude with vested interest of the state in maintaining the pretence of full employment just around the corner.

Nor at Interskills did we wish to take the opposite and defeatist approach of offering only 'coping' skills for unemployment.

> Even if there is no short-term prospect of increased employment there is still a need for vocational preparation. Unless we offer good quality vocational preparation we are surely condemning young people to unemployment and denying them any chance, however slight, of finding a job. Alternative ideas of 'preparation solely for unemploy-ment/leisure' whereby we do not try to prepare young people for work means that we are arbitrarily defining the boundaries of a young person's future and effectively deciding on their behalf that they will not work. In other words we are denying them the fundamental Right to Work.
>
> Community Schemes Resource Unit 1981:1

What we tried to do was to offer scope for the development of dual use or transferable skills, which could increase the young person's control over her environment and which could be used in or out of formal employment. Interpreted in this way transferable skills do have a radical and progressive use, and should not be seen only as an answer to the capitalist's prayer for an adaptable (and pliable?) workforce. There are many skills which can be used both in the context of employment and unemployment, many of which also come within the remit of social education generally with its emphasis on personal development. These skills can be divided into two main groups: organization/communication skills and practical/vocational skills.

Organizational and communication skills are learnt as much through the processes of a scheme that encourage choice and self determination, as through its content. They can also be developed within more structured courses. One of the 'curriculum developments' requested by the trainees and staff at Interskills was a job-hunting skills course which, in spite of our own doubts about running such a course in the context of 80 per cent school leaver unemployment, proved to be an ideal vehicle for the development of communication skills as well as positive response to trainees' own demands. The course helped to build confidence, particularly in formal situations, and allowed experimentation with role-playing and self presentation through practice interviews and the use of video. The content of the course was similar to many others run within YOPs, including letter-writing, formfilling, mock interview and telephone practice. The crucial point about the style of the job-hunting courses was that they were not run on a 'deficiency model', *i.e.* on the assumption that trainees lacked certain skills which, if acquired, would make them instantly employable. The context for the course was an honest approach outlining the seriousness of the unemployment situation in the area and a recognition that job hunting skills could only marginally improve job chances. However, the course was not simply an effort to improve impossible odds. It was designed to help trainees think through what they really wanted out of life in the next few years in the light of an assessment of personal and wider economic circumstances. The staff running the course also worked hard to build up the confidence of the trainees and belief in themselves as possessing abilities and qualities which were of value – even if such qualities were not demanded by the current job market.

Many of the organizational and communication skills learnt were 'transferable'. Skills in written and oral communication and the ability to operate in formal situations are valuable in increasing a young person's power and control over the world in which she lives. They can be used in order to apply for jobs, to file social security appeals, or to organize a pressure group, a sports club, or a union branch.

The vocational and practical skills offered on the scheme were also taught with 'dual use' in mind. While not denying young people their right to work, we also acknowledged the likelihood of unemployment. The scheme offered vocational training in Arts and Crafts, Basic Maintenance Skills, Catering, Office skills and Community Care work. All these areas of work are those in which – theoretically at least – jobs may be found. Yet they also involve skills which may be used in other ways – for self-employment, voluntary work, community or political activity, or simply for creative enjoyment. New skill areas were added to the scheme with this kind of transferability or dual use in mind. None of the skills offered involved high capital investment; they all possessed the possibility of development by a young person as a leisure or self-employment activity without much money or specialized premises. Many of them were also 'survival' skills whose minimum aim was to help trainees 'cope' with a difficult world.

This approach to the teaching of transferable skills requires a strategy that involves an emphasis on resources rather than fixed curriculum, since it develops through constant dialogue with the trainee about her own plans for the way in which she wishes to use these skills in the future. The linking of skills to the complex of aims held by the trainee herself also has implications for assessment. The main purpose of assessment at Interskills was not to benefit some mythical future employer – but was for the benefit of the trainee. For this reason it was a joint process in which the trainee was helped by the supervisor to reflect on her practice and to increase her own awareness of its strengths and weaknesses. In this situation, all written reports or assessments were shown to the trainee concerned. As a matter of principle no records were kept that could not be seen by the trainee. It is always necessary to remember that merely equiping trainees with a collection of skills, however 'transferable' in theory, is insufficient in practice if the rationale behind them is not understood by the learners. In other words the assumptions on which the scheme staff and management bases decisions about the development of skill areas offered in different sections do need to be made explicit to the trainees.

The case for more and better skill training for young people is a reasonable one. Britain has the dubious reputation of providing less post-16 education than most other countries in Europe. 'In Britain 40 to 50 per cent of young people who have reached the minimum school leaving age go into jobs where there is little or no systemically-planned training or further education'; by comparison the figure for France is 19 per cent, and for Germany it is 6 per cent (Labour Party Draft Discussion Document 1981:12) However, the argument for more training has been deliberately allowed to confuse and mystify the separate issue of youth unemployment and its causes, and has by implication put much of the blame for the situation back on to young people themselves. Skills are necessary if only to allow young people to add to their income from supplementary benefit, but they should be taught within a context that recognizes that they will not 'solve' the problem of unemployment.

Introducing Concepts of Alternative Work

If youth training schemes are to go beyond the traditional concepts of social education – self determination, the acquisition of personal, social and practical skills etc. – they have to tackle directly the central questions of unemployment and job creation. Community Projects were in a unique position to identify areas of social need and find new ways of meeting them. It is a sad comment on many schemes that they merely filled gaps in the social welfare system, often unimaginatively. They simply reproduced the old patterns of social relations that put young workers at the bottom of the pile – in unskilled jobs under external discipline and control. Radical practice should involve the exploration of job creation, the development of jobs and projects to meet the expressed needs of the community, and the development of new models for the social relations of work that give greater status and more meaningful work experience to young people. The complex issue of alternative work can be tackled in two ways: at the individual level, through the discussion and encouragement of self-employment, and at a collective level, through the establishment of new projects by the scheme itself.

At Interskills positive alternatives to employment were an important theme of discussions and visits during the Lifeskills course. Voluntary work and community activity, developing a leisure 'culture' of unemployment, self-employment and co-operatives were all covered during the course. A few trainees did attempt to develop ways of supplementing their income by using their skills, either during or after their time on the scheme. However, it is unlikely that many young people are going to become successful entrepreneurs with their lack of capital and work experience; as the story of one trainee illustrates:

> Ted, the Maintenance skills supervisor, told me this morning that Phil's "business plans" had come to a sad end. He had an advance for materials from his first customer last week, for the wood to make a coffee table. Hower, Phil had simply put the cash in his pocket, and this morning he found that he'd gone and spent it – without buying any wood. He's living on his own and finding it hard to manage on a trainee allowance.

Although more practical encouragement could and should be given to those few young people who want to attempt this individual route out of the unemployment trap, it is not an 'answer' to mass unemployment. Such individual enterprises are risky for the very reason that they are tied to the profit-and-loss game of the market system. If an alternative approach is taken which starts from the perspective of needs – rather than profitability – then the scope for the development of meaningful alternative work is huge. Training schemes are in a unique position to take this perspective – rather than apeing a free enterprise system just at the point when so much of it is collapsing. The scheme on which I worked developed a number of projects based on the needs both of the trainees and the community. It is perhaps significant that these projects were concerned with basic human needs; shelter – a young people's hostel project; food – the catering project; clothing – the crafts project; and child care – the Family Centre project.

The hostel project was developed in response to the need of many trainees for accommodation. The housing problems of single young people had always been chronic, but were being exacerbated by the absence of job income and the consequent prolonged dependance of their families. The most acute problems were those of young people who had been in Local Authority Care – several of whom were literally homeless for periods of time while on the scheme. A house was eventually obtained through a Housing Association and, initially, formed a project for the maintenance skills section who put in carpets and fittings. After conversion the hostel was able to accommodate five trainees. Due to the different nature of its primary function – accommodation rather than ongoing training or employment – the hostel project was separate from the main scheme in terms of management and funding.

The craft section was initially set up to provide general training in artistic skills through production of craft goods for the scheme shop. However, it gradually evolved in response to trainees' needs as it became clear that there was a market among the trainees themselves for clothes and accessories, which were fashionable but realistically priced. These products, relevant to trainees' needs, provided a more valuable training than making craft goods for a competitive and fluctuating gift trade. Dress-making and tailoring were also skills which could be of use either at a 'survival' or self-employment level once the trainees left the scheme. The catering section was set up two years later as a more conscious attempt to meet trainees' immediate needs, in this case for cheap, good food, by running a small canteen for trainees and ex-trainees which provided meals at little more than cost price. Catering was also seen as a dual use skill – valuable as a 'survival' skill, but with the potential for employment or self-employment.

Perhaps the most ambitious 'alternative work' project that fulfilled a clear community need was the Family Centre established by the scheme on a new housing estate at the edge of Coventry. The estate was a long way from the city centre and a considerable distance from any shops or community facilities. It housed many families with young children including a high proportion of single parent families; and also old people. After consultation with tenants – through meetings and surveys – the scheme obtained a house on the estate and established it as a Family Centre, accommodating pre-school activities, an emergency day care service for under fives, a mothers' group, an advice and support service, and a weekly pensioners' club. The Family Centre was staffed by one supervisor, a part-time playgroup leader, an assistant employed under the Community Enterprise Programme, and up to six trainees. In addition to meeting pressing community needs, it provided a sound training base for community care trainees, enabling close supervision for a period before they went to 'outside' placements. It also enable them to see and understand the links between the service they provided and the community.

All these projects combined the meeting of real rather than commercially stimulated needs with meaningful and challenging training and work for young people. They created work/training situations which encompassed a full and varied range of tasks for every trainee. Many of these were 'transferable' in the widest sense, from organizational and planning tasks, to the practicalities of hygiene and 'cleaning up'. They offered real responsibility through meaningful relationships with the customers or clients – who were either other young people or the mothers and children of the neighbourhood, and they illustrated to the young people concerned in a vivid practical way the existence of necessary and important work to be done.

Most economic research indicates that with de-industrialization and the decline of jobs in the manufacturing sector, the service sector has the potential for growth (Jenkins and Sherman 1978 and 1981). Community projects have been in a good position, to develop innovatory services as well as providing the training and skills that will be needed in the future. However, it has been pointed out that:

A crucial factor in whether or not the service sector will fulfil its potential to provide future growth in employment is the extent to which the political climate supports growth in public sector expenditure as a proportion of the Gross Domestic Product, or takes the view that such jobs are a burden to the productive sector of the economy impairing future investment and growth.

Community Schemes Resource Unit 1981

There is always the danger that projects such as hostels or family centres merely plug gaps in the welfare system, by substituting trainee run projects where there should be provision by the state which creates employment for qualified staff. This danger can be avoided to some extent so long as first priority is given to the quality of training offered to trainees. Where a clear case of social or community need is shown up by projects then there is a role for schemes to play in enabling their customers, the community, to press for state-run provision (see Stares 1980 for a discussion of ways of assessing the community benefit of schemes). However, the most important role for community projects in this context is that of actively raising questions with trainees and others concerning the reasons for the lack of paid jobs within the present system to serve these very real needs. By illustrating the contradiction of un-met need in a situation of high unemployment, community projects can demonstrate in a practical way that unemployment is not a technical problem but a political one.

Political Education

Young people already have low political status within society and this has been exacerbated by unemployment which has extended their period of dependence on the family. The danger of a further year or more of traineeship is that it marginalizes young people even further – isolating them from the wider community within a 'ghetto' of their unemployed peers. Community Projects have a part to play in breaking down this isolation and allowing young people to fulfil a variety of roles – both within the scheme and the community – which provide them with status and a sense of worth. Even in times of full employment the jobs done by many young people (and indeed many working class people, particularly women) tend to be low status, boring and repetitive. They are usually offered little or no responsibility, and are on the receiving end of orders and externally administered discipline. Too many training schemes for the young unemployed, particularly WEEP courses merely replicate these conditions.

An 'alternative work' approach, in the context of a philosophy and practice of self-determination, shows ways of reversing these roles and explores models for new social relationships of production. Trainees have the opportunity to prove themselves reliable and capable of exercising sensitivity, understanding and technical skills. They are offered the status of creative workers rather than passive consumers of a pre-packaged training course.

They are teachers as well as learners, service providers as well as receivers, organizers and decision-makers not simply cogs in a machine. Only by taking a variety of roles can they become fully participating members of the community. This range of more positive roles are those that young people themselves look for when they leave school. A survey of school students carried out by the Schools Council (1968) showed that they felt work was preferable to school because it offered: 'freedom and independence' 'less discipline and more treatment as an adult' 'a greater variety of tasks', the opportunity to meet 'more and different kinds of people' and 'to do things they could do rather than struggle unsuccessfully academically'. These findings illustrate the specific ingredients that make up young people's desire for work and status, and provide useful consumers' criteria on which to judge training schemes.

Our experience showed that trainees did appreciate the opportunity to meet with a variety of people within the community, particularly those concerned with unemployment – trade unionists, members of political parties, unemployment campaign organizers and the older unemployed. Discussion and dialogue with such people could sometimes prove depressing as it revealed the complexity of the issues involved – but it could also be helpful in showing trainees that unemployment was a problem that could be shared, and to which there might be collective, rather than individual, solutions. Apart from opening up informative discussions, such people provided valuable links with political parties and the labour movement which, on reflection, should have been developed much further. The trade union movement has had an ambivalent and increasingly antagonistic attitude towards MSC programmes, particularly WEEP, which has been wholly justified in many cases. But this has left young people with little practical (as opposed to rhetorical) support from trade unionists a fact which was finally recognized by some unions, notably NUPE, from 1981 onwards – when they began to recruit YOP trainees in some areas. Up to that point however, trainees who wanted to join a union had nowhere to turn.

One of the problems faced by political or union activists trying to organize around employment issues is the isolated and atomized nature of the unemployed. Youth training schemes offer a valuable forum where trade unionists can meet with young people and open up a dialogue in which both sides can learn a lot. The unionization of trainees would give them a channel of communication with the working community, a way out of their 'ghetto', that would be independent of the scheme itself. For how ever liberal and 'enlightened' a scheme's staff may be, they ultimately have authority – they represent the management – and thus find themselves in an artificial situation when it comes to encouraging certain forms of collective action, such as Trainees Councils, within the schemes. But they still have an important role to play in political education – in raising questions about the causes of unemployment for example. Unionization on its own will not achieve anything for young people unless a groundwork of political skills and information has been laid.

Issues of pay and conditions are the obvious focus for action by trainees through unions. Young people cannot play a full part in the community while they are still forced to be economically dependent. The demand for a living wage, whether in work or training, is a pre-requisite for a more equal distribution of income, work and leisure in a post-industrial society. Such a demand challenges the whole relationship of income in relation to 'jobs'. It also challenges the myth of a rapid return to full employment in the form we have known it in the past. Clearly, training schemes are not the agencies through which to make such demands; they are demands that have to be taken up through the unions (see Hannington 1977:44 and 122–129 for a description of the demands of the National Unemployed Workers Movement in the 1920s and 30s). It has been pointed out that social education (and I would include here political education) is not something that can be 'received' by young people or anyone else 'from a group of State employed personnel' within the confines of a training scheme or college of further education (Beresford 1980:4). Perhaps like freedom it has to be fought for and achieved through action within the wider community.

Community Projects, through their processes and styles of work, and their links, both practical and political, with the community, have a crucial role to play in raising these questions with unemployed young people and encouraging reflection on the situation they find themselves in. Such questions may be uncomfortable ones for government, the MSC, and many institutions involved in the unemployment business. That does not mean they should not be asked.

Bibliography

BALL, C. and M. (1979) *Fit for Work? Youth, School and (Un)Employment* London, Writers and Readers Publishing Cooperative.

BERESFORD, S. (1980) *From Social Education and Social and Lifeskills Training to Social Justice and a Real Say for Young People* Battersea Community Action (unpublished).

BRELSON, P., RIX, A., and SMITH, G. (1981) *Trainees Come First – The organizational structure of Community Projects YOP schemes* London, Manpower Services Commission.

CENTRE FOR CONTEMPORARY CULTURAL STUDIES (1981) *Unpopular Education – Schooling and Social Democracy in England since 1944* London, Hutchinson.

COMMUNITY SCHEMES RESOURCE UNIT (1981) *Scope for Skills – Vocational Preparation in YOP Community Projects* Edinburgh, CSRU.

CRAIG, G., MAYO, M. and SHARMAN, N. (1979) *Jobs and Community Action* London, Routledge and Kegan Paul.

DAVIES, B. (1979) *In Whose Interests? From School Education to Lifeskills Training* Leicester, National Youth Bureau.

DAVIES, B. (1981) *The State We're In – Restructuring Youth Policies in Britain* Leicester, National Youth Bureau.

HANNINGTON, W. (1977) *Unemployed Struggles 1919–1936* London, Lawrence and Wishart Ltd (Reprint).

HOPSON, B. and SCALLY, M. (1981) *Lifeskills Teaching* London, McGraw Hill.

JENKINS, C. and SHERMAN, B. (1979) *The Collapse of Work* London, Eyre/Methuen.

JENKINS, C. and SHERMAN, B. (1981) *The Leisure Shock* London, Eyre/Methuen.

LABOUR PARTY (1981) *The Education and Training of the 16–19 age group* Draft Discussion Document (Unpublished).

MANPOWER SERVICES COMMISSION (1981a) *Review of the third year of Special Programmes* London, Manpower Services Commission.

Mary Hopkins

MANPOWER SERVICES COMMISSION (1981b) *A New Training Initiative: A Programme for Action* London, Manpower Services Commission

MORGAN, D. (1981) Youth call up: social policy for the young *Critical Social Policy* Vol. 1 No. 2 pp. 101–110.

NATIONAL COUNCIL FOR VOLUNTARY ORGANISATIONS, EMPLOYMENT UNIT (1982) *Worksheet Feature No. 16* February 1 – The New Training Initiative – Information and Issues London, NCVO.

NATIONAL COUNCIL FOR VOLUNTARY ORGANISATIONS, EMPLOYMENT UNIT (1982) *Worksheet Digest No. 16* February 1 London, NCVO.

STARES, R. (1980) *Community Benefits of MSC Special Programmes* London, Manpower Services Commission.

TRADE UNION RESEARCH UNIT (1980) Occasional Paper No. 63 *Youth Unemployment, State Intervention and the Trade Union Role: Some Emerging Issues* Oxford, TURU, Ruskin College.

WILLIS, P. (1977) *Learning To Labour: How working class kids get working class jobs* Farnborough, Saxon House.

YOUTHAID (1980) *Quality or Collapse?* – Report of the Youthaid Review of the Youth Opportunity Programme London, Youthaid.

Inside the Work Introduction Course

Rob Fiddy

With some effort Sharon pushed herself up onto the cupboard, shuffled herself back a few inches and leaned against the wall. She pulled her long cardigan about her, and picked up a copy of The Sun:

> "Right then – Star Signs", she said. "What're you Rocky"?
> "Sagittarius".
> "Sagittarius, right ... 'Things are looking up at work, opportunities for promotion will arise and....'"
> "... off!" said Paul, who was known to the others as Rocker. "You must be bleedin' jokin'."

Sharon and Paul were two of the twelve adolescents[1] of between sixteen and eighteen years old who had enrolled on a Work Introduction Course set in a College of Further Education, Central College, in a provincial town in the East of England. Work Introduction Courses (WICs), sometimes known as Work Preparation Courses, constitute the remedial provision for unemployed school leavers, around 15 per cent of places,[2] and are organized and funded by the Training Services Division of the Manpower Services Commission. WIC students spend one day a week on a commercial or industrial placement, and the rest of the week in the classroom studying numeracy, communications, life and social skills and basic work skills training. The WIC is aimed at, according to the Trainer's Handbook:

> those young people, often lacking in self-confidence and motivation who cannot otherwise benefit fully from other opportunities under the Youth Opportunities Programme and who require a small amount of numeracy and communication instruction to enable them to take a short training course, go on a Work Experience scheme or enter normal employment.
>
> MSC 1980:1

Or, as the Careers Officer I spoke to said of her area: 'For the WIC I'm looking for somebody who needs help with reading and writing, confidence, or who just lacks a worldly feel about them ...' Prospective students must also have been unemployed for at least six weeks. The Trainer's Handbook goes on to say that: 'In England and Wales some of these young people will have been classified by schools as ESN(m) and this is the lowest level for which the WIC can cater' (MSC 1980:1). The Holland Report emphasizes that unemployment amongst young people is not an individualistic problem in that 'success or failure in getting a job is often a matter of luck and frequently determined by factors well beyond the control or achievement of the individual ...' (MSC 1977:7).

Nevertheless, a message behind the WIC, as with much of the provision for unemployed school-leavers, may be that young people's employability is a matter of training. Is the implication that the fact that the youngsters are unemployed is a consequence of personal deficiency, not the shortage of jobs? Does the 'fault' lie with the individual and is it possible through being trained in skills which the employed have received and the unemployed have missed, to improve the individuals employability? In other words, is not the logic behind a scheme which seeks to improve employability by skills training one which clearly sees unemployment amongst young people in terms of their lack of individual attainment? Setting aside for the moment the apparent paradox that a thirteen four-day a week course can succeed where eleven years of full-time education have apparently failed, the communications and numeracy classes offered by the WIC are of benefit, at least potentially, for the illiterate and innumerate. In the same vein, that which *Unpopular Education* calls 'the Orwellian sounding Life and Social Skills' (CCCS 1981:22a) can be of use to the socially inept. Basic work skills training for WIC youngsters are designed to be 'within the capabilities (of) the target group, and related to the types of jobs which are likely to be available to them in the local labour market ...' (MSC 1980:10). The Trainer's Handbook explains that WICs are not designed to necessarily place their graduates into work. In fact, as the Careers Officer went on to say, 'WICs have been fairly successful with students moving on to something else, generally a Work Experience on Employer's Premises (WEEP) course. I can't remember any young people leaving the WIC for a job!'

Since WEEP schemes also emphasize employability as one of their aims, WICs may be seen as a pre-requisite to the employability process for those who 'lack that worldly feel about them.' The Careers Officer gave her explanation for the lack of success in finding WIC graduates jobs in terms of a changing labour market. I asked her what would have happened to youngsters like those on the WIC in her area before the advent of high levels of unemployment amongst school-leavers: 'Years ago they would have gone into some form of low level job', she said. 'The kind of jobs that are no longer around ... I think companies are finding out that they can do without these sorts of people. They don't need people to do these jobs.'

If employers are discovering that they no longer need people for 'low level jobs' then there seems little point in instructing WIC students in work-oriented skills. Moreover, if selection for a WIC means that the individual has been identified as one who needs to complete that course before going on to a WEEP to begin to be made employable, then this very selection may label the individual as one who would have difficulty in holding down a job. As David Raffe has pointed out, the selectivity of Careers Officers, MSC representatives and FE lecturers in placing youngsters on various YOP schemes has enabled potential employers to discriminate between the graduates of these schemes 'much as they have at other times discriminated between the pupils from different schools' (Raffe 1983). What then of the unemployed youngster who fails to be selected for the WIC, or those who are selected, but who fail to graduate?

Sharon and Paul, along with their contemporaries on the WIC, entered Central College with expectations based much more on myth and hope than on an understanding of the rhetoric versus the reality of such a course, or a knowledge of its rationalization, its history or its projection. What follows is an attempt to portray, through their comments and opinions, the experience of one set of students, teachers and administrators in one particular situation. Although thus both geographically and temporally confined their experience may resonate throughout the existing, and indeed into the future, provision for unemployed school-leavers.

> *'At first I didn't fancy this course because I'd heard that you had to be quite dippy to be on it'.*

This statement by one WIC student indicates that the ability to discriminate between the various provisions for unemployed school-leavers is not entirely confined to potential employers. I was interested in how the students came to be WIC candidates. The initial selection was made by the Careers Officer. She explained to me that the WIC was filled by:

> "... going through the register of those that had been identified already, a register of those that we thought might be suitable ... A lot of them will have been seen by our specialist officers for the handicapped who go to the special schools, and so a lot of them will have been recommended like that. Also other careers officers might well identify them as they see them in school as possible WIC candidates ... We went through the register and identified about twenty ... people we thought might be suitable. We wrote to them and advised them to come in and discuss it, which in fact proved quite sucessful, and we ended up with about a dozen...."

Paul remembered getting a letter from the Careers Office: 'They sent a letter through saying that if I didn't do something about getting a job they were going to suspend my dole money.' Financial sanctions for not going on a course were not in fact at this time in operation. It is possible that an element of coercion in joining the WIC was mentioned by some as a means of rationalizing their presence in what they saw as low status situation, rather than it being a belief. Nevertheless, it was identified by several of the students I talked to. Carol's story was similar to Paul's: 'I got a letter from the Careers Office saying if I didn't come on the course me money would be stopped.... So I was forced to come on it'. Doug also said that he felt under some pressure: 'If you've been on the dole for a year they chuck you off if you haven't had a job within that time. So you've got to find a course.'

Paul was a bit peeved because this opportunity to introduce him to work was interfering with his place in the black economy. I asked him what he had done after he had received the letter from the Careers Office:

"I went down to see them. They said, 'Are you interested in this course?' At first I said 'No', but then I said, 'Well I'll give it a go'. Well I came up (to the College) to see Harris (the WIC tutor) and he said, 'Well, you know, this course is for people who can't find jobs very easy' and he thought I couldn't find a job very easy and so he took me on. . . . But I'd been working with this bloke on Artex ceilings for six months, while I was on the dole, but I couldn't tell them that otherwise they'd 've taken all me dole money away and probably fined me."

There were many positive reasons for being on the course as well, not least the promise of paper qualifications: 'It was my old man's idea for me to come on this course', said one of the boys, 'I started swagging money off me mum. I kept on asking her for money and she never had any and me old man says "If you want money you want to go on that course and that'll help you get a job because you get certificates after it."'

Most of the students on the WIC at Central College left school with no qualifications at all or in a few cases on or two low grade CSEs, referred to by one of the teachers as 'kiss of death qualifications in this kind of economy'. The idea of the WIC giving them 'certificates' proved very appealing to many, perhaps as a way of recouping from their lack of success at school which some saw as a prime reason for their unemployment. The course was also seen by some in terms of an immediate pay rise: '. . . (they said) we'd get £23.50 a week (now £25.00) – that's more than the dole for me and at the end we'd get a certificate. . . . I weren't too keen on the idea 'cos I didn't like school, and I thought this would be more or less like school . . . but that's different when you get here'.

The Careers Officer recognized the problem of prospective WIC students not wanting to go back to school: '(The WIC) is sometimes very difficult to sell. We've actually got to get them in and sit down and talk to them and tell them that it really isn't like school . . . and that there'll be a lot going for them if they can just get themselves into college'.

One of the things that was actually 'going for' the WIC students was an opportunity for personal development: 'I don't honestly know how they do it', continued the Careers Officer, 'but they get these youngsters much more able to cope with life. . . . Sometimes I think well, perhaps they should have done this at school, but it seems at school that it's all too easy to be put on the side and not noticed'. Some of the students were less impressed than others about the dissimilarity of the WIC to their last educational experience. 'It ain't much different from school', I was told, 'we still get woodwork and that'. Woodwork, in conjuction with leatherwork made up the 'basic-skills' training element of the course, 'there is one difference though . . . we get paid for being here'.

Carol also thought money made a difference. '. . . if you take time off here your money get stopped'. If students were absent from classes a proportion of their allowance from the MSC was deducted by the WIC tutor. Carol also had positive things to say about her WIC experience in relation to school however. 'You're not told to sit down and shut up like in school. School was more strict'. 'Oh yeah', added Tracy, 'they treat you like a sort of person, an adult here.... I suppose they're trying to sort of help you to grow up, so that when you go out to work you can behave like an adult ... that's what it's about ... helping you to adjust, sort of thing, to being a sort of adult. In school you're just a kid, if they send you a letter they address it to your parents....' I asked Paul what he thought about the course making people more mature in thirteen weeks. 'You can't get more mature in thirteen weeks', he said. 'Maybe in a year, but not in thirteen weeks.'.

'Mr. Harris says I'm employable now'

Tracy realized that one of the aims of the WIC was to help her become a 'sort of adult'. If she felt that she was employable now then she had certainly felt less so when she had left school, and was not that why she was out of work? Certainly she felt that she had changed since her schooldays:

> "I used to be really shy at school", she said, "I used to be really quiet... I don't know, I've just got more confidence, you know.... I've sort of come out of meself.... I don't think I spoke up enough at school. I just used to sit there and shrink into the seat, but I suppose that I've realized that I've got to get on ... when I used to go for jobs I used to be really mousey ... but ... I've got into the habit now and that don't bother me anymore.... I don't think that would've happened without this course".

Tracy felt that her WIC experience had increased her job chances. She assessed the usefulness of the exercise in terms of her increased potential market situation. When I asked her what she thought the course was for she replied, 'To help me get the job that I want'. Most of the students saw the WIC in terms of work preparation. Their comments on its purpose ranged from the already mentioned optimistic Tracy, via Carol, who felt it was to 'Help me get a job', to the more cautious Paul, who said it was, 'To get you used to work and to get on well with people', and Steve who thought the WIC would, 'Get me a better skill to help me work better I suppose. I dunno ... I suppose I'm looking for it to give me a better job afterwards'. The Careers Officer, as mentioned before, had no such aspirations. Nor did David Harris, the WIC tutor: 'I think all a course like this can do is to start sowing some seeds. I think it builds confidence and that's a bit of progress....'

That part of the WIC rhetoric which specified it as being primarily a stepping stone to further courses had largely not been communicated to the students. This is not to say that there were no realistic comments about the course's purpose however. 'It's better than nothing', I was told. 'It's better than sitting at home all day watching silly kind of "Going to Work" programmes on the telly". Many of the students, like Tracy, thought the course was a crash course in employability. Particular lessons and venues for work placements were evaluated in terms of future work rather than personal development. If they did feel that they had 'come out of themselves' then this was often only seen as useful in getting a job.

This attitude was not confined to the students. Many teachers, whilst realizing that personal development was a useful by-product of the thirteen week experience, saw their role purely in terms of increasing the students' employability by filling in some missing element. 'Is that why they're all out of work?' one teacher said to me. 'Is it just the bright ones who get picked and these get left behind?... Does it show up in interview I wonder, I mean Tracy's a hard working girl, and very nice, and smartly dressed, and from a nice background with lovely parents and sister....'

'It doesn't matter, at the end of the day, what you teach'

Leatherwork classes and a woodwork workshop make up the basic skills training element of the WIC curriculum at Central College. These particular vehicles for basic skills training were chosen as a pragmatic response to filling the timetable with the available skills. Mrs. Stannard is the leatherwork teacher. She had joined the College when the town's shoe industry was flourishing and had spent many years sharing her considerable talent with the clicking knife. She had a particularly good relationship with the WIC group. As one of the boys said of her, 'She's much more ... hum, I can't put a word, a name on it, but it's something like "sensitive", or some big word anyhow'. Mrs. Stannard was one of the teachers who interpreted the students' unemployment as a direct consequence of their personal lack of ability: 'They're very despondent, they've got no prospects, they've got no work. The only way I can get to them and help them is to find out the type of person they are and get to why they wouldn't get employment, and why they couldn't hold a job down'. One of the ways she felt she could accomplish this was through concentrating on the work ethic:

> "When they go into industry, which is where I suppose most of them will end up, they'll have to conform to rules.... I try to make it as near to the work situation as I can with leatherwork ... it's got to be the timing, the taking orders and a strict routine. Leatherwork is just a means to an end, it could be anything, but leatherwork helps to motivate them, it helps them to learn to take orders."

Of course, as far as instilling the rules of the workplace was concerned, Mrs. Stannard was quite correct in proclaiming her subject as 'just a means to an end'. Most of the students had not realized this about leatherwork however. Sharon preferred it to woodwork because:

> "We've got a better chance of a job with leather than wood – girls I mean. But for the boys that's different ... they could get a job in a timber yard or something. We've probably got more chance of working in a handbag shop.... You have to know something about leather even in a shop.... If I thought I could get a job with wood then I'd be more interested in wood-work. I mean I'm not likely to get a job as a carpenter".

Like Mrs. Stannard, Mr. Morris saw his teaching in the workshop in terms of preparation for the work place, in this case the factory production line: 'I thought, well if they're going to go into a job and they've just come from school it's obviously a work approach', he said. 'I am totally – as far as I can be

– work orientated. Thus, the organization of production, with time sheets and bonuses and so on'. Mr. Morris' workshop was set away from the main buildings of the College. At the start of each class the student designated as 'timekeeper' for that week noted down the arrival time of the rest of the group on a specially prepared form. Each of the students had a role to play, and they changed round weekly. One would be a storeperson, one foreman, or shop-steward or quality control and so on. Mr. Morris always played the part of manager. I asked him what the role-play was for:

> "Well, take the foreman's role. The difficulties that a foreman may have in dealing with personalities. They are actually doing their job rather than telling people what they must do because they're a bully, or that they don't like you. . . . One of the major aspects of these kids in their ability or inability to hold down a job is in their experiences with personalities. Now they can realize that to be a foreman is a role that someone else is playing".

Bonuses, in the form of being allowed out of 'work' five minutes early, are awarded by Mr. Morris for conscientiousness and good time-keeping. Similarly bonuses can be deducted for being late or messing about. A sign above the door in the workshop reads **FACTORY**, and other signs around the room lay down the rules for the various roles to be played. Those students who do not have a specific role are designated 'Employees'. They too have a sign:

EMPLOYEES
YOU SHOULD WORK AS HARD AS YOU ARE ABLE
YOU MUST FILL IN YOUR TIMESHEET AND HAVE IT SIGNED
YOU MAY APPEAL TO A TRIBUNAL IF YOU HAVE A GRIE-
VANCE
ANY BAD TIMEKEEPING OR BEHAVIOUR WILL LEAD TO A
LOSS OF MONEY

The workshop is set out like a production line with each student completing one facet of the work. One saws wood into shapes, another sands the pieces, another screws them together.

The subtleties of the factory simulation may have been overlooked by many of the students as shown by Sharon's comment earlier, but this is not to say that the workshop sessions did not have any impact.

> "We did similar things at school", said Paul, "it's not likely I'll get to be a quality controller when I get a job. Anyway it's boring . . . I don't want to work in a factory. Mr. Morris keeps going out for a cup of tea and when we said that weren't fair he said, 'That's what work is like'. I think we get too much of that (6 hours a week) I'd rather do more leatherwork".

I pointed out to Paul that he might not get a job in leatherwork either:

> "Yeah", he said. "But at least I can make something useful and take it home".

> "Can't you do that in the workshop?"

"Dunno ... I've never asked ... anyway we never finish anything and if we do it's not ours".

"You mean it belongs to the College?"

"Nah, I mean it's not yours ... I mean ... look, we all do a bit of the same thing don't we. So if we make say, twelve tool boxes ... if we all wanted to take one home we'd have a box that someone else'd made, not like in leatherwork where you choose what you make for yourself and it's yours. You just do the same all the time in woodwork".

"Maybe that's what it's like in a factory", I said.

"Yeah?... Well you can stuff it then".

There was a certain irony in Paul's final comment in that Mr. Morris' 'total work orientation' in the workshop had simulated alienation alongside the mass production process. There was also a contradiction in the implied philosophy of the basic skills training elements of the WIC. Both Mr. Stannard and Mr. Morris saw the students' unemployment in terms of their personal characteristics, and both saw their roles as that of increasing the students employability by working at their self-confidence and autonomy. The strategies they chose to accomplish this however emphasized 'learning to take orders', and the routine of the production line.

Not all the WIC teachers agreed with the work-centred approach. Sandie Smith, a part-time Life and Social Skills teacher, said she was ideologically and politically very cynical about the course. "I find it impossible to say to these youngsters, 'This is to prepare you specifically for work' because even if they did come away being better prepared for work there still aren't enough jobs, so I think you can't have it designed to do anything directly related to work." Although there were parts of her teaching which were, on the face of it, work-oriented Sandie Smith put forward the view that they had additional purposes. 'It doesn't matter at the end of the day what you teach, what's important is the attitudes that you perpetrate and the skills that they acquire. Like when we do job interviews. It's not just so that they can succeed better in an interview, it's so they can answer questions about themselves ... it's the art of communication'.

Once again the 'means to an end' argument was proving elusive. Doug was more cynical about the usefulness of the exercise: 'We do too much of that job interviewing stuff', he said. 'I bet there isn't one kid on this course who hasn't had plenty of practice in failing interviews.'

Mr. Morris and Mrs. Stannard on the one hand, and Sandie Smith on the other, reveal two sides to teaching unemployed youngsters. One one side are the conservative arguments: that youngsters should be pushed as high up the employability ladder as possible and that unemployment should only be seen as a temporary setback, both in national and personal terms. Unemployment can be overcome by increased effort and educating for unemployment would be disgraceful. On the other side are the radical arguments that education will not create jobs and that an alternative identity to that found through work must be offered to unemployed youngsters, an identity which is fulfilling and worthwhile. A complication to the argument, as far as WIC students are concerned, is found in the Careers Officer's previous comment that '... companies are finding out that they can do without these sorts of people....' This is a comment which begs the question of what is the purpose of giving WIC students instruction in 'learning to take orders' and the production line process if it was admitted that there were no suitable jobs anyway. That these were the jobs that were no longer around. Her answer was in terms of a revision of education for work rather than alternative to promoting the work ethic. "How are we all actually going to live if we can't work? I think schools do tend to think they know what education is about, and they don't ever seem to talk to employers to find out what they actually should be teaching".

Doug also had difficulty in envisaging life without work. At the end of the WIC he was anticipating going on to a WEEP course if he didn't get a job. I asked him what he thought might happen after the WEEP:

"Dunno", he said. "I'll get a job by then I suppose".

"What if there aren't any jobs to be had?", I asked.

"Well I want to work.... I suppose if I keep on looking and hanging around I'll get one".

"Have you ever thought that there might not be jobs, I mean that you may never work?"

"You mean never?... Well you've got to work...."

Jenny Evans, the WIC numeracy teacher, made a comment on life without work: "I don't know whether these kids have actually had it put to them that they might not get a job. I mean, that there may not be jobs for them. I mean that does impinge on their perception of what is going on.... You see the kids see being unemployed as a temporary thing and, of course, that's what we keep telling them."

> *'What's this course about as far as you're concerned?'*
> *'Getting told off', said Steve.*

Youngsters can be rejected from WICs, both initially on the grounds of ability, the lowest level for which the WIC can cater is ESN(M.), and during the course on the grounds of behaviour.

Four hours of the WIC were timetabled for Horticulture in the same workshop as Mr. Morris used for woodwork. The class started at 10.00 am. The girls entered the workshop and the boys stayed outside, a performance I had witnessed before. The teacher began his lesson while the boys were still outside. He said to them once, through the open door, 'Why don't you come in lads?'. They replied that they were smoking and there is no smoking in the workshop so they had better stay outside until they had finished their cigarettes. After a good ten minutes they trooped in and began to bang chairs and generally misbehave. The teacher told three of them to leave. One left immediately and, after a few minutes of argument with the teacher, he was followed by the other two. Instead of disappearing, as I had expected, all three boys hung around outside the workshop door banging on pipes, belching loudly, shouting and even rolling stones into the room so that they rang against the chairs. The teacher did his best to ignore them and the lesson, on a variety of subjects associated with the reproduction of plants, continued until 11.00 am.

"Horticulture is a waste of time", said Doug the next day. "He just rabbit on don't he?".

"Tell me about when you got thrown out", I said.

"Well we meant to do it 'cos we don't like that leasson. We're trying to do it every week ... there's me, Rocker (also known as Paul) and Steve outside having a fag 'cos it says 'Highly Inflammable' in there. The bloke said come in, but we said we'd got a fag on and what about if this place blow up ... look who's responsible, so we finished them and went in and he go 'Take a chair', but Rocker – he went a bit too far and the bloke chucked us all out".

"But when he chucked you out Steve went at once, and you and Paul stayed behind ...", I said.

"I know", said Doug, "but I wanted to find out why I got chucked out".

"But you said you wanted to get chucked out...."

"Yeah, but when I get chucked out I want to know why".

"Why did you hang around after you were kicked out?"

"Don't know", he said. "We didn't have anything to do. We didn't have any money for anything to eat and anyway the bloke said wait ... we just hung around mucking about, throwing bricks and spitting ... and aiming things through the door ..."

I asked Doug if anything had happened about the incident:

"Nah", he said. "Not about that, but later that day Steve was bunging coke cans at me and I stood beside this car so he wouldn't do it, but he bunged one and it hit the car and the owner stood there watching us, and she went and told Harris and I don't know what's gonna happen now.... I don't care, I want to leave anyhow ... as long as they chuck me out and I don't chuck meself out".

"Why would you prefer to be chucked out?".

"Because then I can get the dole. If I sack meself, sort of thing, they don't give you any money for eight weeks".

I wondered about his parents:

"Well they want me to have a job 'cos they don't think I'm doing very well here.... I come home and say 'Another row today' and they say 'Oh, what again?'. On Tuesday when I tried to get meself chucked out they said, 'Well you shouldn'y try to get yourself chucked out, you should wait until they chuck you out, like don't bother to go to your placement 'cos that'll go against you."

"But you said to me before that you wanted to be a motorcycle mechanic and your placement is at a 'bike garage isn't it?"

"I haven't got a placement", said Doug. "I was going to Smiths (a local motorcycle dealer and workshop) but I said to me parents that I wanted to leave the course and they said that it would be better if I did leave. They could see I weren't getting on very well, and that I was gonna get meself kicked out anyway.... Me Mum 'phoned up Smiths and the bloke said that he couldn't give me any training on that day, and that's what the placements are for isn't it? He was just going to make me sweep floors and that i'nt training.... I thought I'd be doing some mechanics".

"You never went to find out what it was really going to be like?"

"Nah", he said. "He told me Mum on the 'phone and she didn't think I'd stick it...."

Unlike Doug, Paul had no desire to be expelled from the WIC: "If I get chucked off me old man'll kill me ... It can't help you too much if you say you got chucked off this course".

Within a week of the horticulture and coke-can incidents, Paul and Steve were thrown out of a numeracy lesson. I asked the teacher what had happened:

"Paul and Steve were helping me collect a video from another department.... Paul pushed the video against a wall, went tearing after Steve and rugby tackled him in the corridor, screaming, 'You effing so and so' at the top of his voice, whereupon they grappled on the floor. Somebody came out of the staffroom ... and blew up at *me*. I got upset and when we got back to the classroom I took it out on the two of them and threw them out of the class".

Later that day I spoke to Steve about the fight. I wondered if anything had happened.

"I've been told that I will very likely get chucked off the course for what happened this morning and the coke-cans", he said.

"What then?"

"Dunno", said Steve, "go back on the dole more'n likely".

I asked him how he felt about that:

"Not very happy", he said.

"So you want to stay on the course then?"

"Yeah".

That Friday Steve was told that he was to be expelled from the WIC. Paul and Doug were given warnings and another chance.

I talked about the situation with David Harris, the WIC tutor who had expelled Steve.

> "Although Steve has been kicked off now, and I suppose is at a loose end", he said, "the same problem would have applied to him at the end of his thirteen weeks.... There was no evidence that he was willing to change ... that's why he's gone and the other two have stayed.... I think Steve has a psychological or physiological problem – that is hyper-activity".

If Steve was 'hyper-active' he had little opportunity to channel that energy after leaving the course. Several times during the ensuing weeks he returned to Central College to hang around in the corridors, and to get into WIC lessons if the teachers did not mind. On each occasion I asked him what he was doing with himself, and on each occasion his answer was the same, 'Not a lot'. I asked David Harris if there was any follow up on WIC youngsters after they had left the course. 'No', he said, 'but to me I don't think that's particularly important. What's important is what you can measure, what improvements you can see while they're here". Several of the WIC teachers did express concern over what happened to the students after they had left the course. One of them summed up her fears for me: 'I have this awful feeling that at the end of their time here they just fall into this dark pit."

The dangers of 'the dark pit' were more apparent for WIC failures than for those who graduated to a WEEP scheme, who at the very least had another six months of relative security in terms of 'something to do'. To be expelled from a WIC is to fail the initial test, to be demonstrably unsuitable for a WEEP course which itself aims at improving the employability of its students. Being expelled from a WIC may well be the equivalent of being labelled as unemployable. 'Graduating', on the other hand, ascribes the dubious status of being in the position of needing a thirteen week course in order to be on a par with other unemployed youngsters, awaiting a course in employability.

'OK, we've got problems ...'

Several members of the WIC staff expressed some surprise over Steve's explusion. For some the first knowledge they had of the incident came from the rest of the group when they asked if anyone knew why Steve was absent. Although there are familiar problems of inter-departmental communication in a busy and overcrowded college, one of the major reasons for the lack of communication on the WIC is the number of part-time members of staff. As the part-time numeracy teacher said to me of the part-time life and social skills teacher: "I didn't meet Sandie until we went on a course together. Her name was on the list I was sent. I contacted her because she lived near me, to see if she wanted a lift. It was only when we were driving down and chatting about what we did for a living that we realized that we taught the same kids on the same course". Part-timers are easier to employ during a freeze on full-time appointments in the face of continuing cut-backs in expenditure in further education. Anyone teaching over twelve hours a week can claim 'associate lecturer' status, with the ensuing benefits of holiday and sick pay. Part-time staff cannot claim these benefits and, as a consequence, few lecturers are taken on to teach more than twelve hours week. Because, in order to earn a living, part-timers often teach at more than one location in the town during the week they are seldom all available to be able to meet and discuss the WIC. A further obstacle to meetings is lack of motivation however. Many staff, who might otherwise have opted out, have no alternative to teaching on courses for unemployed school-leavers in a period of unprecedented cuts in education, with one of the few areas of expansion being MSC-sponsored courses. In the case of the WIC this situation is aggravated by the fact that many of the students are 'difficult' and demand and require further reserves of patience and commitment.

The WIC is also seen as being of low status. Officially, in that it is of least value in terms of points under the Burnham Scheme – with a result that lecturers who specialize in such courses have little chance of promotion and thus less time for administration and counselling, let alone less remuneration. Informally, the WIC is also seen as low status in that it attracts students of a calibre previously often not seen in Colleges of Further Education ('is it the bright ones who get picked and these get left behind ...?') a situation sometimes resented by uninvolved members of staff who may perceive a consequent eroding of their academic standing by association. Also a common complaint from the WIC teachers I spoke to was that their colleagues have no appreciation of the difficulties of their task.

Problems of communication are not confined to within the College however. I asked the lecturer in charge of courses for unemployed school-leavers about his relationship with the MSC:

> "Depends which bit you're talking about," he said. If we take the TSD, who are responsible for the WIC, then my relationship with the local man is reasonable ... he doesn't really understand what's happening ... he's an administrator. He has forms to fill in and that's what he does, he fills them in. . . . He sees a set of regulations which, as long as they're applied, is fine by him, he's not concerned with the curriculum in any way. (The regional monitors) have more interest in what's going on, but again not a gigantic amount ... they go and see a lot of courses but they don't teach on them. So coming back to my relationships. . . . I do very often find myself in a defensive position which means not saying to them, "OK we've got problems, we're not sure how to work them out, help us". We just say, "Look", you know, "it's OK".

David Harris, the WIC tutor, also mentioned the MSC's lack of teaching experience: 'They know nothing. They make judgments but they've never been in the classroom to my knowledge. They make all sorts of bloody irritating judgments without actually being there!'

The traditional autonomy of the teacher may be seen to be threatened in some way by working with representatives of the MSC. Certainly courses sponsored by the MSC are visited by 'outsiders' far more than any other existing provision in Further Education, a situation which may be seen as akin to an inspection, one undertaken, however, by figures who, unlike HMIs, are not seen as having any educational expertise. This may account for the resentment of the MSC involvement in the College and the reticence of the staff to share problems. Certainly the lecturer in charge was able to identify problems within the WIC:

> "We're incredibly under resourced in terms of staff.... There's a gigantic strain on the course tutor, I mean the job that David Harris does is almost impossible.... There's so much new work as far as FE is concerned – a simple example is paying the kids – the corridor type counselling is new in its magnitude, I don't see lecturers from other departments doing that.... A WIC tutor is a very demanding and difficult job, particularly when the system by which you get credit in education, by exam successes, or even by students saying 'You're doing a fantastic job', or by colleagues saying 'That went down really well' is all too often denied. ... That's not just here, it's in every college I've had contact with...."

'She's been bored at home on the dole for months, and now she's doing things and meeting people – she's a lot happier – that's what matters'

It was Carol's father who summed up one of the course's main attractions in the above comment. He told me that he was not concerned with his daughter becoming more employable or not, or with my interpretations of the usefulness of the course. He was concerned that his daughter had been at home since leaving school and 'fed up' until she got the opportunity to go to the College for a few weeks. It is all too easy to over-state the importance for the students of courses such as the WIC and to overlook the undeniable fact that many of them are motivated by nothing more than filling their time. (It's better than nothing, better than sitting at home watching silly kind of 'Going to Work' programmes on the telly'). It is also undeniable that many students benefit greatly from their experience on the WIC in terms of 'coming out of themselves'.

The observer of WIC courses such as this may, as I did, react negatively to the emphasis on employability, conformity and the work ethic, but it is important to note that for the students these values were what they had come to expect. Their school teachers had already told them repeatedly how important these things were, so they were not taken by surprise by the amount of time spent on them. The problem is not whether WICs make students feel more employable or more competitive in job hunting, but how these students then cope with continuing unemployment. And how long can you go on selling a deficit model to young people who will remain surplus to economic requirements?

Notes

1 Although situations are contextualized by my interpretations of my observations all direct speech is verbatim from tape recordings and has been cleared for use by the

people concerned. Similarly, all names and locations have been changed.
2 1981 figures.

Extracts from this chapter have appeared in *The Times Educational Supplement* 19 March 1982:21, and *Youth In Society* February 1982 no. 63 pp. 18–20.

Bibliography

CENTRE for CONTEMPORARY CULTURAL STUDIES (1981) *Unpopular Education* London, Hutchinson.
MANPOWER SERVICES COMMISSION (1980) *Work Introduction Course Trainer's Handbook* London, HMSO.
MANPOWER SERVICES COMMISSION (1977) *Young People and Work* (The Holland Report) HMSO.
RAFFE, D. 'Education and employment: Does YOP make a difference (and will YTS)' in GLEESON, D. (Ed.) *Youth Training and The Search For Work* Routledge & Kegan Paul (forthcoming)

WEEP: Exploitation or Advantage?

Howard Williamson

Preamble

The data discussed in this paper are the product of an area case study. It is important to emphasize that the area studied still had, at the beginning of the research period, a relatively low level of unemployment though it accelerated rapidly during this period. The data therefore relate to a specific time (1979–80). The area also had a very small ethnic minority population. Therefore, while the comments in the paper are intended to contribute to, and open up the debate about WEEP provision, the empirical data from which the arguments have been developed should not be generalized without careful consideration of their applicability to different circumstances.

Introduction

In 1976, the government established the Work Experience Programme (WEP) in an attempt to stem the growing tide of unemployment amongst the young. Anticipating that 100,000 young people would be unemployed that year, WEP was planned initially to cover 30,000 young people (Gregory and Rees 1979:8). Unlike the Job Creation Programme which had been launched in 1975 and had set the precedent for allocating considerable sums of government money for tackling the problems of the young unemployed, the Work Experience Programme was designed to permit unemployed young people with no experience of work to gain experience in a real work environment. Through such a measure young people would secure that much-needed experience without which employers would not consider them for a job, and thereby cross the bridge to work. Fears that the scheme might provide employers with cheap labour were allayed through the designation of young people on WEP as

This paper draws on research data from a study of school leavers and the Youth Opportunities Programme carried out by the Department of Social and Administrative Studies, Oxford University. The research was sponsored by the Manpower Services Commission, but the views expressed here are solely those of the writer.

'trainees' receiving an allowance, and a concomitant requirement that schemes should provide counselling and careers guidance as well as, if possible, training in social and life skills. The 'bridge to work' offered by the Work Experience Programme was considered to be reasonably successful: according to Lasko (1978:297), two-thirds of trainees found work after WEP, two-thirds of these with the employer who had given them experience.

The Work Experience Programme was essentially an urgent but temporary response to the presenting problem of youth unemployment. When increasing concern about the greater permanency of this problem led to the Holland Report's[1] recommendation of an integrated programme of work, education and training for the young unemployed, it was not surprising that the new Youth Opportunities Programme (YOP) was constructed in 1978 around the already established nucleus of the Work Experience Programme. Indeed, the Work Experience on Employers' Premises (WEEP) element of YOP has, over the three years of YOP's existence, comprised at least three-quarters of the 'work experience' component of YOP and two-thirds of the Programme as a whole[2]. In 1980–81 the highest percentage increase in entrants was in the WEEP element of YOP. The 74 per cent increase took the number of WEEP entrants to nearly a quarter of a million, from 139,000 in the previous year. Unlike most other elements of YOP, which have various 'remedial' under-stones, WEEP has carried on in the tradition of WEP, aiming to provide a bridge to work and to break into the often cited vicious circle of being unable to 'get a job without experience, but can't get experience to a job'. Further-more, it could offer employers the chance to provide opportunities to young people whom they would not have considered for permanent positions and might as a result break down their prejudices against certain groups (such as the unqualified, girls or ethnic minorities) when they observed that such young people could prove reliable and competent. Indeed, one mechanism by which YOP could act directly as a 'bridge to work' was through WEEP trainees being taken on permanently by their WEEP employers (though the Holland Report noted that if WEEP came to be regarded by employers as a 'normal avenue of recruitment' (1977:36), then it might be necessary to review the basis of funding such opportunities).

The success of WEEP in the early days of YOP was equal to that of its predecessor WEP: similar proportions of trainees found work afterwards, many with the same employer. In 1978–79 employers were still recruiting substantial numbers of young people, youth unemployment was nowhere near the levels it was to reach later (though it was considerably higher than in 1976, but YOP was concealing the gravity of the situation) and the apparent 'success' of WEEP was attracting widespread praise and only muted criticism. WEEP, after all, was also the cheapest form of YOP provision, with only marginal administrative costs on top of the allowance paid to trainees. It was acknowledged that WEEP tended to take the 'better' YOP entrants, but this was explained primarily through the *need* of less eligible young people for more sheltered provision and training and more concentrated, personalized support. Only rarely were the assumptions about the needs of the young unemployed seriously questioned (cf. Atkinson *et al.* 1982); popular and official accounts were concerned with overall numbers – of places, entrants and places filled – not so much with the distribution of opportunities or the distribution of entrants. Increasingly, however, the spectre of exploitation has gathered over WEEP. Despite some still favourable assessments, it has been observed that WEEP opportunities are skewed towards the service and distribution sectors of the labour market, most often in smaller non-unionized enterprises, frequently offering little or no training – in fact little more than a taste of unskilled work (Youthaid 1981:18). The 'success' rate of WEEP, when measured in terms of the number of trainees getting jobs afterwards, has declined (Dawes *et al.* 1982), and even the Manpower Services Commission has acknowledged that perhaps 30 per cent of WEEP sponsors are using WEEP trainees as a substitute for permanent employees. Admittedly there are still some positive features about WEEP – even the critical pressure group Youthaid (1981:18) has stated that WEEP may still be 'an excellent training ground'. Nevertheless, the view that the scheme is being abused has become increasingly prevalent as the rate of recruitment after WEEP has declined and, one must note, as employers have become more attuned to the 'free labour' opportunities afforded by WEEP. As one advertisement put it, 'And the great thing about the opportunities programme is that for six months employers will have a willing pair of extra hands about the place absolutely free'[3].

My argument in this paper will be that one cannot make bland generalizations about WEEP precisely because it embodies such diverse opportunities. Nor must judgments about its value be based upon assessments of different aspects of WEEP in isolation, such as numbers securing afterwards or trainees' subjective comments on its usefulness. A synthesis of such material must be developed which will allow conclusions to be drawn at a number of levels. For example, even if WEEP is one grand arena for the exploitation of the 'cream' of unemployed youth, this does not mean that *only* employers benefit from it. Some young people may still do well out of it, but one must ask which young people, how and why? The paper discusses the extent to which WEEP opportunities exploit or benefit young people who participate in them and asks whether the structure of YOP – and of WEEP within it – effectively excludes certain groups from the theoretical advantages of WEEP over other elements of the Youth Opportunities Programme.

Allocation 'Policies' on YOP

In almost all cases young people seeking places on YOP are 'filtered' through the Careers Service, whether or not the initiative first came from elsewhere (for example, friends or neighbours). Allocation within YOP, however, is not a mechanical process based upon the objective characteristics of prospective trainees, but the product of a complex interaction between these characteristics, various perceptions and assumptions about applicants made by Careers staff, and the occupational aspirations of young people, which indicate the greater suitability of a particular form of YOP provision. So although allocation decisions will be based to a large extent on such objective factors as qualifications or health problems, these may be modified by Careers Officers' views about young people's interests, hopes and 'prospects' (essentially subjective judgments concerning personal stability, disruptiveness, self-presentation, etc.). Within this framework, Careers staff will attempt to provide an opportunity which matches the individual's work interests. The final constraining factor, however, is obviously the availability of certain types of work opportunity in YOP, sometimes only in certain elements of YOP.

As a result of this *combination* of factors which affect allocation procedures one cannot assert categorically that some individuals are more likely to be deliberately excluded from WEEP opportunities than others. Let me take the example of young people of West Indian origin. One might wish to argue that they are less likely to enter WEEP as a result of discriminatory practices by WEEP employers or, similarly, as a result of being channelled by the Careers Service into non-WEEP forms of YOP in anticipation of discrimination against them by employers. A more liberal and favourable argument is that Careers staff believe that West Indians are more interested in further education and therefore YOP college courses are more 'appropriate' opportunities. Furthermore, in the Oxford research, most West Indian male YOP entrants went to a training workshop to do carpentry. The 'liberal' argument here is that West Indian boys often aspire to carpentry work (which was indeed the case in our sample) and the workshop was the only segment of YOP in the research area which could offer them this opportunity.

It is therefore problematic to present a unitary argument for allocation within YOP: the advocates of YOP (following Holland) might maintain that each young person is given an opportunity most suited to his or her needs; the critics are more likely to argue that places have to be filled whoever comes along. There is *some* truth in both viewpoints. With these issues in mind, I will now turn to some of the data from the Oxford study concerning who entered WEEP.

Who Enters WEEP?

In the study of 607 1979 school leavers, a total of 112 young people entered YOP. Sixty of these joined WEEP schemes, a proportion rather lower than the national one. Twenty seven trainees 'progressed' on to a second YOP scheme, twenty of these on to WEEP and of the six individuals who went on a third scheme, two entered WEEP[4]. Only seven young people went on more than one WEEP scheme; one girl actually went on three.

A disproportionate number of girls joined WEEP schemes, partly because the female YOP entrants had better qualifications and partly because of the lesser availability of alternative opportunities within YOP. It was also because of the *greater* availability of sales and clerical WEEP places, reflecting the skewed distribution of WEEP opportunities in the labour market. One Careers Officer, commenting on the decline of both job and YOP opportunities for boys in the manufacturing sector, observed:

> "... whereas in terms of work experience schemes on the girls' side ... there isn't a short supply of work experience schemes for shops and offices and, you know, you can get some low level girls taken on in supermarkets, for example, in filling shelves and so on...."

Approaching three-fifths of all 82 WEEP placements were indeed in shop and office work and over four-fifths of girls' placements were in these sectors. It might be argued, however, that since many girls 'aspire' to such work and since WEEP is the most likely of YOP schemes to lead to work afterwards[5], these 'appropriate' placements were giving girls an advantage over boys. I shall show below that this was not always the case.

Black trainees, in contrast to girls, were noticeably under-represented on WEEP, yet their qualifications were no worse than those of the white trainees. Less than a fifth of the black trainees went on WEEP as a first scheme and even of those who went on to a second scheme, relatively few progressed on to WEEP. Finally, WEEP entrants generally had better qualifications than typical YOP entrants, though as noted above some poorly qualified girls did get places on WEEP. Of course, even the 'better' trainees were only 'well qualified' in relation to unemployed young people: they were at the top of a broad band of generally poorly qualified and often disadvantaged young people from which YOP trainees are usually drawn.

In short, then, WEEP entrants were more likely to be female, white and better qualified than typical young people who joined YOP. The low representation of poorly qualified boys and West Indians on WEEP highlights again the complexity of allocation processes. A substantial majority of YOP entrants in the Oxford study were enabled to do work in which they had expressed an interest, although few were given a choice about schemes. This suggests tentatively that low qualified white boys could be accommodated to their satisfaction (at first) in training workshops and community service projects doing mechanics, carpentry, painting or bricklaying; similarly, West Indians initially welcomed the opportunity to get *training* in carpentry at the training workshop or in mechanics or office or sales work at the local college. Placements throughout YOP then were, in all but a few cases, viewed initially as satisfactory and appropriate by trainees (and, of course, by careers staff). But what were the reactions of young people once they had actually experienced the work they were expected to do on WEEP?

Reactions to WEEP

"It's useful but it don't help me to get a job"

"What I am doing is a load of rubbish ... if he is trying to say I am going to learn something from that, I'm not ... (but) they keep you on here ..."

"I have learnt quite a bit really.... I like it here and I'd like to finish what I am doing here first, so I will have the experience behind me...."

"... trolley bashing and rubbish clearing ... I didn't like the work I was doing but they put the glitter on it before I started and I wanted shop work at the time...."

These quotations from WEEP trainees clearly do not exhaust the range of possible reactions to participation in WEEP but they do illustrate that young people have diverse motivations for joining YOP and use different criteria for assessing the experience of WEEP. Even 'exploitation' does not *automatically* generate negative connotations. However, central to most trainees' assessment of their WEEP experience were the twin aspects of the quality of training and the perceived likelihood of getting a real job afterwards, preferably through being kept on. One of these aspects might be 'traded' for the other; they did not have to be complementary. But there were other dimensions to WEEP which are reflected in the quotations above.

'It's useful but it don't help me to get a job'

Rather than being a 'foot in the door' or a 'bridge to work', this comment suggests that the route to work may be rather more oblique, and the experience of WEEP may have a more indirect, if any, effect on job-getting potential. *But nor is WEEP exploitative.* It is viewed – like many trainees view other elements of YOP – as a constructive alternative to unemployment, as YOP was intended to be, combating the isolation of the dole and perhaps improving an individual's inter-personal relationships and self-confidence. In these ways, it is useful, despite the poor remuneration and the relatively low chance of it helping the individual to get a job. Both of the following individuals did not believe that their specific experience would greatly improve their chances of getting a job; nevertheless, they talked favourably about WEEP:

> "Well I am mostly talking to people because I am very shy actually. I am never that close to people so I have learnt to speak to people"

> "... that taught me how to get on with people because when I was serving I was having a chat with the customers and that, and I was getting on better with them."

Thus not all young people denigrate the value of WEEP if it is not seen to lead to a real job, but for most WEEP's contribution to an improvement in their job prospects is of prime importance, as the following example illustrates quite clearly: WEEP may be 'rubbish', but there is a job at the end of it.

'(it is) a load of rubbish ... (but) they keep you on here'

One senior staff member, in an organization which took a substantial flow of WEEP trainees and which had a policy of offering permanent employment to them once they had done six months on WEEP, made the following illuminating comment about the regulations governing the provision of WEEP places. Officially, trainees were supposed to be moved around departments in order to experience different work and to acquire a range of transferable skills, but ...

> "We found that those people we did move around we were less likely to keep. They never got to know a job thoroughly enough to become conversant with it. They never became part of the team of that department....
> So now I try to keep them in one department. This way I get a full

picture of what they are capable of doing.... I think there is a great deal of advantage to these youngsters and to ourselves as well, because after the six months we retain a higher proportion of staff that way than if they are swapped around. The Manpower Services are not too happy about it, but I think if they look at their records they will find that it has worked out better....

If we can place a lot of these youngsters after the six months I think this is far more important than giving them bits of experience in different types of work".

I have quoted this manager at some length because it suggests that some WEEP employers are operating on a different and often more specific concept of 'training' than the MSC's use of the term. This employer, for example, was undoubtedly 'training up' the young people on WEEP until they could make a positive contribution to the company. This might well be interpreted as 'substitution', though the manager in question claimed that his firm could not afford to train young people at its own expense and without WEEP would make do with either fewer workers or part-time older, experienced workers. Nevertheless, the firm was still clearly making use of labour provided free by the MSC. So was the firm which employed the boy whose comment introduced this section. That firm gave its WEEP trainees the most monotonous tasks to do, but once trainees were taken on permanently (which was company policy) their work became more pleasant and varied.

The former company, then, was training WEEP kids to an acceptable level of competence; the latter was establishing their reliability and durability. The point is that young people entering such schemes rapidly become aware that they are being 'used' (exploited) but many are prepared to put up with this provided there is a strong likelihood that they will have a real job at the end. These WEEP trainees are willing to 'trade off' a bad time on YOP (and poor money) for a good chance of a job afterwards. This is in strong contrast to those trainees on, for instance, a community service placement scheme where some are prepared to accept that there is little chance of permanent employment afterwards provided the experience is enjoyable and interesting. In this case, the trade-off is reversed.

WEEP trainees adopting a 'trade-off' approach to YOP are simultaneously exploited *and* advantaged; the bargain implicitly struck only breaks down when employers suddenly stop their policy of recruiting trainees, as the following girl explains: 'Everyone kept saying to me, "You'll get a job because everyone does", and it was a bit depressing then to find out that they wouldn't ... well I know now they won't be able to take me on, so it seems pointless to me to carry on doing it.' In such circumstances WEEP trainees feel that employers have reneged on the anticipated 'arrangement'. Not surprisingly, they become resentful when they discover that they have simply traded one bad deal for another.

'I have learnt quite a bit really ... so I will have the experience behind me'

In this, and the following example, trainees' reactions to WEEP are more clear-cut. Here the girl speaking is confident that the experience and knowledge gained on YOP will place her in a more advantageous position in the competition for work. While not necessarily expecting to be kept on, trainees adopting this perspective assert that the (albeit basic) practical 'skills' learned on YOP in a real work situation will enhance their prospects of getting a job in a similar capacity. Such a perspective is most clearly in tune with the aims and objectives of YOP as officially articulated in the Holland Report. By gaining useful experience in a range of work tasks, individuals will be better equipped for working life. Trainees backing this view of WEEP were usually well satified with its provision during their participation in the Programme, though in retrospect many were more critical of the 'training' they had received when – through no fault of their own – they were still unable to find a job.

'Trolley bashing and rubbish clearing'

The most publicized comment on WEEP provision has been related to the potentially (and sometimes very real) exploitative nature of the scheme. Once employers have convinced the MSC of their good intentions and mapped out a persuasive programme of 'training', it is argued that they have *carte-blanche* to use young people as free labour. These young people are off the unemployment register and that is the central concern of the bureaucracy dealing with the young unemployed, so the argument goes. The desperation of the Careers Service to build up WEEP opportunities and the pressures on the MSC which have not permitted its officials to monitor adequately the quality of WEEP schemes, together with an increasing awareness on the part of employers of the availability of a free pair of hands, has merely compounded the problem and reinforced accusations of exploitation. Furthermore, trainees' comments concerning exploitation are usually more incisive than observations about the more positive features of WEEP and so are more often remembered. For example, when asked that he had learned on WEEP and whether it was useful, one boy replied: 'Well, like, I do cleaning. I could leave here and become road sweeper and I'd be pretty good at it, but otherwise up to now – nothing.' Unfortunately, a tape-recording cannot capture the sardonic expression on his face! Other examples include: 'It was really boring sticking little men on pieces of wood for lamps . . . it was horrible'; and 'They seem to think we are no good because we are only Work Experience . . . they give you the worst things to do just because they haven't got time to do it'.

To counter such noteworthy criticisms, it should be emphasised that fewer than a quarter of WEEP trainees were at all negative in their overall assessment of their WEEP experience. Only a handful were wholly negative and while approaching a fifth had mixed views, a majority had generally positive reactions to WEEP.

Some further points concerning trainees' reactions to WEEP may be of interest. One requirement of employers taking WEEP trainees was, as noted above, that trainees should be moved around to get 'training' and experience in different areas of work. After all, they were receiving a training allowance (£23.50 during the research period, now £25), they were not employees receiving a wage. It has often been argued that trainees who were expected to do the same work as permanent staff would 'vote with their feet' about the disparity in levels of remuneration or would assert more strongly their *trainee* status. Yet some interesting twists to this argument emerge from the Oxford research. Certainly, there was general dissatisfaction with the training allowance amongst WEEP trainees (though amongst all YOP trainees in the sample a majority considered the allowance to be a 'fair wage' or said that at least they 'could manage' on it), but there was only rarely discontent about being expected to do the same work as permanent employees. Not only did trainees not mind about doing the same work, but they usually disliked any means by which they were segregated or distinguished from other staff, for example officially in the delivery of 'wages' or unofficially in the attitudes of other employees, as this girl maintained: they treat you as if you are the lowest and you have got to do all the dirty jobs ... they didn't just introduce us by our names, they said 'these are WEPs' ... they could have just said our names instead of 'these are WEPs', which sounds awful.

Compare the following comment by another girl: 'I think it is a very good thing for anybody to go on.... I enjoyed everything.... As soon as you went they made you feel like one of them, they really included you in everything.' WEEP trainees decidedly wanted both social and work-based integration with the regular workforce, probably to 'apparently' escape from the limbo and ill-defined statues of 'YOP trainee'. Although they often still objected to the training allowance, doing the same work enabled them to convince themselves that they had an – albeit temporary-*employment* position: 'I don't think I get paid enough but as long as I am doing something I don't care ... as long as I can say I have got a job to go to at the moment.'

In addition, many trainees believed that they would learn more if they were given a 'real job' to do, rather than if they were excluded from general work and instead given 'odds and ends' to do. This point, then, brings us full circle back to the different conceptions of 'training' held by young people, employers and the MSC.

The Outcomes of WEEP

Having discussed the diverse responses to participation in WEEP, it is important to examine what actually happened to trainees after they left WEEP. Had the critics seen through the veneer of WEEP and identified and exposed its exploitable character? Were the hopes and expectations of the advocates fulfilled?

Just over two-fifths of the 73 placements which had ended had been completed (i.e. trainees had done the full six months); there was little difference in proportion between the sexes. Reasons for non-completion were varied. A fifth found work and a similar number left voluntarily, were made redundant or transferred to another YOP scheme. Five trainees (all girls) were dismissed and three girls left because they were pregnant. An analysis of the progress in the labour market of WEEP entrants from the sample shows that, despite the greater number of girls on WEEP, they were considerably *less* likely to benefit from the most overt advantage of WEEP – that is, being offered a permanent job by the same employer. Whereas a third of the boys on WEEP were kept on and only one subsequently left (through redundancy) before the end of the study, less than a sixth of the girls were kept on and over half of these had left, been made redundant or been dismissed by the end of the fieldwork period. Furthermore, although poorly qualified girls had more chance of getting on to WEEP in the first place they did not do so well afterwards as the poorly qualified boys who entered WEEP. It should be stressed here that these findings may be specific to the nature of WEEP opportunities in the research area and a different picture may emerge elsewhere[6].

The simple facts of job-getting, however, could easily create a quite false image of the effect of WEEP in enhancing job prospects. WEEP trainees might just have fortuitously 'discovered' a job quite unrelated to the work they had been doing on WEEP. In fact we cannot definitely attribute success in job-getting to WEEP except in those cases where trainees are kept on*.

Nonetheless, the extent to which trainees got jobs doing similar work to that pursued on WEEP may be argued to reflect the efficacy of WEEP in improving competitiveness for such work. Most trainees did in fact continue in similar types of work. Of the three-fifths who worked after a WEEP experience, almost two-thirds of both boys and girls did the *same* work as they had done on WEEP. Others had done similar work, or the same work for some of the time; only a quarter found jobs which required quite different 'skills' from those they had in theory acquired on WEEP.

One might argue that those who were kept on by their WEEP employer would automatically be doing the same or similar work. But this was not always so. Some trainees, as I have explained above, were anticipating an improvement in their working conditions and a higher level of work once they ceased to be on WEEP; in contrast, other trainees were taken on as, for example, 'garage hands' having spent six months on WEEP 'training' in mechanics. One final point of interest on this subject is that those girls who did quite different work from their WEEP activities invariably reversed either clerical or sales work. In other words, those doing shop work had experienced a clerical WEEP and vice versa; this may be more indicative of the low level of skill demanded for such jobs than of the transferability of the competence acquired on WEEP!

Why the 'Bias' on WEEP?

It becomes clear that a relatively advantage group – white boys with some qualifications – gets most benefit from participation in WEEP. Even not so well

---

*Even then there is some question of whether – if substitution is so rife – employers recruit to WEEP only those they would previously have recruited to work. As one WEEP sponsor commented to me, 'The young people that I've had in the office I've found quite suitable, the type that I'd probably interview and engage anyway'. This is added confirmation that in general it is the better 'quality' YOP entrants who go on to WEEP.

qualified boys secured some gains from WEEP whereas girls, though well represented on WEEP, tended to make gains according to the level of their qualifications and even then their gains from WEEP were still far more limited than those of boys. On WEEP, then, qualifications appear to count, not only to get on to WEEP in the first place (or be put up as a candidate for WEEP by the Careers Service) but to sustain that success in the competition for real jobs. This is the crux of the matter: WEEP employers retain the right to select their trainees from a number sent by the Careers Service. This means that they can, if they wish, apply exactly the same criteria for screening applicants for WEEP as they would candidates for a real job. Of course, there will be some employers who may select in favour of more disadvantaged young people, but such altruistic impulses may often be outweighed by the consideration of the risk that these young people will require more supervision and yet contribute less to the employing company. What is more, it is not just a question of whether WEEP sponsors might take more disadvantaged individuals, but also of more concealed *pre*-selection policies by the Careers Service. Employers, after all, can only recruit (or reject) those who are sent to them. And the Careers Service may not wish to jeopardize WEEP placements by sending young people whom they (Careers staff) anticipate will be judged 'unsuitable' by employers. Should they adopt this approach, they would be unlikely to send girls for mechanics or other 'male' WEEPs, or blacks for WEEPs at all. This is, of course, a sweeping generalization but there is substantial truth within it. Careers staff can rationalize such policies not only through pragmatic concern with not risking the loss of valuable WEEP opportunities but also by arguing that it is unfair and insensitive to shatter the confidence of unemployed young people even further by sending them for WEEP placements which almost certainly they will not get.

Such a perspective sounds highly critical of an apparently collusive and *laissez-faire* Careers Service and it is easy for non-aligned academics to accuse the Service of simply reinforcing and bolstering up the traditional distribution of opportunity rather than taking a proactive role in breaking it down. But the Careers Service has to a large extent become the fall-guy, being blamed for a situation much of which is outside its control. It cannot force employers to take young people on WEEP; employers can withdraw WEEP opportunities at any time. The Careers Service is concerned primarily with generating placements and slotting as many eligible young people as possible into YOP, and its reasoning that WEEP employers will select trainees according to their traditional preferences and prejudices is clearly often accurate, as the following comment by a WEEP sponsor confirms:

"When we agreed to this Manpower thing we had a right load of weirdos come, all black Rastas, unemployable I call them – they had about half a dozen blacks with them, I haven't got anything against the blacks, but I'd rather employ a white lad to be truthful with you, because I've had a black working for me and he was the biggest rip-off merchant you have ever known in your life . . . you look at them and think no way am I going to take this kid on. I mean, he has got about half a dozen black kids sitting on the wall waiting for him when he comes in, and you can tell he doesn't give a monkey's toss."

Such rationalized racism is endemic in recruitment practices at many different levels, as Lee and Wrench (1981) have shown recently with regard to the intake of ethnic minorities into apprenticeships. But a different kind of rationalization is also a feature of allocation policies by the Careers Service within YOP. Taking a stand on these issues, in the eyes of the Careers Service, would simply reduce the precious *total* stock of YOP places, which seems to be a futile and unjustified exercise when Careers staff can find apparently logical reasons for the placement on non-WEEP elements of YOP of those young people who would probably suffer from the discriminatory practices of WEEP employers.

Conclusions

I have argued in this paper that the diversity which exists in the type and quality of WEEP places precludes any precise conclusions which may be applied to all WEEP schemes. I would maintain that a policy such as WEEP cannot be dismissed simply as 'exploitation' but neither can it radically alter opportunities in the labour market in favour of the less competitive since ultimately employers retain control over recruitment to WEEP. And as WEEP constitutes by far the largest segment of YOP, employers effectively have a powerful, if indirect, constraining role on the allocation of all young people within YOP. The Careers Service partially reinforces the problem since it is concerned primarily with the provision of YOP opportunities for all young people who are eligible for the Programme. As a result, it has an interest in developing and maintaining a sufficient number of WEEP opportunities and consequently it must keep in favour with those employers willing to offer places. Therefore the Service is likely to *pre*-select for WEEP only those young people it believes will be acceptable to prospective employers. By rationalizing the allocation of 'unsuitable for WEEP' young people to elsewhere in YOP in terms of personal choice and individual need, it can deny any *active* collusion with the discriminatory and self-interested practices of many WEEP employers. Nonetheless, with few exceptions, this creates a situation whereby any advantages which may accrue from participation in WEEP are conferred on those individuals who, relative to most YOP entrants, are already most competitive and therefore best equipped for their forthcoming struggle for scarce employment opportunities.

Notes

1 Manpower Services Commission (1977) *Young People and Work*, London, HMSO.
2 The Youth Opportunities Programme is divided into opportunities designed to offer *work preparation* and those aiming to offer *work experience*. These two elements are further divided into a number of schemes and courses offering different types of preparation and experience.
3 This was one of the earliest features promoting WEEP in this way, found in the Wolverhamption Wanderers v. Aston Villa match programme, 27 October 1979.
4 It should be noted that as a result of progression through YOP, some less well

qualified young people will be placed on WEEP if they choose to enter more than one opportunity, but only if employers can be persuaded to take them.

5 For an analysis of the effectiveness of different forms of YOP provision for different types of YOP entrant in terms of job-getting success, see O'Connor (1982).

6 For example, on the basis of a national study, Bedeman and Harvey (1982) suggest that there are only marginal differences between the sexes following WEEP, though they do not give a sex breakdown of those recruited by WEEP employers.

Bibliography

ATKINSON, P., REES, T., SHONE, D. & WILLIAMSON, H. (1982) 'Social and Life Skills: The Latest Case of Compensatory Education' in ATKINSON P. & REES, T. *Youth Unemployment and State Intervention* London, Routledge and Kegan Paul.

BEDEMAN, T. & HARVEY, J. (1982) *Young People on YOP: A National Survey of Entrants to the Youth Opportunities Programme*, MSC Research and Development Series: No 3, London, Manpower Services Commission.

DAWES, L., BEDEMAN, T. & HARVEY, J. (1982) 'What happens after YOP – a longer-term view', *Department of Employment Gazette* Vol. 90, No. 1, pp. 12–14.

GREGORY, D. & REES, T. (1979) *Work Experience: A Case Study Evaluation from South Wales* London, Manpower Services Commission.

LASKO, R. (1978) 'The Work Experience Programme', *Department of Employment Gazette* Vol. 86, No.3, pp. 294–297.

LEE, G. & WRENCH, J. (1981) *In Search of a Skill: Ethnic Minority Youth and Apprenticeships*, (unpublished), University of Aston in Birmingham.

O'CONNOR, D. (1982) 'Probabilities of employment after work experience', *Department of Employment Gazette* Vol. 90, No. 1, pp. 8–11.

YOUTHAID (1981) *Quality or Collapse?* London, Youthaid.

3
Cause and Effect

The Impact of Mass Unemployment on Careers Guidance in the Durham Coalfield

Derek Kirton

The following account of the impact of mass unemployment on careers guidance is based on interviews with twelve careers guidance practitioners, working in schools and the careers service, in three locations within the Durham coalfield.

Since the second world war, the area of the coalfield has been transformed, with the pits all but disappearing, declining from a total of over 200 to under 20 with further closures imminent. They have been 'replaced' by an amalgam of small factories, particularly in clothing manufacture, and outposts of multinational companies (Beynon & Austrin 1980). Such a mix has proved highly unstable, with unemployment levels remaining well above the national average. In the case of youth unemployment this has risen catastrophically in recent years to a situation where only around ten per cent of sixteen year olds found full time employment in 1980–81. The concern of this paper, however, lies with the effect of this collapse on the work of those in careers guidance.

Careers Guidance in Schools

In *Learning to Labour*, Paul Willis (1977) describes the teaching paradigm in terms of the exchange of knowledge for control, with teachers offering knowledge in return for co-operative behaviour on the part of pupils. Despite their high degree of introversion, schools have always sought to underpin this exchange with the stronger logic of the labour market, depicting acceptance or rejection of the paradigm as the key to occupational success or failure. Not surprisingly, it is in careers teaching, with the knowledge and control tied tightly to the world of work, that this relationship is most explicit. As Willis graphically demonstrates, the operation of the paradigm is far from smooth. Its basic tenets, such as the need for qualifications to enter desirable jobs, are subverted by the 'lads', who have very different ideas on what constitutes desirable work (tough, manual) and the 'qualifications' needed to get it (contacts and local knowledge). It could be argued, however, that this 'self-elimination' makes both the practical and ideological operation of the paradigm more effective for the majority of pupils, lessening competition and reinforcing the notion of 'just desserts'. The threat which mass unemployment poses to the paradigm is clearly of a different order. For here, the 'pay-off' for school performance is drastically reduced and may threaten willingness to perform. In this section, I consider how careers staff in six Durham schools sought to meet this threat.

Many of the problems faced by careers teachers are exacerbated rather than created by mass unemployment. Fundamental difficulties arise from the attempt to link individualist ideology to the realities of the job market. Careers guidance theory constantly stresses the need for optimisation of choice, and a non-directive, client-centred approach. 'The counsellor's prime responsibility is to his client and not any organizational body such as the school or the state' (Hayes & Hopson 1975:56–7).

The key to this process is self-assessment, whereby the client (pupil) comes to know his/her strengths and weaknesses, interests and values, and makes an appropriate career choice in the light of these. This inward focus is backed by a variety of psychologistic theories (Super 1981) which, in turn, have been criticized for their neglect of the importance of opportunity in moulding choice (Roberts 1974). Allocation of job entrants within the division of labour must be both efficient and legitimated within an ideology of 'free labour'. Such legitimation is attempted in two main ways. First, prospective entrants are encouraged to 'discover' that they are peculiarly suited for particular jobs, which as Roberts suggests, usually conform closely to available opportunities, but are nevertheless seen as 'free' choices. Second, they are encouraged to accept a competitive order as legitimate, and to recognize the possibility of having to settle for less than the ideal choice. Despite the rhetoric of 'acceptance' of pupils' interests and values there is clear recognition that the guidance practitioner has a duty to adjust these if necessary. As one careers teacher, Mr. Anderson,[1] put it, shortly after talking at length about self-assessment: 'If I got a kid in who wanted to do something he was incapable of doing, then I would put him wise, no question about that.'

Such sentiments were echoed by the other careers teachers. The importance of 'realism' is even clearer when careers teaching deals with work preparation rather than occupational choice. Whereas the latter would entail dissemination of occupational information, through books, leaflets, films, speakers, visits and so on, the former deals with interview practice, application forms or letters, entrance tests and attitudes.[2] Its emphasis is very much on the need to recognize and adjust to employer's demands, or face the consequences. Work experience is often used in this light. Mr. Walsh talked of how they would discuss, 'what happened to little Johnny when he was late for work and the foreman cuffed him round the back of the head, sort of thing. It's bringing the real world into the classroom.' Thus for pupils, the careers curriculum involves receipt of information about 'work in general' including requirements of behaviour and attitude, and more specific information to facilitate job choice, with assistance rendered to make this choice realistic. As I have suggested this is somewhat problematic at the best of times but becomes seriously threatened by the advent of mass unemployment. Careers teachers are well aware of this threat, several of them noting the tendency for youngsters faced with bleak prospects to 'simply give up'. 'There's no carrot to dangle any more'. So how do careers teachers react to this situation?

The differences in both 'philosophies' and programmes indicate that there is no set response, nor indeed any set view of exactly what careers education should involve. However, the common ground between them is also indicative of a certain situational logic; of prescriptions which are both practically and ideologically difficult to escape. I shall attempt, within the limits imposed by space, to do justice to both elements.

One of the most important factors constraining any reaction is the organization of schools. Mr. Prescott told me, 'the school is a machine. It goes on. It's in the business of churning out kids,' going on to suggest that any request for increased timetables space (at someone else's expense) was fiercely resisted. Moreover, progress should mean addition rather than substitution, the dropping of curricular elements being seen as a retrograde step. Another important factor is that a careers teacher has 'responsibility' for a particular group of youngsters. 'If there's any jobs going round here, I suppose I want my pupils to get them before anybody else's, which is a very selfish attitude but then if I'm in a job as a teacher at ... then obviously I've got to.'

Mrs. Thomas, at a nearby school, attempted to compete with Mr. Prescott's long-established work experience programme by only sending top band pupils on work experience so as build her school's reputation. An image of pupils as school representatives and awareness of the school's continuing careers needs are very important in shaping both programmes and opportunities within them. Yet there could be different responses to similar situations. For example, a shortage of work experience places was met by Mrs. Thomas adopting a fairly explicit pecking order built around motivation, proof of knowledge and interest, and so on. Of a lower band group she said: 'it's so difficult to get places there's no way I'd send most of this class. If I send them rubbish, they wouldn't take anybody after that. It seems cruel but I think they should see places as a reward.' Other teachers simply issued forms and trusted to apathy to prevent an excess of applications over places.

Mrs. Thomas' dilemma is part of a wider one, namely the relationship of the respective reward structures in school and work to each other. In one sense, these structures dovetail nicely, school imposing a hierarchy built around qualifications and work attitudes which is then roughly translated into hierarchy of occupational entry. Thus, school certifies and socializes for occupational allocation and work discipline, while they in turn provide back-up for school discipline. The nature of this relationship makes unemployment a double threat in that it undermines socialization in school which in turn undermines the future quality of labour-power.

In another sense, however, as sociologists of education have repeatedly emphasized, the two structures do not fit at all neatly.[3] Where this occurs too visibly, it is usually regarded as dangerous to the paradigm. Mr. Anderson expressed concern about the effect of a local factory employing the sons of its workers: 'Now, kids see this and they'll sharp tell you, "so-and-so's got a job at ... works and he's thick as a plank, and I never even got an interview."' One head teacher I spoke to told me how frustrating all the staff found it when the 'wrong' pupils got jobs, particularly when they were scarce. There was also a recognition that, for some, rejection of school was tied to very positive attitudes towards work. Mr. Prescott, in explaining why certain 'undesirables' were not given work experience placements on the grounds of their being untrustworthy, noted that 'you usually find that the worst kid in school goes out on work experience and you have no bother with them, just because he wants to get out there.'

It appears that the deciding factor here is the perceived effect on the school reward system. Similarly, there is an ambivalence with regard to the significance attached to qualifications and character where these are not positively correlated. As was suggested earlier, perhaps the most fundamental problem posed by mass unemployment is its attack on the exchange paradigm, knowledge for control.

In careers teaching this paradigm operates rather differently from its operation in other subjects in that the control aspect is much more closely bound to future employment requirements. This makes it potentially more vulnerable to the effects of unemployment. In particular, inculcation of the work ethic and its practicalities becomes more difficult as prospects of actual work recede.

Assuming that this does provoke changes in approach, there are two main directions in which change can occur. Either stress on the work ethic can be eased by increasing the 'non-work' elements of careers guidance or work preparation can be stepped up in the hope that the pupils will fare better in the job market and snap up the few available positions. This is further complicated by the debate on how closely education should be geared to the 'needs of industry' anyway (CCCS 1981, Reeder 1979). Careers teachers have traditionally straddled the fence on this issue, appreciating their colleagues distaste for producing 'factory fodder', yet feeling that the attitudes of pupils and parents are much closer to employers than teachers. Once again it is important to realize that there are underlying problems here, regardless of unemployment which are, nevertheless, heightened by its presence.

The careers teachers I spoke to offered very different views on the debate, though all seemed to accept the proposition that education should be closer to work requirements, especially with regard to 'basics'. Mr. Anderson went furthest on this,

> "I'll go and listen to a headmaster saying 'I am not here to provide industry with its future labour force'. Well I maintain he is, and that education is there, at whatever level, to produce either the highly trained ... or the cannon fodder in the factories. This is what education is".

Whatever stance is taken the practical problems remain. What are the 'needs of industry' at a time of unemployment? and for those who wish to move away from a work focus the question is – in which direction? So how are these problems tackled?

Mr. Walsh did so, apparently, by adopting radically different positions on different occasions. At one point he stated that,

> "if we can give them an interest in themselves and in life itself rather than the old Protestant work ethic, sort of 'thou shalt work and if you don't work you're a sinner'. That's out. I mean it's just no good trying to do that sort of thing these days."

Yet later he related how,

"we try to make them realize that there are only a few jobs on the market and therefore, to tell any particular class 'half of you are going to be unemployed. 'Now, do you want to be unemployed?' 'No sir'. 'Right, then you've got to do something to make sure that you're the one who gets a job instead of somebody else. So what we're trying to bring back, I suppose, is a kind of competitiveness that has been lacking."

Another problem was that teachers saw it as their duty to help pupils cope with the disappointments of not obtaining employment. 'It's unfair to build up hopes too much, but I try not to let them get depressed. It's not their fault they can't get a job'. Mr. Prescott elaborated on this when he said, 'to look at themselves as being a failure if they don't get employment is very, very wrong and I've got to try and show that.' Another careers teacher emphasized that there was no point making people more competitive, 'because it's not a matter of trying hard, it's a question of what's available.' Yet, equally, all insisted on the need to inculcate positive attitudes focussed on employment. As Mr. Prescott remarked, 'I've still got to teach for those people that could look for employment.' The dilemma was certainly felt, often acutely, but almost invariably the practical outcome was towards more postive, competitive solutions. Why should this be so? I would argue that the answer lies chiefly in the structural location of careers teaching, the particular options within this location and the consequences of choosing other options.

In spite of the oft-repeated rhetoric (e.g. Moor 1976:133) calling for mutual reconciliation of the respective emphases of education and industry, there is no doubt that if there is to be any movement, it will be of the former towards the latter rather than vice-versa. Youth employment theorists may muse along the lines of 'perhaps it is the jobs themselves which should be changed and not the people' (Keene 1969:63) but this is hardly on the agenda, at least not in the sense Keene intends. Careers teachers are faced with a situation where, in broad terms, the labour market is unalterable, but pupils are not. Moreover, there are the needs of schooling itself, to fill regular timetable slots constructively, to maintain discipline, to gain results with 'their' pupils and to conform to the perceived wishes of colleagues, parents and so on. Thus, despite considerable recognition of its problems, it is the positive solution which tends to win out. This pattern manifests itself in various ways. A generation (and class) gap between employers and many youngsters with regard to dress, hairstyles, attitudes etc. was frequently noted, with the careers teacher professing as much if not more sympathy with the latter. Practical resolution of the problem was to promote pupil conformity without taking direct responsibility for doing so. For Mr. Walsh, this meant saying to pupils. 'O.K., we want you to be yourself, but if you want the job you've got to be somebody else. You've got to act, to dress up. You're acting a part when you go for that interview'. Despite the obvious contradiction both elements are important. 'Being yourself' is an important component of the ideological world of consumer sovereignty, free labour and democracy. Thus its negation, in the face of the necessity for the propertyless to work, is usually somewhat apologetic in tone.

Mr. Prescott talked of being uneasy about moulding youngsters in this way and acting as an 'establishment figure'. Yet he resolved this problem by getting the same inculcation across in a 'reasoned' rather than 'authoritarian' way. Mr. Anderson resolved the 'who's values?' dilemma by making an implicit distinction between types of middle class values, those of the educationalists who mistakenly saw pupil motivation in terms of the thirst for knowledge, and those of employers whose instrumental view was more in line with the pupils themselves.

A further indication of the underlying pressure for a positive approach was given in the delight with which certain teachers greeted isolated examples of jobs remaining unfilled for want of qualified applicants. Concrete examples of 'missed opportunities' from the real world were clearly manna for the positive approach and consequently received far greater attention than any number of contrary examples. Skilled vacancies were especially prized in that the opportunities lost were greater, and because of their greater capacity to reinforce the paradigm. There was also considerable reluctance to damage motivation by dealing more than fleetingly with unemployment or even the Youth Opportunities Programme for which most of the pupils were destined. The notion that preparation for unemployment is both practically difficult and morally wrong has many adherents. Baxter (1973:119) having noted that the requisites of a worthwhile careers programme become 'all but impossible' in areas of high unemployment goes on, 'but I hope we shall never "educate for unemployment" which is a contradiction in terms and the sort of defeatism-realism we can do without.'

For one deputy head, a similar perspective was justified both positively and negatively. Confessing that he had 'baulked at the idea of teaching people to be unemployed', he continued, 'everybody wants to work because that's still the thing that gives purpose in life. Now once you take that away and say to people, "well, you are just not going to work", what do you put in its place?' Some, such as Mr. Prescott, dealt with unemployment at the end of the programme where it could do least damage to the whole.

As regards YOP, only Mr. Anderson said he made it clear to pupils that it had distinct disadvantages, namely its temporary nature, often with little change of permanent employment, the possibility that its 'training' may not be recognized, and that being on probation was a double-edged sword, allowing youngsters to prove themselves 'incapable' as well as capable and therby creating extra pressure for them. He felt this last point to be particularly important where employers had the option of a steady stream of trainees. More typical was Mr. Prescott, who, despite a local keep-on rate of under 5 per cent summed up his approach as follows;

> "I try to stress it as a training scheme. It gives you experience. It might
> be a passport later on because you've had six months experience.
> Insofar as showing its drawbacks I wouldn't think I'd deal with that
> very much, unless they brought it up."

One teacher worked very hard, and he felt, successfully on the positive aspects of YOP. All negative views were challenges to be overcome, quibbles about the level of payment put down to 'high expectations' (this apparently included the proposed NTI allowance of £14.40 per week). In other words, the positive perspective often shows an almost boundless willingness to 'sell' official packages and preserve correct attitudes among future workers. Often in higher classes, YOP was never mentioned at all, much to the annoyance of some pupils.

The Careers Service

Without doubt the major influence on the recent development of the careers service has been the massive growth of YOP. Its pervasive impact has led to changes both within the service and in its external relations. The rise of YOP has been accompanied by the increasing appointment of unemployment specialists who do, in effect, the work of ordinary careers officers minus their school involvement. In certain cases, unemployment specialists who have no careers qualification have been appointed and this has led to friction between them and mainstream officers, partly over respective salary gradings but also over their differing 'philosophies'. A district careers officer, Miss Robinson, talked of the two week 'D of E' course for unemployment specialists, 'Where they're D of E-ized and they haven't quite got the philosophy that we've been given on our courses namely that it's very much the kids that matter, not numbers.' This swipe was aimed less at the unemployment specialists and more the Manpower Services Commission, who were seen as replacing the careers service's traditional 'client-centred' orientation by a numbers game where the emphasis was on placement *per se* rather than the suitability of particular placements for their occupant trainees.[4] As Miss Barton put it, 'Careers officers tend to think that a bad scheme is worse than no scheme. Other people tend to think that any sort of occupation is better than nothing'.

Almost all those I interviewed felt these divergent principles to some extent, although there were differing views as to how serious a problem this was and the extent to which unwelcome pressure could be avoided.[5] As to external relations, there had been two major effects of YOP. First, through monitoring trainees' progress, an increased contact with employers but contact in increasingly stereo-typical form. Second, an inevitable increase in the amount of contact with youngsters, given that all progression to YOP is via the careers service, that almost all unemployed youngsters are at least offered schemes, and that a succession of placements or offers may mean several visits to the service. The effect of these changes will be discussed later, but one perceived effect of coping with this greater volume of work was that the service had 'put itself on the map'.

As in the case of careers teaching, it is worth considering the degree to which unemployment and counter-measures such as YOP create new and distinct problems and how far they merely aggravate existing ones.

Those in the careers service recognize that they are overwhelmingly regarded as a job placement agency and seem reasonably happy to accept this role. Yet under such an umbrella designation there are various possible approaches to the task. These vary according to the weight given to, on the one hand, job-seekers' interests and 'characteristics' and, on the other, 'manpower needs'. Clearly there are many factors which pull the former towards the latter but the precise manner of their combination is always negotiable with careers officers among the chief arbitrators. The question of whether a bad scheme is better than no scheme is a case in point. One unemployment specialist (also a qualified careers officer) thought not and made no attempt to fill the small minority of schemes she considered to be 'bad'. Most careers officers and, indeed, many MSC monitors had tried to have particular schemes improved or scrapped, where training requirements or other stipulations were being flagrantly violated. A cynical view of this might be to regard it as a sop to consciences and/or a feeble attempt to maintain credibility as monitors, citing as evidence the large amount of abuse (substitution, displacement, probation, skivvying) which is allowed to go unchallenged.

Perhaps it would be fairer to say that any programme which seeks to keep youngsters closely in touch with a labour market which has no use for them is inevitably riddled with contradictions and that this has important consequences for careers guidance workers.[6] To understand those consequences requires consideration of the ideological and practical orientation of careers officers and the way they are affected by the disappearance of full-time jobs for school-leavers.

There are various factors which support the idea that the 'client-centred' approach is the 'starting point' for the work of careers officers. First, such an approach has a considerable weight of tradition behind it, reflected especially in training. This is important, for while it is true that there has always been the 'ulterior motive' of adjustment to the labour market, this has usually been done in such a way as to conform as closely as possible to the job-seeker's stated interests. Second, such a focus is encouraged by individual interviews, case records and caseloads. Thus, those who are interested in particular types of YOP schemes are given priority when places are available, while the disciplinary approach to unemployment is less in evidence.[7] Third, there is little doubt that officers do try to be 'non-directive',[8] and that their annoyance at bad schemes is both genuine and based on concern for their charges who suffer on them. Finally, there is no reason to suppose that they do not derive their maximum satisfaction from helping youngsters along their chosen paths.

Nevertheless, regardless of unemployment this starting point is tempered in two senses. One is that of 'realism' and, like their teaching counterparts, careers officers seems to feel they would be doing no favours by failing to adjust aspirations. The way in which this is done reflects the uneasy amalgam of realism with a non-directive approach. 'I'd tell someone they were being unrealistic and point out the problems that they would encounter.' The philosophy tends to remain constant across a range of practical direction. Miss Robinson, for example, would say to youngsters,

> 'Look, unless you get rid of that pink bit I am not going to submit you
> for the following apprenticeship, because I know that the employer
> will not accept you. Fair enough, have as many pink bits in your hair
> as you like, but if you want an apprenticeship with this firm ... you
> have no chance."

The other tempering factor is the ill-fit between an emphasis on growth, development, and fulfilment through work with the sizeable number of jobs which offer precious little in that line.[9] This has led some guidance theorists such as Hayes and Hopson (1975:31) to suggest that, 'it is very inadvisable to lead students to believe that work *is* always or *should* always be intrinsically satisfying.' Yet how well does this square with their assertion eight pages on that, 'work provides the individual with an opportunity to express himself.'

The problem here is how to construct a general theory of career development across the enormous range of intrinsic job satisfactions under the capitalist division of labour.[10] The 'solution' appears to be either to adopt contradictory positions to cope with specific issues or to push the responsibility back onto the job-seeker, who according to Daws (1970) should consider 'how much of myself do I wish to define in occupational terms', a valid question taken in the abstract, but also a convenient ideological device for handling the contradictions of career development theory.

Whatever problems may arise from the question of the importance of work in relation to satisfaction, they pale into insignificance when the question is posed in relation to mass unemployment. Too great an importance may lead to depression and disillusionment, too little importance to a loss of work discipline which may prove difficult to restore even with draconian social security measures.[11] In either event, there is considerable potential for criminal or political deviance. 'Balance' is called for, but as with careers work in school such balance tended to veer in a very positive direction. To understand how this actually operates it is useful to begin by outlining the relationship of YOP to the labour market.

No one would argue that YOP is anything other than a poor substitute for 'proper jobs'. Yet, even as a pale shadow of the real labour market, it has features which are of great importance for the practice of careers guidance. In areas such as Durham, where YOP has in effect become the labour market for young school-leavers, efforts have been made to provide opportunities across the board of local employment. It has been said of places such as Consett that there are virtually no workplaces which do not have YOP trainees, and it can be argued that in many ways this new 'labour market' is rather easier to enter than the old one in conditions of full(er) employment. First, the six month duration of schemes both increases turnover and hence 'opportunities' and also means that employers may be more 'lax' in whom they take on. Second, despite an undoubted incidence of substitution, there are many YOP schemes which are obviously surplus to any conceivable requirements. This applies to both WEEP (Work Experience on Employers' Premises) and non-WEEP elements of YOP, with the latter, although further removed from the labour market, often providing more thorough training. Third, there is the selection procedure for YOP with its rather strange mix of the 'guaranteed offer' and shortlists of applicants drawn up by the careers service (employment assistants) from which employers choose their trainees.[12] The important aspect of the selection procedure for our concerns, is that it is largely done on an interest basis *i.e.* those who have expressed interest in a particular type of work are usually given priority. Once again this has the effect of producing a closer correspondence between expressed interest and placement than would occur in the ordinary labour market.[13] In turn, these factors have a profound influence over the way in which the service handles YOP.

First and foremost, the 'equivalence' of old and new labour markets means that in day-to-day terms the traditional approach of the careers service can be maintained and even enhanced. One careers officer suggested that 'basically it's the same as what I've been doing for a number of years, the only thing is that now, instead of reviewing people at work, permanent jobs ... we're reviewing kids that are on schemes.' Others noted that, 'instead of having a row of vacancies to go through it's a row of schemes' or that, 'you come up with a job recommendation ... and that's going to be the same for a proper job or for YOP. So that side doesn't change a lot ... what we end up with, what we decide that kid is going to follow through, is the same for YOP as for a job.' As overarching guidance role allows for great adaptability with regard to the precise nature of the guidance, or rather it's setting. The scope for 'enhancement' derives from the ideal workings of careers guidance and the fact that, in a certain sense, YOP allows a closer approach to them. It has been claimed (Moor 1976:162) that times of severe unemployment create a special need for 'highly trained and knowledgeable careers advisers.'

In similar vein, a district careers officer contended that,

> "the matching process seems to me to exist more strongly now than it did in the past, because YOP is supposed to cater for the needs of young people. So we make an effort in school to establish what the need is going to be, and then the MSC are, strictly speaking, required to cater for that need in terms of YOP.'

However rare 'tailor made' schemes might be, then very idea marks a departure from previous practice, and is in closer accord with a genuine 'match'. Another factor is that, as mentioned earlier, involvement with youngsters is both 'widened' and 'deepened'. This makes the goal of guiding youngsters through their transition from school to work more of reality, especially if thoughts of the long term future can be shelved. Previously, reviewing was generally restricted to letters enquiring after the recent school-leaver's occupational well-being, many of which were not answered. In the words of Mrs. Broom, 'it was all a bit hitty-missy.' Under YOP trainees' well-being can even be pursued into the factory.

None of the above analysis is intended to suggest the blossoming of a love affair between the careers service and YOP, but it is worth recognizing those aspects of YOP which serve to make its implementation more palatable to the service. The other major factor in the adoption of a strongly positive approach to YOP and the work ethic generally, is that officers did not translate their reservations about YOP into action. All the officers I spoke to were well aware of the abuses of YOP (cheap labour, substitution, minimal training etc.) and aware that even in the unlikely event of such abuses being eliminated, the programme was far from ideal for young people. Miss Barton's answer was to encourage youngsters to see YOP as, 'the light at the end of the tunnel,' having made them fully conversant with the immense difficulties of finding a job.

> "We have a lot of reservations about YOP but I think you've got to present it in a positive manner no matter what you think you yourself ... I think you've got to work within the system. It's the best we've got right now".

It seems that it is an extremely large step to translate negative views into negative acts and that this leads to various forms of rationalization, including denial of viable alternatives and confinement of contrary thoughts to the non-work self. Mrs. Broom saw the main enemy as fatalism. 'I think it's wrong for the pupils to say "well, I'll do anything. I'll wait 'til I leave school and then see what you've got in YOPs".' She was insistent that youngsters should be strongly encouraged to have clear preferences and to pursue them vigorously through YOP and whatever remained of full-time employment. Again, as with careers teachers, incidents justifying the positive approach were relished, however isolated and unrepresentative they might be. Similarly, appreciation of the bizarre effects of competitive solutions to systemic crises could co-exist with an apparently uncritical acceptance of the need to promote such solutions. At one point Miss Barton pierced its logic.

> "I mean it's become outdated hasn't it, that you were going to improve your skills, improve your knowledge, improve your training so that you would stand a better chance of getting a job. But if everybody's being improved, there's still no more jobs, it's just better people competing with better people."

Yet, a short while later, she declared, 'it always amazes me that when jobs are short that kids ... don't do everything they can to get that job.'

Conclusion

The object of this study has been to examine the operation of 'structural constraints' on the consciousness and action of careers guidance practitioners based in the Durham coalfield. Clearly, a more adequate account would require the use of 'client perspectives' and consideration of relationships both within schools and the careers service (especially hierarchical relations) and between them and other agencies such as the MSC and employers. This, however, was precluded, partly due to space and partly due to some of this material being beyond my own research concerns and hence not gathered in any systematic way. Of necessity my aims have been more humble, focussing on constraints as perceived by practitioners. In particular, I have attempted to show constraints operating via their presentation of fairly sharp, dichotomous alternatives which render substantial 'non-conformity' very difficult. Moreover, that they tend to be mutually reinforcing as in the case of the variety of pressures towards adoption of a positive approach to YOP and the work ethic. Against this, however, it has been stressed that careers guidance practitioners have been able to put their own interpretation on directives from above, albeit with MSC tolerance. I have also tried to examine how within these parameters consciousness relates to action. For this occurs not only in the sense that a variety of devices are employed to legitimate action despite awareness of its problems and contradictions,[14] but also that ultimately idealist beliefs can be of considerable importance in 'fine-tuning' action. One good example of this would be the efforts of careers guidance practitioners to create space for their aims of 'client-centredness'. This would appear to be one way of handling ideological contradictions; by 'accepting' one set of imperatives at one level, while oppositional notions are relegated, either to another level of operation where they can be both vigorously pursued and safely contained, or to a realm outside the 'work self'.

Given YOP's scheduled replacement in autumn 1983 by the Youth Training Scheme it is perhaps worth offering a final comment on the likely effects of this on careers guidance. It seems unlikely that the schools will be much affected by YTS *pre se*, though the possibility of some wider transformation in the whole area of transition from school to work should not be ruled out. As to the careers service it seems that little will change, with the New Training Initiative's commitment to greater guidance and counselling provision largely confined to the level of rhetoric. There is no indication of additional staff appointment for this purpose, which suggests a level of involvement close to that in YOP. Equally, the type of involvement will almost certainly remain the same, given that YTS occupies a position within the transition from school to work fundamentally similar to YOP. It is therefore argued that the above analysis will generally be as applicable to YTS as it is to YOP.

Notes

1 Unless otherwise stated all names in this section refer to careers teachers, those in the next section to careers officers.
2 Work experience straddles these two areas. On the one hand it aims at allowing sampling of a particular type of work for future reference but also is thought useful as an introduction to work discipline and habits per se.
3 There may be any number of reasons for this including discrimination on grounds of class, sex and race, 'cultural capital', use of contacts, regional location, employers refusal to use qualifications as the main criterion for employment, educational prestige and so on. (See *e.g.* Halsey *et al.* (1980), Karabel & Halsey (1977), Dale, *et al.* (1976), Cosin *et al.* (1977), Deem (1980)).
4 This textbook version of career guidance, while expounded somewhat tongue-in-cheek, is nevertheless an important influence on the work of the majority of careers officers.
5 There was one curious exception to this where a district careers officer complained about a member of the MSC link team being over-zealous in his monitoring duties.
6 The twin aims of realistic work experience and avoidance of substitution exert pressure in opposite directions. Realism demands performance of regular, non-superfluous work tasks, having others dependent on their performance and so on, yet if employers come to rely on YOP trainees it can be argued that substitution must have occurred. One-off tasks are useful for avoiding substitution but often provide minimal training or realism. Schemes are not supposed to be used as probationary employment but as this is almost the only way schemes are likely to demonstrate that they improve employability, they are generally regarded as virtually the ideal of scheme operation. However, 'probation' usually means closure of schemes which conflicts with the desire to maintain places, while ongoing places are likely to entail some degree of substitution. Perhaps the awesome scale and insurmountable nature of these problems (allied to the 'attractive' features of YOP) largely account for their being ignored.
7 Pressure to take YOP schemes does occur, of course, but this is normally through the requirement to 'keep in touch' with the careers office, and consequent discussion of schemes, rather than via ultimata to take particular schemes.
8 While not denying that pressure or influence is often exerted, dressed up as 'choice', there are nonetheless important differences in the way this is done.

9 Similar sentiments have been expressed in the education and industry debate.

> In recent years the social environment in a number of schools, with more emphasis on personal development and less on formal instruction, has been diverging from that still encountered in most work situations, where the need to achieve results in conformity with defined standards and to do so within fixed time-limits call for different patterns of behaviour. The contrast is more market where changes in industrial processes have reduced the scope for individual action and achievement.

Training Services Agency 1975:15

10 This is not to imply that jobs hold a set amount of 'intrinsic satisfaction' regardless of their occupants, but the general point is undeniable. An extreme 'relativism' in this area can be very convenient for those who wish to see the capitalist division of labour as at least potentially in line with workers' desires.

11 The material necessity for the propertyless to work limits the weight of ideological factors but these nevertheless remain significant.

12 These contradictory aims, workable in practice only due to the existence of various large training or community projects which are not too choosy about whom they take on, reflect the essential tension between some vague unarticulated 'right to work' (or more cynically, keeping the reserve army well-oiled) and upholding the selection prerogatives of employers. Against any over-simplistic notions of state agencies as capitalist puppets, it must be stressed that careers officers were often keen on moving towards a position where they would select the trainees, and often tried informally to persuade employers to agree to this. Within the careers service there was some unease about the use of selection procedures and in particular whether to favour employers by selecting the 'best' youngsters for interview or to adopt more client-centred methods. The mediating role played by the service in the 'hiring of labour' certainly creates ideological problems insofar as responsbility for employment can only partly be passed off to the employer. Yet, equally, the debate this has aroused in some offices further demonstrates that the careers service is not entirely willing to simply toe the MSC line.

13 This is not to argue that such expressed interest are markedly less linked to ultimate opportunities, merely that once expressed there is often a better chance of their being 'realized' under YOP than in the ordinary labour market.

14 One interesting example of this came from Mr. Walsh, who made great play of his promotion of equal opportunities for the sexes and in certain areas undoubtedly acted this out. Yet at the same time he ran a rigid, sex-divided option programme with child care, home management, and hygiene-beauty-grooming for girls; motor mechanics, building studies and metalwork for boys. He appeared to see nothing incongruous between this and his assertion that, 'as far as I'm concerned, a girl can be a fireman, an engineer, or whatever she likes, a boy can go and nurse children. It doesn't matter to me.' As ever, it is crucial to see the relationship between an ideology of self-determination and capitalist social and economic divisions, in this instance on the basis of gender.

Bibliography

Beynon, H. & Austrin, T. (1980) *Global Outpost* Working Paper, Durham University.

Centre for Contemporary Cultural Studies (1981) *Unpopular Education* London, Hutchinson.

Cosin, B., Dale, R., Esland, G., MacKinnon, D. and Swift, D. (Eds.) (1977) *School and Society* London, Routledge and Kegan Paul.

Derek Kirton

DALE, R., ESLAND, G. and MACDONALD, M. (Eds.) (1976) *Schooling and Capitalism* London, Routledge and Kegan Paul.

DAWS, P.P. (1970) 'Occupational information and the self-defining process,' *Vocational Aspects of Education* XXII No. 52, pp. 71–9:

DEEM, R. (Ed.) (1980) *Schooling for Women's Work* London, Routledge and Kegan Paul.

HALSEY A.H., HEATH, A.F. and RIDGE, J.M. (1980) *Origins and Destinations* Oxford, Oxford University Press.

HAYES, J. and HOPSON, B. (1975) *Careers Guidance* London, Heinemann.

KARABEL, J. and HALSEY, A.H. (Eds.) (1977) *Power and Ideology in Education* New York, Oxford University Press.

KEENE, N.B. (1969) *Employment of Young Workers* London, B.T. Batsford.

MOOR, C.H. (1976) *From School to Work* London, Sage.

REEDER, D. (1979) 'Education and Industry: a recurring debate,' in BURNBAUM, G. (Ed.) *Schooling in Decline* London, MacMillan.

ROBERTS, K. (1974) 'The entry into employment: an approach towards a general theory', in WILLIAMS, W.M. (Ed.) *Occupational Choice* London, George Allen & Unwin.

SUPER, D.E. (1981) 'Approaches to occupational choice and career development', in WATTS, A.G. SUPER, D.E. and KIDD, J.M. (Eds.) *Career Development in Britain* Cambridge, CRAC/Hobson.

TRAINING SERVICES AGENCY (MSC) (1975) *Vocational Preparation for Young People* London, HMSO.

WILLIS, P. (1977) *Learning to Labour* London, Saxon House.

Social Behaviour and the Young Unemployed

Sue Bloxham

Youth unemployment is running at unprecedently high levels with no apparent signs of decline. In January 1980 there were 128,000 under eighteens unemployed in the UK, almost half of which had been out of work for more than three months (*Dept of Employment Gazette*: February 1982). In addition many thousands of school leavers and young people are participating in the Government's special employment programme. In December 1981, it was estimated that the number of people covered by these schemes was 657,300 (*Guardian* 23 December 1981).

The task of this paper is to consider the socio-psychological consequences of unemployment or precarious or substitute employment for the young people concerned; particularly the mass of young people who are not part of established sub-cultures; who are not on the streets; and who live in the roads, suburbs and small towns where the vast majority of people have jobs. I shall particularly concern myself with the extent to which the experience of unemployment causes individuals to change their social behaviour or lose social confidence; at a time when the development of social relationships is an essential part of their progress to maturity.

The second task of this paper is to explore the strength of the arguments for including training in social skills as a central part of most special measures for the young unemployed. That is: the validity of the arguments by which it has been decided that the consequences or causes of unemployment for young people can be linked to a lack of 'Social and Life Skills' and to what extent such training is a valid part of the Youth Opportunities Programme.

PART 1

The Consequences of Unemployment

Sinfield (1981:37) makes the point that research into the psychological consequences of unemployment is tenuous. He suggests that they have not been rigorously researched and the results of what research there has been tend to indicate a too unitary view of individuals' responses to the experience of unemployment. It is clearly the case that the massive unemployment the nation is experiencing at present is such a recent phenomenon that it has yet to give rise to a large body of academic research. What research there has been is succinctly reviewed by Hayes and Nutman (1981:9–19) and suggests various stages or phases in the transition from employment to acceptance of unemployment. They suggest that 'There is a great deal of similarity both in the nature of the cycles put forward and in the categories and concepts used to describe the phases in these cycles' (page 16). Kelvin argues that the experience of unemployment can be understood at two levels; firstly, the physical and practical circumstances such as shortage of money, boredom and loss of social opportunities at work; and secondly, its psychological consequences such as resignation, depression and loss of self confidence (Kelvin 1981:8). On first approaching the problem of the consequences of unemployment for school leavers, it is difficult to decide to what extent their experiences are likely to match those of the older unemployed for whom 'work' has become an established part of their lives. Hayes and Nutman (1981:53–54) suggest that school leavers' experience of unemployment will be dependent to some extent on each individual's 'anticipatory occupational socialization'; that is to what extent their 'background and early socialization have encouraged the development of a public persona in which the occupational self-concept forms an important part.' However, they continue to argue that the psychological consequences and 'psycho-economic pressure' for young people will generally be less than that of people who were previously employed full-time. They base this argument on school leavers' recent experience of coping with extended leisure time and the relatively smaller effect of low income. School leavers are unlikely to be the bread winner of the family and although they may feel badly off in comparison with their employed counterparts, they have little, if no, financial responsibility to others.

It is difficult to argue that young people do not have to fill long periods of unorganized time during their schooldays and a number of writers have suggested that they often have to develop strategies for dealing with boredom. (Corrigan 1979, Kitwood 1980 & Willis 1977). Likewise, my own and others' experience in youth work and and related fields supports the view that surviving with a shortage of cash is part and parcel of adolescence for many youngsters. The constant cadging and sharing of cigarettes and 'hassling' to borrow 10p provide day-to-day reminders. Therefore, having to cope with boredom and lack of money are not experiences restricted to worklessness during youth. However, I consider that viewing the consequences of unemployment as less important for young people on such a basis ignores the complex changes that accompany the transition from 'pupil' to 'worker'. Values, attitudes and behaviour which were appropriate during schooldays cannot be assumed to continue into the period after they have left school. Kitwood (1980:239) makes reference to this point in his recent study of adolescent values: 'For those who experience it (unemployment), the roles and values relevant for an earlier phase are not adequate' and Hayes and Nutman (1981:53) also suggest that values have an important part to play when they say: 'The extent to which the views of others will affect the unemployed school leaver's self-image will be a function of the individual reference group and the attitudes of significant others'. It is this question of the values attached to work; the emotional investment in employment; that I shall pursue here.

The Value of Employment

The role of work in our society has been the subject of argument and discussion for many decades. Despite differing views as to its intrinsic or functional value; its satisfying or merely expedient role, there is little question of the acceptance of the 'value' of work in our society (Kelvin 1980 & Watts 1979)

> Work may have different meanings for different people, but as well as these different meanings it also has an important shared meaning for most people in society. Being a member of the work force, enjoying the status of worker, leads to considerable positive re-inforcement and satisfaction irrespective of the nature of the job. The Protestant work ethic is still with us but in a disguised form. It has been secularized.
>
> Hayes and Nutman 1981:45

However, can we assume that adolescents also value work?

In the post-war period there has been considerable argument as to whether young people absorb and internalize the adult culture and its values. Musgrove (1964), for example, suggested that the extension of compulsory education and the concomitant lengthening of the time during which young people are segregated from adult society would lead to the creation of a potentially deviant population and, therefore, young people, deprived of status and held in low esteem, would become a force of social change. It is this idea of the young emerging as a new 'class' with values in opposition to the 'consensus' adult society which has been portrayed in both academic and popular literature and has lad to them being considered as a social problem.

However, more recently both psychologists and sociologists have tended to oppose this viewpoint of youth as a more or less homogenous class with separate values (Wilmot 1960, Jefferson and Hall 1976, Brake 1980, Kitwood 1980 & Cockram and Beloff 1976) and have argued instead that, on the one hand, most young people do not 'enter a tight or coherent subculture' and, on the other hand, the subcultures that do exist are 'localized and differentiated structures *within* the parent culture' (Jefferson and Hall, 1976:13). Their distinctive pursuits are marginal and largely to do with fashion markets. As a consequence, socio-economic class continues to be of central importance in determining the life styles and life chances of adolescents. A wealth of empirical evidence supports this view that the values, aspirations and lifestyles of the majority of young people are derived from their culture and neighbourhood. Can we be assured that this continuity of values applies to the value of work as 'employment'?

The evidence of a variety of studies conducted over recent years suggests a positive attitude to employment amongst adolescents (Ashton & Field 1976, Kitwood 1980, Burger 1977, Sawdon *et al* 1979, Ince 1971). Young people are keen to leave school and start work (Sawdon *et al* 1981b:9). Data from a current longitudinal study I am conducting with sixteen and seventeen year old school leavers from one school district in the North West supports this view. The young people were all experiencing difficulty finding work once they had left school. Amongst the fifty six young people interviewed in the November/December after leaving school, 86 per cent offered other reasons apart from earning money for having a job. 28 per cent valued work for the enjoyment, interest or pleasure it gave them as expressed by Jane:

I: "Do you think the only reason it is worth going to work is to earn money?"

Jane: "No, not really, all sort's of work's interesting I suppose, its just an interest int it. I mean if you didn't want to go to work, you just say you can't get a job and go on the social for a while wouldn't yer"

A further 27 per cent valued work as a means of avoiding boredom and being occupied. As Derek replied to the same question: 'Not really 'cos if you don't go to work you'll get bored pretty easily won't you, you get sick and tired of it.' Twenty five per cent saw employment as an opportunity to learn something, to get a 'trade' or 'experience'. A typical response of this nature to the question was Andrea's:

"No it's sort of like a hobby isn't it if you like doing something . . . like when I used to work at P – I used to get 50p an hour and me other mate used to get 90p an hour but she was just behind the shop counter and people used to say to me you've got a trade in your hand, you know, you're learning something, she's just behind the shop counter, she's not learning owt"

Work is also appreciated by some young people as an opportunity to meet and get on with other people. As Simon replied:

I: "Do you think money is the only reason for going to work?"

Simon: "No I don't see it that way, I see work as taking me off boredom all day. See if I never went to work I'd be sat at home watching telly or laying in bed and no-one to . . . all the rest of me mates working or on a Government Training scheme so I'd be lonely. I think I would rather work than not work anyway even if nobody else was working".

This reason was offered by 18 per cent of the young people. Employment was also valued by 11 per cent of the respondents as a means of getting out of the home. For example:

I: "Do you think money is the only reason for going to work?"

Ann: "No not really, there's nowt to do at home, you all look forward to leaving school and then when you leave school you don't know what to do with your time"

and Kate: 'Well you enjoy yourself . . . you're away all the time, you're not bored sat at home all the time'. A smaller proportion of the young people appreciated work as a means of gaining personal satisfaction and feelings of achievement. This was mentioned by five per cent. Stan replied to the same

question: 'Getting satisfaction out of the job, you've got to have an ambition
... when you've finished, you can say I've done that.'

In addition, employment was seen by individual youngsters as a means to
avoiding becoming 'like a cabbage' or feelings of shame at having to claim
social security. These comments also illustrate the extent to which the young
people saw work as fulfilling more than one need and, as the following
example shows, identified employment as a central purpose of their lives:

I: "Is money the only reason it is worth going to work?"

Stuart: "No, getting experience, that's what its all about, I think, well
I think anyway, the money, comes in handy but getting on with
people and just doing the job, spending your time usefully, to me's the
best thing anyway".

Evidence of ambivalence to work (Ince 1971:49, Parker 1974:71–73 and
Philips 1973:415) can be understood as less of a rejection of having a job, *per
se*, but more of an attempt to improve ones employment circumstances; that is
wages or type of work. Therefore periods of voluntary unemployment are
seen as coming *between* jobs and not as a long term alternative to work. The
evidence that young people are often selective about what work they will do is
not consistent with the argument (Fromm 1966) that young people want work
at any cost. However such 'fussiness' gives no indication of a rejection of the
value of work but more of a recognition (even if an incorrect one) of the
different status, future prospects and interest involved in different types of
work. As a school leaver amongst my sample explained:

I: "Do you think it matters what you actually have to do at work;
would you have taken anything that was offered to you?"

Keith: "Yer, well mainly as long as it isn't factory work."

I: "As long as it isn't factory work? Why don't you fancy factory
work?"

Keith: "Me Dad works in one and he doesn't like it so..."

Nevertheless the impact of unemployment on opportunity to choose is also
recognized:

I: "Would you have taken anything that the Careers Office had
offered you, to fill in?"

Sandra: "I'd have taken pretty much anything, I wouldn't have cleaned
loos or anything like that, I'd have done anything, you know, shop
assistant, anything like that really. I think they were pretty intent on
finding me someat that would help me with me nursing, that was my
original idea but when I found how difficult it was to get a job, I'd
have taken anything really, 'cos I was beginning to get really bored".

And as the longitudinal study of school leavers conducted by Youthaid reveals
(Sawdon *et al* 1981a:146), in the present employment climate, job stability
amongst young people is very much the norm.

Thus we have a situation where, although young people may not invest 'employment' with expectations of satisfaction and pleasure, they do value it and aspire to achieve it on leaving school. As one youngster in a recent study (Wilcox *et al* 1980:7) said: 'When you're at school, you're still a boy really, even if you are staying on, but the day you start working, they start treating you like a man. You can make your own decisions all the time.' I consider that the 'value' young people place on 'having a job' is an important factor in developing an explanation of their experience of unemployment, and the influence it has over their social behaviour.

Self Esteem and Unemployment

The 'self' is one of the objects towards which one has attitudes (Rosenberg 1965:5) and on which one makes evaluations. These attitudes and evaluations are, to an important extent, derived by social comparison with relevant others whether through comparative appraisal or reflected appraisal (Stroebe 1977:81). This is: comparing attributes and actions with those of other people or interpreting what others think and how they react to oneself.

Self esteem has been defined in terms of 'evaluative attitudes towards the self' (Coopersmith 1967:28) and the link between how an individual sees himself and how he evaluates his actions and attributes can be found in his 'self values' (Rosenberg 1965:243). Thus definitions of success occur within a personal frame of reference and self esteem cannot be judged in relation to overall socio-cultural standards but only with regard to a person's effective environment and values (Rosenberg 1965:124 & Coopersmith 1967:243). For example being a successful student will only contribute to a person's self esteem if he values that quality and if he thinks success or failure at that activity reflects on his competence and effort. Consequently self esteem can be understood by relating an individual's evaluation of his achievements with regard to his aspirations; his aspirations deriving from self values as to what is important and feelings of personal failure to live up to aspirations leading to loss of self esteem. (Coopersmith 1967:29)

The experience of unemployment amongst young people is certainly reported as a feeling of having failed at something essential (Schneider 1977:44). However, do young people perceive that failure as a reflection of personal characteristics and thus a threat to their self esteem?

Initially, as Frith (1980) points out, provision for unemployed young people was premised on the assumption that the central cause of youth unemployment could be located in the inadequacies of the young people themselves. They were seen as leaving school with insufficient skills and inappropriate attitudes. However, as unemployment increases steadily and opportunities for young people wither away, there are few writers who do not regard the problem as at least cyclical and possibly structural (Watts 1979:16). Unfortunately, the evidence presently available, suggests that, as yet, there is little recognition amongst young people or their families that this is the case and that the individual is not largely responsible for his failure to find work.

In respect of the unemployed in general, Heinemann (1978) points out that worklessness is a socially discredited situation and work is a social norm. Therefore unemployment is seen as a fault of the individual. It is considered less as a collective fate; as a social, economic and political problem, and more as an individual failure.

With regard to the young unemployed, an International Labour Office report notes that 'Economic reasons behind recessions are not always understood by youngsters and often they attribute their unemployment to personal failure' (Schneider 1977:44). Various empirical studies confirm this view (Heinemann 1978, Wilcox *et al* 1980:13). Fifth year pupils in a Sheffield study appeared 'to have little understanding of the broad economic issues associated with rising unemployment' and their 'reasons why they might not find work are grounded in the perceptions of their own personal inadequacies and failures' (Wilcox *et al* 1980:13).

My current research also tends to confirm this internal attribution for unemployment. Forty nine recent school leavers were asked for their reasons for not having found permanent work. They gave a total of 66 different reasons, twenty six (39 per cent) of which located the cause directly in personal failure such as not trying hard enough to find a job, 'nicking off' school too frequently or not getting sufficient exam passes. A further ten (15 per cent) reasons located the cause in the young people themselves, but with characteristics for which they could not be held responsible such as being too young or not having any experience of work. Three (four and a half per cent) other reasons were also personal such as not having had time to find a job yet or not having wanted to work at the time (for example having been on holiday). Only fifteen (23 per cent) reasons were external to the young people; for example the shortage of jobs or state of the national economy. This evidence is all the more surprising given that the unemployment rate for under eighteens in the North West at the time (October 1981) was 25 per cent.

A Youthaid study of young Londoners (Youthaid 1981b:12) confirms this attitude. The report says that 'general concepts of the problem of unemployment were highly individualized, focussing on personal characteristics very much more than any shortage of jobs in the economy' and although respondents had experienced great difficulty and frustration in looking for work themselves, they located the causes of youth unemployment largely with the inadequacies or lack of effort of young people themselves, with less than a third mentioning a shortage of jobs as a reason.

This is reinforced within their families where young people encounter attitudes of personal blame for worklessness. In one study (Youthaid 1981b), less than 10 per cent of the adolescents felt that they had been given support or encouragement by their parents, and some youngsters complained of hostility and arguments as a consequence of their failure to find work. These attitudes are reiterated in a recent German investigation and in a study located in an area of traditionally high unemployment, the North East (Youthaid 1980:32): 'Only four in ten of the young people could expect a tolerant or helpful attitude on the part of their parents.' Finally, in their Sheffield study, Wilcox *et al* (1980:11–12) remark that amongst the fifth form pupils in their sample 'Echoes of their parents' views on unemployment surfaces strongly and the stigma attached to being out of work and claiming 'dole' in à society committed to the intrinsic value of working is very real.'

Given the importance, mentioned above, of an individual's immediate social environment in defining criteria of success and failure, it is clear that family attitudes to unemployment will influence adolescents' own views of the reasons for their worklessness.

Thus, it appears, we have a situation where the young unemployed not only feel that they have failed at something they value, but also feel that this failure is a reflection of their own lack of ability or effort and, consequently, we might expect to see a relationship between repeated failure to find work and a lowering of self esteem. This relationship, between unemployment and self esteem, has to some extent become taken for granted in the literature on the subject. For example a Youthaid report (Sawdon *et al* 1981b:9) states: 'In the early 1970s it became clear that our society could no longer offer to all its citizens the income, status and self esteem of a decent well-paid job' and Gurney (1980:175) points out that 'One of the most commonly held and plausible beliefs about the impact of unemployment is that it results in a lowering of a person's self esteem.' However, there is also limited empirical evidence as well as intuitive opinions to support the relationship between unemployment and low self esteem (Heinemann 1978, Presdee 1981:8, Gurney 1980, Tiffany *et al* 1970).

Social Behaviour of the Young Unemployed

Undoubtedly, the relationship discussed above requires further research; however, I suggest that it may provide a possible key to understanding the social behaviour of the young unemployed because as Kelvin argues 'If work is crucial to the concept which an individual has of himself, it will also be crucial to his relationship with others (Kelvin 1981:2).

Evidence points to a correlation between level of self esteem and preference for social participation. As Burns (1979:231) has argued: 'Those with low self esteem, through previous interpreted life experiences, anticipate failure and rejection (and) this saps motivation to interact with others'. Empirical studies of self esteem, particularly with adolescents, tend to support this view. Rosenberg (1965:169), for example, points to 'interpersonal threat' as a strong feeling amongst low self esteem teenagers who see themselves as awkward and uneasy in interpersonal relationships and thus tend to avoid other people 'or at least fail to take the initiative in establishing contacts with them' (p. 173).

As Duck (1977:76) says, a person's mechanisms 'for deducing what to expect from other people' are influenced by his own personal 'history of interactions where he has learned how other people respond to him personally'. Therefore, an individual's tendency to interact will depend on whether he expects it to be a rewarding experience on the basis of past experiences. Consequently, people with low self esteem, anticipating failure, can be expected to be anxious about social encounters especially if they expect further evaluations to be involved; as, for example, when going for an interview for a job. Thus self esteem is an important characteristic in influencing individual's inclination to interact with others.

It is hardly surprising, therefore, given the additional barriers of reduced structured social contact and shortage of cash, that writers have reported a tendency amongst both adults (Davy 1981:30) and young people to lose friends, to become isolated and to have difficulty with social relationships (Burger 1977:116–117, Crocker *et al* 1980:5, National Youth Bureau 1981:2,

Brannen 1975:67, Youthaid 1981b:12 & Institute of Careers Officers 1979:6–7). In fact, Heinemann's research tends to confirm that isolation amongst unemployed youngsters stems less from rejection by or loss of contact with friends and more from the choice of the unemployed individual who, he argues, has less wish for contact with others (1978: Chap. 10).

It is easy to understand why youngsters efforts to find employment gradually tail off (Crocker 1980:12) as they experience one rejection after another, and why, despite valuable attempts to attract them, they make little use of social facilities offered to them such as drop-in centres and youth clubs (Bl *Annual Report* 1980–81:11 & 27). The 'Just the Job' research report (Gladstone 1979: para 7) highlighted this issue when it revealed that it was the more motivated and parentally encouraged young people who tended to make use of its services. Likewise we must realize that although some youngsters do make use of provisions for the unemployed, it is possibly those who have been hardest hit by the experience of worklessness who are sitting at home in front of the television or wandering aimlessly around the shopping precinct.

German and British research also points to this isolation being particularly prevalent amongst girls, possibly through choice and possibly because they are expected to make a greater contribution to the running of the home (Burger 1977:115–117, Youthaid 1981b:12).

I have argued that the evidence shows that young people 'value' employment and that it would appear that they feel responsible for their own failure to find work. This failure at a valued activity leads to loss of self esteem and thus a diminishment of social contacts or reluctance to initiate new relationships.

The duration of unemployment for young people may be fairly short. As the Sawdon *et al* (1981b:9) study points out, the employed and the unemployed are not two different groups of people. 'Rising unemployment means rather that they will have to wait longer for a job when they leave school and when they change jobs, they will have to wait longer before entering a new one.' On this basis, one might argue that although the consequences of unemployment are serious for young people, the experience is likely to be transitory or intermittent and, therefore, presents less of a social problem. Undoubtedly, this appears to be the premise on which official provision for the unemployed is based with little or no emphasis on assistance with managing the experience of unemployment or changing attitudes to the unemployed. However I would argue that loss of self esteem and the concomitant lack of confidence in social relationships are of vital significance when they occur during adolescence by virtue of the important function of adolescent social relationships as preparation for adult social roles.

Adolescent Friendship

The changing function of friendship during adolescence has received little attention. Nevertheless, a small number of studies of teenage friendship and other more general investigations of adolescent behaviour and acquaintance reveals, at least, a fairly consistent pattern to teenage friendships (Wilmot 1960, Douvan and Adelson 1966, Dunphy 1963).

Parsons (Parsons & Bales 1956:38) posits a requirement of childhood and adolescence wherein the individual must learn progressively more roles than his 'family of orientation' can offer him; a view confirmed by Douvan and Adelson (1966:174) who see peer relations at adolescence as part of the preparation for adult friendship. They suggest that kinship intimacy is too likely to continue earlier patterns of relationship and thus maintain the 'self' at the *status quo*. They report three phases in female adolescent friendship moving from the early relationship centring on activity, through a stress on security and loyalty onto the more relaxed friendship with the emphasis on personality and shared interests that emerges with late adolescence. They argue that by late adolescence, the opportunities available in earlier relationships have enabled the girl to acquire the rudiments of social skill and there is less need for, or investment in, like-sexed friendships. At this stage heterosexual relationships are likely to take on more importance. Coleman's (1980:91) research tends to confirm their view. He suggests that empirical findings support the notion that young people have different needs at different stages and these needs are reflected in friendship patterns.

Further evidence that adolescent friendships prepare adolescents for a future 'heterosexual role' is presented in a study by Dunphy of Australian teenagers (1963). His research points to a progressive development of peer group structure from predominantly unisexual to heterosexual friendship groups and eventually to groups of loosely associated couples. He argues that patterns of behaviour within the groups encourages development towards a mature sexual role as the adolescent proceeds through a series of successively more complex systems of relationships.

Friendship serves the purpose of validating an individual's thoughts and feelings (Duck 1980). The discovery of people who share our attitudes and feelings is a rewarding experience as it implies that what we think is social acceptable and valid. During childhood and adolescence, we gradually learn to identify aspects of others' personality more subtly. Consequently as an adolescent's personality develops, he is particularly likely to mix with friends who are at a similar stage of personality change and who can confirm and validate the changes he is undergoing (Duck 1980:229). Loss of friendship at adolescence deprives people of this personality support and the opportunity to practice social skills needed in future relationships. Heinemann (1978) agrees that social behaviour requires a common learning and behaviour *milieu*. When contacts are limited, important learning opportunities disappear. The 'natural conditions for role playing', learning 'common norms and value attitudes' and the 'horizon of common experiences' are lost (1978: Chap. 10).

Therefore, what evidence there is, suggests that friendship during adolescence is developmental and serves a progressive function as an active support for the tennager in the more towards satisfactory adult social relationships. If an adolescent's lack of self esteem coupled with the restrictive social opportunities of unemployment cause him to avoid awkward, competitive or novel social situations, he will be denied opportunities to progress in his social skills. Skills which as Hopson and Scally (1981:16) point out, are of ever growing importance as regular employment changes and geographical mobility put greater stress on the ability to satisfactorily 'create, maintain and end relationships'.

This relationship, I have described, between unemployment, social behaviour and development of social skills has important implications for government provision for the young unemployed. In the second part of this paper I shall explore the nature of social skill training within such provision and discuss the significance of the case put forward in part I to the development of that provision.

PART 2

State Provision for the Young Unemployed

Successive governments over the past decade have been aware that youth unemployment cannot merely be ignored in the hope that the kids will hang on until the jobs arrive. Morley-Bunker (1981:5) suggests that the emphasis in the provision for the unemployed on the youngest end of the range stems in part from 'anxiety about public order' and it is not surprising that part of the government reaction to recent urban disorder has been an expansion of services for the young unemployed through the Youth Opportunities Programme (*Guardian* 28 July 1981).

When YOP was first established it was recommended that further education should be included in each scheme and all WEP trainees have the right to be released to attend classes (Comm. on Scottish Affairs 1981: para 46). A particular aspect of further education within YOP and theoretically part of virtually all the various schemes (MSC 1981a: chap 2), is 'Life and Social Skills Training' (LSS). It is generally offered as an 'off-the-job' training component of WEP schemes and features in the curriculum of most short training courses.

Although Life Skills has a history of use for work with 'The mentally handicapped, with prisoners and even with those seeking help with personal and behavioural difficulties' (Davies 1979:4), the term 'Life and Social Skills Training' was only brought into use by the Manpower Services Commission in the mid-seventies (Joels 1981:75). It has developed as an element of YOP schemes, and many other industrial training schemes, on the basis of a 'recognition that the acquisition or possession of technical skills is not sufficient for young people to be successful at work' (FECRDU 1979:21). Therefore, course objectives are derived from assumptions about the 'demands made on young people in the work place and the community at large' (FECRDU 1979:21) which they might have difficulty satisfying because through extended education or lack of adult employment they have been deprived of the contexts where the skills might have developed naturally.

Life and Social Skills as a subject has been defined as 'The discovery of social tools to assist in the achievement of individual goals, to stimulate motivation, to enhance self esteem' (Pearn and Munene 1978:16). On a more tangible level, it is described as learning *social* skills, for example, relating to others in face to face contact, on the telephone and by letter; and *coping* skills such as dealing with everyday equipment and procedures, for example claiming social security, using a public telephone and completing forms (Stanton 1980:6).

A review of specific course outlines (Intowork 1980, YMCA 1980, Crichton-Miller 1981) and MSC documents (MSC 1981a & MSC 1973) reveals LSS curricula to invariably include 'job search' and job interview skills in addition to a range of other training such as 'how the job market works' (Crichton-

Sue Bloxham

Miller 1981:235), the 'legal system, civil rights, police and consumer rights' (Intowork 1980:27), mixing in, taking orders, communication, making friends and resisting provocation (MSC 1973:3).

The emphasis in such training is firmly work-oriented, both in its official direction (after all MSC is an organization established to deal with *employment* matters) and in its practice (FECRDU 1978). An example is a report on a YMCA run LSS course which remarks: 'Every session had an element related to work, this being the continuous theme running through the course' (YMCA 1980: para 4.4) Nevertheless, extending the boundaries of the curriculum into less work-oriented areas *is* endorsed in as much that 'a satisfactory personal life encourages work motivation' (MSC 1981a:12).

However, the training offered on LSS courses, although heavily work-oriented, is not vocational training as such, but a training in more general skills and attitudes which are considered to be useful in the work place. Joels (1981:78) points out that behavioural skills cannot be learnt without the accompaniment of appropriate information and attitudes. For example, learning good 'time-keeping' requires as much a positive attitude to work as it does ability to set an alarm clock! The ITRU (1979:18) study of young workers identified good 'time-keeping' as 'arising from their generally responsible and mature attitude'. Likewise, failure in communication with supervisors; not listening to or forgetting instructions and not querying orders that they didn't understand; was linked in many cases with 'attitude rather than ... cognitive blockage' (ITRU 1979:17). Consequently, a central aim of LSS courses is training in the 'appropriate' attitudes needed for success in basic skills at work. For example, assisting young people's communication skills is premised on an encouragement of favourable self attitudes on the basis that such attitudes will give trainees the confidence to approach and talk to other people. Therefore, courses are designed with specific personal development objectives, both in terms of attitude to self; encouraging self awareness, self confidence and self esteem (Findlay 1980:274); and in terms of improving skills in making and coping with interpersonal relationships.

I have argued in Part 1 that both these areas; that is attitude to self and ability to cope with personal relationships; might suffer as the result of unemployment or precarious and substitute employment. However, the view that MSC courses are therefore able to remedy, or give aid with, the psychological disadvantages of unemployment must be set against the background to their courses and the underlying values that the content expresses.

Originally government provision for unemployed young people was aimed to help the least able and least qualified because it was that group who initially felt the major impact of youth unemployment in the mid-seventies (Sinfield 1981:69). The provision was aimed at alleviating the perceived causes of that unemployment. The A–Z study (ITRU 1979) of the differences between improvers and non-improvers among young unskilled workers clearly reveals the importance employers place on attitudes to work, personal relations and communication skills in achieving success in the work place and the courses were designed to foster those skills. However, despite the massive growth in youth unemployment, extended across a much wider achievement range, government special measures still identify the young people, and their lack of skills, as the problem rather than directing provision towards solving the

124

problems that the young people face (Morgan 1981:108). 'Most of them are as competent as their parents were when it comes to day-to-day basic skills. What they most obviously need is a full-time secure job and more than £25 a week' (Starr 1982:11). Nevertheless, YOP continues to take a 'deficiency' view of the causes of youth unemployment, arguing that training in basic skills is needed to help young people's employment prospects. This 'deficiency' view is inadvertently transmitted to the young people by the curriculum of LSS courses because 'job search' remains as an essential ingredient of such courses and it appears from what has so far been published that the approach intended for the forthcoming *New Training Initiative* is not very dissimilar. The White Paper declares that training should 'Foster skills in communication (*interview* for example)' (HMSO 1981: para 26 – my emphasis).

The futility of teaching unemployed young people how to look for jobs that don't exist is clear: raising standards of 'job search' neither creates jobs nor helps young people to do the work once they've found employment. In addition, there are other implications of this emphasis on work in the content of LSS courses. On the one hand, the value of work is strongly reinforced amongst the trainees and, on the other hand, as Morgan points out, they are 'through the training programme, encouraged to believe that it is their own inadequacies which create unemployment' (1981:109).

If, as I have argued, unemployed youngsters lack of self esteem, and concomitant unwillingness to subject themselves to further chances of rejection as might occur in new social relationships, stems partly from their allegiance to the 'value' of having a job; then there is little logic in attempting to alleviate these problems via a course. A course which, through its overwhelming bias towards the value of work and the students inadequacies in obtaining it, only serves to reinforce their failure and the *importance* of the task they have failed at. In other words, to tell a young person that he could benefit from a course that will give him skills to help him find work, firstly reiterates the value of having a job and, secondly, has the effect of informing him that he is responsible for his own predicament: he can't write neatly enough, he doesn't dress smartly enough, he doesn't show enough enthusiasm, he doesn't express himself well enough at interviews and a myriad other lessons he learns. It reinforces the young person's own feelings of inadequacy that may have led him to devalue himself in the first place. Thus, MSC recognizes that personal development is an integral part of the progress towards satisfactory adult employment and states that such a development is a central aim of its Youth Opportunities Programme. Yet the form of its provision for this aspect of its courses is such that it may well serve to negate itself. Social and Life Skills training may in fact be contributing to a failure to acquire social skills.

This discussion, therefore, posits two problems for the future of LSS training in programmes for the unemployed. First, the need to recognize that although course organizers and teachers may understand the economic background to unemployment, it is often not clearly explained to trainees. As the likelihood of getting a job after YOP decreases, the importance of this for the psychological well-being of trainees takes on a new significance. Hopkins, writing from the Interskills Community Service Scheme in Coventry, recognizes and tackles this dilemma:

The economic background of unemployment is often dismissed as being too abstract and distant from the individual to be of interest. Our experience showed that with the right person and an informal discussion approach based on local information, this is not the case, and that in fact it can provide a boost for trainees by putting the 'blame' for unemployment squarely on society and thus remove for some of them the guilt and lowered self-esteem that accompany unemployment

Hopkins 1980:15.

The second, and more fundamental, problem of current LSS courses is their encouragement of adherence to the 'value' of work amongst the very young people who are at present unable to achieve that status, and whose future employment prospects are dismal in comparison with previous generations. Present policies are designed to establish the individual in work and by doing this 'society has effectively decided that it is not necessary to develop and pursue policies designed to help the individual adjust to and cope with a state of sustained worklessness' (Hayes and Nutman 1981:6). The evidence suggests that there is no lack of desire to work amongst our young people. If some youngsters do show less than enthusiasm at the prospect of a job, is it our place to deter that attitude and foster motivation towards something that they may have difficulty attaining. The rushed introduction and hectic operation of LSS courses has perhaps prevented organizers from considering this issue but as Jaap and Ware argue, YOP should be designed 'to equip the individual with living and social skills to enable life to be conducted irrespective of the unemployment situation' (1980:2). It would be difficult to argue that that is what presently takes place!

Bibliography

ASHTON, D.N. & FIELD, D. (1976) *Young Workers from School to Work* London, Hutchinson.

BALL, C. & M. (1979) *Fit for Work* London, Writers and Readers Publishing Co-operative.

B1 YOUTH UNEMPLOYMENT DROP-IN CENTRE (1981) *Annual Report 1980/81* Leicester.

BLYTHE, J. (1979) *Teaching Social and Life Skills* Coombe Lodge Report Vol. 13, No. 7. Bristol, Coombe Lodge.

BRAKE, M. (1980) *The Sociology of Youth Subcultures* London, Routledge & Kegan Paul.

BRANNEN, P. (Ed.) (1975) *Entering the world of work* London HMSO.

BURGER, A. & SEIDENSPINNER, G. (1977) *Jugend unter dem Druck der Arbeitslosiokeit* Munich, Juventa Verlag.

BURNS, R.B. (1979) *The Self Concept* London, Longman.

COCKRAM, L. & BELOFF, H. (1976) *Rehearsing to be Adults* Leicester, National Youth Bureau.

COLEMAN, J.C. (1980) *The Nature of Adolescence* London, Methuen.

COMMITTEE ON SCOTTISH AFFAIRS (1981) *Youth Unemployment and Training Vol. 1* London, HMSO.

COOPERSMITH, S. (1967) *The Antecedents of Self Esteem* San Francisco and London, W.H. Freeman & Co.

CORRIGAN, P. (1979) *Schooling the Smash Street Kids* London, Macmillan.

CRICHTON-MILLER, N. (1981) 'ICFC's Work and Learn Programme', *The Training Officer* August 1981.

CROCKER, F., FLETCHER, S., FOSTER, J., HALL, R. & SQUIRES, A. *Camden Unemployed Girls Project Report 1980.*

DAVIES, B. (1979) *From Social Education to Social and Life Skills Training: In whose interests?* Leicester, National Youth Bureau.

DAVY, D. (1981) 'The Psychological Aspects of Long-Term Unemployment', *Network*, August.

DEPARTMENT OF EDUCATION AND SCIENCE (1980) *Education for 16–19 year olds* London, HMSO.

DEPT OF EMPLOYMENT GAZETTE. (1982) February.

DEPT. OF MANPOWER STUDIES (1982) *A Comprehensive Youth Training Programme for 16/17 year olds in Northern Ireland* Dept. of Manpower Services and Dept. of Education (N.I.).

DOUVAN, E. & ADELSON, J. (1966) *The Adolescent Experience* New York, Wiley.

DUCK, S. (1977) *The Study of Acquaintance* Farnborough, Saxon House.

DUCK, S. (1980) 'With a Little help from my friends', *New Society* 30 October.

DUNPHY, E. (1963) 'The social structure of urban adolescents', *Sociometry* Vol. 26, No. 2.

FINDLAY, I. (1980) Day Release Life and Social Skills Provision for WEEP Trainees. *Coombe Lodge Report* Vol. 13, No. 7.

FRITH, S. (1980) 'Who's to blame', *Youth in Society*, February.

FROMM, F. (1966) *The Fear of Freedom* London, Routledge & Kegan Paul.

FURTHER EDUCATION CURRICULUM REVIEW AND DEVELOPMENT UNIT (FECRDU) (1978) *Postal Survey of FE provision for the Young Unemployed* London, FECRDU.

FURTHER EDUCATION CURRICULUM REVIEW AND DEVELOPMENT UNIT (1980a) *Beyond Coping* London, FECRDU.

FURTHER EDUCATION CURRICULUM REVIEW AND DEVELOPMENT UNIT (1980b) *Developing Social and Life Skills* London, FECRDU.

GLADSTONE, D.E. (1979) 'The Evaluation of 'Just the Job': A summary! Exeter University.

GURNEY, R.M. (1980) 'Does unemployment affect the self-esteem of school leavers?', *Australian J. of Psych.* Vol. 32, No. 3.

HAYES, J & NUTMAN, P. (1981) *Understanding the Unemployed* London, Tavistock.

HMSO (1981) *A New Training Initiative-A Programme for Action.* Command Paper 8455.

HEINEMANN, K. (1978) *Arbeitslose Jugendliche* Darmstadt, Luchterhand.

HOPKINS, M. (1980) 'The boom stops here', *Basic Education* January.

HOPSON, B. & SCALLY, M. (1980) 'Teaching Lifeskills for living in a post-industrial society', *Careers Journal* Vol. , No. 1.

INCE, D.E. (1971) *Contact* Leicester, Youth Service Information Centre.

INDUSTRIAL TRAINING RESEARCH UNIT (1979) *The A–Z Study* Cambridge, ITRU Publication SY4.

INSTITUTE OF CAREERS OFFICERS (1979) *Young People and Unemployment* Bromsgrove, ICO.

INTOWORK (1980) *Life and Social Skills from the Inside* North Tyneside Into Work Ltd.

JAAP, T. and WARE, H. (1980) 'Survival training', *Training* Vol. 6, No. 9, November.

JEFFERSON, T. & HALL, S. (1976) *Resistance Through Ritual: Youth Subcultures in Postwar Britain* London, Hutchinson.

JOELS, C. (1981) 'Life and social skills in ASHTON, D.N. & BOURN, C.J. (Eds.) *Education, Employment and Young People.* Vaughan Paper No. 26. University of Leicester.

KELVIN, P. (1981) 'Work as a source of identity', *Brit. J. of Guidance and Counselling.* Vol. 9, No. 1.

KITWOOD, T. (1980) *Disclosures to a Stranger* London, Routledge and Kegan Paul.

Sue Bloxham

MANPOWER SERVICES COMMISSION (1973) *Instructional Guide to Social and Life Skills* London, Manpower Services Commission.

MANPOWER SERVICES COMMISSION (1981a) *The Youth Opportunities Programme and the Local Education Authority* London, Manpower Services Commission.

MANPOWER SERVICES COMMISSION (1981b) *Using Residential Experience in YOP* London, Manpower Services Commission.

MORGAN, D. (1981) 'Youth call-up: Social policy for the young', *Critical Social Policy* Vol. 1, No. 2.

MORLEY BUNKER, N. (1981) 'In the streets but not dancing', *Time Out* 1–7 May.

MUNGHAM, G. (1976) (Ed.) *Working Class Youth Culture* London, Routledge & Kegan Paul.

MUSGROVE, F. (1964) *Youth and the Social Order* London, Routledge and Kegan Paul.

NATIONAL YOUTH BUREAU (1980) *Drop-In Centres Information and Resource Pack* Leicester, NYB.

NATIONAL YOUTH BUREAU (1981) *Youth Unemployment Facts and Figures* Leicester, NYB.

PARKER, H.J. (1974) *View from the Boys* Newton Abbot, David and Charles.

PARSONS, T. & BALES, R.F. (1956) *Family, Socialization and Interaction Process* London, Routledge & Kegan Paul.

PEARN, M.A. & MUNENE, J. (1978) *Increasing Employability: An evaluation of the Fullemploy Training Scheme* London, Runnymede Trust.

PHILIPS, D. (1973) 'Young and unemployed in a northern city' in WEIR, D. *Men and Work in Modern Britain* London, Fontana.

PRESDEE, M. (1981) 'Education for the dole', *Youth in Society* May.

ROSENBERG, M. (1965) *Society and the Adolescent Self Image* Princeton, Princeton University Press.

ROUSELET, J. (1975) Les jeunes face au travail, *Autrement* Part I.

SAWDON, A. & TAYLOR, D. (1980) *Youth Unemployment: A background paper* London, Youthaid.

SAWDON, A., TUCKER, S. & PELICAN, J. (1979) *Study of the Transition from School to Working Life Vol. 1* London, Youthaid.

—— (1981a). Vol. 11.

—— (1981b). Vol. 111.

SCHNEIDER, G. (1977) *Youth Unemployment In Industrialized Market Economy Countries* Geneva, International Labour Office.

SINFIELD, A. (1981) *What Unemployment Means* Oxford, Martin Robertson.

STANTON, G.P. (1980) *Developing Social and Life Skills* London, FECRDU.

STARR, A. (1982) Life classes, *Guardian* 13 April.

STROEBE, W. (1977) 'Self esteem and interpersonal attraction' in DUCK, S. (Ed.) *Theory and Practice of Interpersonal Attraction* London, Academic Press.

TIFFANY, D.W. (1970) *The Unemployed: A Social-Psychological Portrait* Englewood Cliffs NJ, Prentice Hall.

WATTS, A.G. (1979) The Educational Implications of Unemployment, *Coombe Lodge Report* Vol. 12, No. 1.

WILCOX, B., DUNN, J., LAVERCOMBE, S. and BURN, L. (1980) *Anticipation of Employment and Unemployment: Views of Pupils Likely to be at Risk in the World of Work.* EEC Transition from School to Working Life Project, Sheffield Ed. Dept.

WILLIS, P. (1977) *Learning to Labour* Farnborough, Saxon House.

WILMOT, P. (1960) *Adolescent Boys of East London* London, Routledge & Kegan Paul.

YOUNG MENS' CHRISTIAN ASSOCIATION (1980) *YMCA Youth at Work Service: MSC, WEEP Courses Oct.–Dec. 1979* YMCA.

YOUTHAID (1980) *Jobless: a study of unemployed young people in North Tyneside* London, Youthaid.

YOUTHAID (1981a) Quality or Collapse London, Youthaid.
YOUTHAID (1981b) In and Out of the Programe London, Youthaid.

Acknowledgements

I would like to acknowledge the support of the Social Science Research Council for my research study of the social behaviour of unemployed adolescents and the assistance given me by Henry Chignell in translating German and French texts.

Race, Riots and Unemployment

John F. Schostak

In Elizabethan times John Hawkins was knighted for his success in the slave trade. For centuries Britain has had a shameful relationship with black people, exploiting their lands and defining them as racially inferior (Bolt 1971). Today, although there are no longer slaves in Britain, racial discrimination persists (*c.f.* PEP1967, 1976), and has frequently exploded into violence (e.g., Richmond 1961; Lawrence 1974; Scarman 1981). However, today being young black and unemployed cannot easily be separated from being young, white and unemployed. We have again entered an age of mass unemployment but there are differences from previous ages, for this is also the 'age of affluence'. It is the age of mass consumption and the young will not easily forgo their share of today's enjoyments. Indeed, black revolt today cannot be easily disentangled from youth rebellion in the consumer society, nor can rebellion be disentangled from the awareness of individuals that they have a right to expect a decent standard of living and quality of life. Today's problems are therefore not a temporary aberration in social history but are part of an historic expression of the rights of groups and of individuals to expect certain kinds of rewards from their labour, to be recognized as having certain rights and freedoms of expression and to have a life-style of their own deciding. Today's problems were, therefore, sown centuries ago in the desire to create classes of people who could be made to work for the benefit of the rulers of powerful nations. The racist attitude is one dimension of the desire to hold power over another, whether those others are workers, peasants, children, women, the poor, or the 'racially inferior'. The various dimensions of the desire for power over others form a common framework. This framework forms a basis for the interpretation of racism, youth rebellion, and violence in employer-employee relations and provides for actors a common frame for action either to suppress or to resist suppression.

Something of the growing awareness of a common framework of action uniting youth can be seen in the differences between the riots of 1919 in Liverpool, the riots of 1958 in Nottingham and the riots erupting in a variety of cities in 1981. This is not to say racism is not still a major motivating factor in social behaviour today but to say the seeds for a new awareness are germinating. In this paper I will argue that the government's responses to youth unemployment avoid addressing the causes of unemployment and

131

John F. Schostak

blame the unemployed by defining them as inadequate. This is done for purposes of social control in order to preserve existing power relations. This, however, continues the tension which leads to social unrest. First, therefore, I will illustrate the changing face of rioting by comparing the earlier Liverpool and Nottingham riots with the recent street rioting of 1981, placing it into a context of systematic resistance against discrimination whether social or racial. Secondly, the motivations for rioting will be illustrated in the words of young blacks and whites as they search for solutions to their predicaments. And finally, the responses of government to the present situation will be examined to see the extent to which they adequately meet the needs of the young in general and the blacks in particular.

Racial Conflict – Liverpool 1919 and Nottingham 1958

In the host country the immigrants have a place if they are either slaves or skivvies but as Richmond (1961:237) writes:

> When work was scarce white seamen were apt to express hostility towards coloured seamen, and the disturbances which broke out in Cardiff and Liverpool and on a smaller scale in east London, Tyneside, and Glasgow, after the First World War, were a reflection of the growing sense of insecurity which was felt by white seamen, who resented the competition of coloured colonials.

Richmond goes on to give a description of racist rioting:

> The disturbances of 1919 followed a similar pattern wherever they occurred. A relatively minor incident between one or two men, probably under the influence of drink, provided the spark that set off the inflammatory situation. In Liverpool the coincidence of a sudden increase in the number of Negro immigrants after the First World War, and the first signs of the post-war depression in the shipping industry, led, in May and June 1919, to serious disturbances. The climax was reached when a Negro was drowned in a scrimmage on the docks and the police had to make several baton charges on the crowd.

The racial conflicts were fought out upon the stage created by the 'invisible hand' of market forces. The market forces of the demand and supply of labour by their very impersonality erase the history of the origins of particular economic situations. Forced into competition for jobs, white and blacks fought each other. The solution was not to change the system but:

> The upshot of these disturbances was a campaign for the repatriation of coloured colonials in Britain and a number, in fact, took advantage of schemes to pay their passage to their home town. Others remained in Britain in hopes that the prospects of work would improve, but on the whole they were disappointed.

Indeed, a study by Jones (1940) found that blacks in Liverpool suffered high unemployment, poverty, and poor housing with rents being relatively higher than for whites.

The 'invisible hand' of market economics, however, aided by the benevolent hand of 'Keynesian' governments, began to create a new economic climate. During the 1950s and 1960s the demand for labour was so great there were shortages of supply in the lower paid occupations, particularly in the service industries. Thus, many blacks were drawn to this country by the lure of a new life. The PEP Report (1976) asked of a sample of 3,292 people defined as coloured, 'Why did you come to Britain?':

> Over half of them (57 per cent) say that they came to Britain to get work or to earn money, and this is the most frequently mentioned reason for coming. Although the men tended to be pioneers in the migration, there is an important minority of them (16 per cent) who came to join their families. The other main reasons given by men for migrating are to seek a better future or life for the family (17 per cent) – which may be a rather more idealistic way of expressing the need for work – and education (13 per cent). An important minority also moved for political reasons (8 per cent).

The total of black immigrants according to the report was at most two and a half per cent of the British population. Yet in the minds of racists the figure appeared larger. And Britain was an essentially racist society as the events and the aftermath of 1958 made clear.

Despite increasing affluence, the hostility remained as Lawrence (1974:2) describes concerning the 'Race War City' (*Daily Sketch* 1 September 1958) of Nottingham:

> . . . in 1957, there was an ugly clash between West Indians and whites in the Employment Exchange during which knives were drawn. The first of the 1958 disturbances took place on 23 August. On leaving a pub at closing time a crowd began to argue and brawl and within a few minutes a number of West Indians had stabbed four local people. Another squabble broke out a short distance away and two more people were stabbed. By 11 p.m. a crowd of 1,500 had gathered and its hostility was directed against any coloured people still on the streets. As a result, the reinforced police force either escorted coloured people home or took them into protective custody. Crowds gathered in anticipation of more trouble the following Saturday. Until 11 p.m. the police succeeded in preventing any further outbreak of violence. Then sections of the estimated 3,000 strong crowd began to attack the police – presumably in retaliation for the protection they had afforded coloured people the week before. Although on this occasion no-one was seriously hurt, large numbers of people were arrested. The following Saturday, at about the same time, after a group of West Indians had been escorted home by the police, a smaller crowd began to attack several houses in which coloured people lived. They broke down a brick wall, used the bricks as missiles, and smashed several windows. The tenants replied by throwing bottles at the crowd. Once again the police acted firmly and the troublemakers were dispersed.

As Lawrence goes on to point out, the official view in Nottingham was that there was no racial discrimination anywhere to be found in the city. He quotes Katznelson's view that 'the pre-1958 illusion of harmonious race relations has been restored, but in my view it remains, unfortunately, merely an illusion.' The PEP Report of 1967 further reinforces the view of Britain as a racially divided country. However, the response of government was to reinforce racial discrimination through the Commonwealth Immigrants Act 1962 of which Kapo (1981) writes:

> The Commonwealth Immigrants Act had blown the guts out of the 'mother country' hallucination, in which blacks and Asians had been romanticizing, thumping the idea into guesswork that the black position here was very arbitrary. The act concurred, by rendering unthinkable the psychic idea of peaceful black, brown, and white rapport in the near future.

He goes on to describe how the newspapers ran headlines on blacks dominating house buying, on black depravity and so on, and how clubs immediately enforced a colour bar against blacks. He recounts his horror when:

> Hatred was taken further and in 1963, among many repulsive incidents, came an event which startled me: Junta Singh, an Indian in Birmingham, had his grocery store bombed. The bombers had carefully packed a fire-extinguisher with explosives and planted it in the doorway of his shop.

Racial hatred and acts of violence continue still in this country systematized in the hate campaigns of the National Front, The British Movement and so on, and instilled in the youth culture of 'skin heads' – but changes have also begun to occur.

The Surprise Eruption of Street Rioting – 1981

Of course it was no surprise the street riots occurred but many behaved as if it were. There had been a long build up as can be seen in Clutterbuck's (1978) book in which he catalogued the mounting violence in Britain. Most years since 1966 have seen at least one major national industrial dispute involving strike action or work to rule. In 1967 unemployment climbed to 600,000, there was a dock strike and the pound was devalued. The 1970s saw a series of major strikes which led to the Heath government falling in 1974; and in that year oil prices quadrupled. In 1975 there was one million unemployed and unemployment rose to nearly one and a half million in January 1976. 'Right to Work' marchers at West Hendon injured 41 policemen and at the Notting Hill Carnival of 1976, 250 people were injured of which 120 were police. In 1977 the Socialist Workers Party attacked a National Front march in Lewisham; in Birmingham the Socialist Workers Party attacked police guarding a National Front by-election meeting; and at the Notting Hill Carnival there were further disturbances. In 1978 the National Front initiated its 'School's Campaign' to stimulate racial hatred. In 1980 there were the riots at St Pauls in Bristol.

These are but a few of the incidents from the 1960s and 1970s in Britain.

Yet, the 1981 riots came as a surprise! Teddy Taylor, Tory MP for Southend East (*The Sunday Express* 12 July 1981) wrote:

> Most people have watched the reports of the outbreaks of violence and rioting throughout our cities with a mixture of disbelief and alarm. Even a few years ago the possibility of our policemen having petrol bombs thrown at them by school children and crowds of adults and teenagers helping themselves to goods from looted shops would have been regarded as stupid alarmist talk.
>
> And there is no way in which the riots can be classified as being only a racial problem. It is true that the rioters in Brixton and Bristol were overwhelmingly black. But many of the vandals and looters in the last week's outbreaks were white and most worrying has been the number of very young people involved.

Rather than proclaiming racial conflict new explanations had to be found in the face of evidence that black and white youth had side by side looted and burnt with the common enemy being the police.

Taylor saw the riots as 'simply the cumulation of a rising tide of crime and violence which has been destroying our nation's reputation as a peaceful and law-abiding place to live in.' Robottom (in Tutt 1976:40–55), in a study of the history of violence in this country argues that without an historical framework it is difficult to argue against the assertion that:

> violence is on the increase in our contemporary domestic society, especially when they are supported by supposedly definitive evidence in the form of statistics or by being related to some other putative historical trend such as a decline in parental authority, an increase in personal income, a waning of religious and moral sanctions and so on. A simple answer would be that, despite the existence of figures, we do not know enough of the facts to make a quantative investigation of the amount or intensity of violence in English history.

He goes on to show that 'the further one goes the more the use of violence is inseparable from other features of social activity and political organization' in the history of our country. On the evidence, it could be argued that violence is less today than in earlier years. He writes 'The central thesis of this essay is that both public and specialist awareness of violence – itself a term which has only recently gained its connotations of capricious and deviant behaviour – has increased as the major threat has declined.' Certainly, the violence is there, but whether the riots were 'simply the culmination of a rising tide of crime and violence' is very much open to doubt, historically. In short, 'What history teaches us, if we are prepared to learn, is that violence is not atypical or anomalous; on the contrary it is usual and endemic in the historical development of all nations; virtually every study points to the fact that violence has been pervasive, and sometimes chronic, as far as history records' (Tutt 1976:28). Tutt goes on to write that violence has a positive side since 'tyrants have been banished and despots deposed by violent methods.' If we are to believe Freud (1979) the whole of civilization is built upon the rebellion of the sons against their fathers, that is, upon the revolt of youth against the repressive authority of age. Heer (1974) has written a history of youth rebellion which clearly shows its pervasiveness throughout history; thus, for example:

> Risings and disturbances in English schools were not uncommon in the first years of the French Revolution. In 1793 Winchester College was held in occupation by its pupils for two days. The Red Flag was flown on the Middle Gate.

Youth rebellion is the energy of social change. But 'it is the fate of revolutionary youth movements to flare up suddenly, in bright, upright flames, which are then stamped out, or die down of their own accord-sometimes both together.' It could be argued that black youth today are in the vanguard of youth rebellion – rejecting Babylon (the white world) and white parental authority, choosing, instead, their own leaders. White youth too, are rejecting the old ways. Thus, in the face of their discontent in the 1981 riots, Boyson, the Junior Education Minister, argued for a return to more authoritarian modes of discipline (*The Daily Telegraph*, 11 July 1981):

> Liberalism has in our time been enfeebled by sentiment and corrupted by egalitarianism. Tradition, the cement which helps to hold society together, has been scorned as restrictive and replaced in many cases by naive arrogance.
>
> The gradual undermining of authority was also at the root of present-day problems. More children would have to be taken into care if the authority of parents continued to be undermined, resulting in good homes falling apart.
>
> Similarly, if we destroy the authority of the headteacher and his staff, society will reap dragon's teeth in the form of juvenile revolt.

Typically, there is an excitement in riots, a carnival spirit where:

> The Carnival King – normally a slave – reigns for a day or a week. All the usual patterns of authority are reversed in games, dances, orgies. Passions and instincts are given free rein. Like characters on a stage, the victims are tried and marched to the guillotine between cheering crowds.
>
> Heer 1974:38

Heer thus characterizes the youth rebellion of virtually any period of history. It is against the Carnival King that the austere authority of Boyson fights. Thus, there was the response of the Home Secretary in introducing the 'short sharp shock' for young offenders. This involved subjecting them to a harsh physical routine for a short period of time in a detention centre. Harsh physical punishment in the training and upbringing of children is a long and venerable tradition, not only in England, but the world over (*cf.* De Mause 1974). Caning in schools is still not entirely abandoned. It can be argued that the authority of the headmaster is founded either upon acts of violence, or threats of violence in those schools were caning is still allowed. Even in those schools where it is not allowed, the authority of the headmaster is founded upon a variety of threats involving the ability to administer sanctions and founded upon the fact that children are, in effect, compelled to come to school.

Children are under the eye of authority at school. And on the streets they are under the eye of the police. Insensitive policing was considered by many to be one of the major cause of the 1981 riots. Both black and white complained of being harassed by police activities. Landau (1981) has shown that for young blacks, police treatment is more severe than for young whites. Moreover, Phillips (1981) suggested that due to police treatment there was a 'criminalization' of blacks where they expected to be stopped, questioned, picked up, chased, held, beaten up. That is, they expected to be treated as would be criminals. Brogden (1981) quoted a young Liverpool 8 black as saying: 'It's not "sus" that leads to hassle with the police, but the number of times that we're searched on the street – round here it's a crime to be black.' The 'sus' law refers to the 'suspected persons offence' which empowers police to pick up a person on 'suspicion'. Both the 'sus' laws and the 'stop and search' powers of the police were contentious issues during the riots. Waller (1981) in his analysis of the Toxteth riots concluded: 'The character of policing in Toxteth, particularly police relations with young blacks, is one of the keys to an understanding of Liverpool's part in the general disturbances'. It was this relationship with the police that made the 1981 riots so different to earlier riots. Waller goes on to say:

> The element of 'race' in the 1981 disturbances is difficult to objectify. Indirectly, a memorial of the past was afforded by the very building used by the Liverpool 8 Defence Committee, the Charles Wooten Centre for Adult Education, named after the black victim of the 1919 conflict. How many caught the association, or what meaning they placed on it, is inestimable. Not that symptoms of racial tension have been absent in this district. The first surge of the now protractedly high unemployment, in the late 1960s and the early 1970s, uncovered signs of racial polarities as workless youths organized themselves into gangs whose identity was differentiated by colour.

Certainly, the racial tension is there as it was in other districts. But the social conditions were affecting both black and white – and both black and white had a common enemy.

Of Brixton, another major centre for the riots, The Scarman Report (1981:11) concluded:

> Many of the young people of Brixton are ... born and raised in insecure social and economic conditions and in an impoverished physical environment. They share the desires and expectations which our materialist society encourages. At the same time, many of them fail to achieve educational success and on leaving school face the stark prospect of unemployment. Many of these difficulties face white as well as black youngsters, but it is clear that they bear particularly heavily on young blacks. In addition, young black people face the burden of discrimination, much of it hidden and some of it unconscious and unintended. Without close parental support, with no job to go to, and with few recreational facilities available, the young black person makes his life on the streets and in the seedy commercially run clubs of Brixton. There he meets criminals, who appear to have no difficulty in obtaining the benefits of a materialist society.

Discrimination is itself a violent act, it demeans the individual, creates a sense of worthlessness, sets the stage for hostile acts. The necessary pre-condition for such discrimination is a society built upon social inequalities; during periods of increased competition for resources and jobs, violence must flare. Whether we have Boyson's 'Tradition of Inequality tempered by Liberalism without Sentiment' or any other variety of inequality, discrimina-tion will develop, *must develop;* hence we must have a Boysonian form of Liberal Discrimination enshrined within the laws of the land and the institu-tions of government. We are all deep in the nightmare of discrimination in all its forms, and of racism in particular.

Laws now define immigrants as outsiders. The latest is the British National-ity Act of 1981. As Wilenius illustrates and concludes:

> The proposals of the Nationality Bill have been taken as confirmation of all the worst fears: *'I'm going to have to get this qualification because you know the way things are going with this Bill, and Maggie, she is extreme . . . I reckon in a couple of years I'll be thrown out of the country.'*

True or not, the fear is there. Black people have all the problems of young whites in this age of mass unemployment, and more besides. Yet, when the rioting begins, we are always surprised. Why are they not grateful for the opportunities we give them?

In Search of Opportunities

In the face of three million unemployed, a forecast of 203,000 unemployed 18 year olds for autumn 1982, with 328,000 men between 20 and 24 unemployed in June 1981, with 20,000 university places cut, with education spending in general reduced, one may ask, what opportunities for the young are there left which the young can realistically take? During a study in a Northern comprehensive school I asked over 100 pupils what they would do when they left school. The following response by four fourth year girls is typical[1]:

Angie: Dunno, probably on the dole.
Carol: On dole, there's no jobs is there?
Mary: That's what all the fightin' in Toxteth's for.
Sue: It 'appened down here somewhere, there's one last night.
Mary: Yeah, it was all down here last night.

Riots and unemployment were clearly linked in their eyes. This area is virtually all white but noted for crime and violence and, of course, massive levels of unemployment. Only 11 per cent of the school's leavers found real jobs by December 1981. The label of racial conflict cannot be applied here. Perhaps it was 'copy cat' rioting? Perhaps, but this does not explain why usually peaceful individuals – parents and teachers – while deploring the violence could also say, 'perhaps it's the only way to make them listen.'

Some fourth year black boys in a London school were also the subject of my study but upon a smaller scale involving primarily participant observation, connected unemployment to the rioting in the following way:

Alex: About three quarters of my mates are unemployed. They just
'ang around, they just 'ang around the Boy's Club all night.
Ray: Yeah.
Alex: An' all day.
Ray: They 'ang around um.
Alex: An' they complain.
Ray: Amusements an' things...
JFS: And there's nothing for them to do?
Ray and Alex: No.
Ray: But when there's riotin', when there's riotin' they go to that 'cos
that's the only thing they can do. There's nothing really to do.

Opposed to the boredom of 'nothing to do' is the excitement of the riots – to
be 'Carnival King' for the day. Both the New Town of the Northern
comprehensive and London are characterized by gangs – as are most other
similar areas. Gang activities are a means by which to generate excitement – a
fact long known (e.g. Thrasher 1927). Without the means by which to buy
commodities individuals alone or in gangs will seek other means to get them.
As one sixteen year old London white boy said: 'I mean, it's a natural mutual
feeling now, isn't it? If you can nick something, nick it, without gettin'
caught. It's quite natural'.

Both New Town and the deprived areas of London and other cities are the
creation of market forces in conjunction with governmental initiatives. The
conditions of industry and government have created between them, and
continue to perpetuate, a climate of opinion where of stealing it can be judged
as 'quite natural'; and of riots, 'that's the only thing they can do'. But the
shame of New Town is that it was *purpose built* to take the slum families of a
nearby city (Schostak 1982a, 1982b).

In New Town, as I said, there are few blacks – Darren Baily is one of the
few. I do not have space to go into his case study in detail here but I can give
the bare outlines. Darren is a natural leader, a boy who creates his own
opportunities. The deputy head of the school said of Darren 'Darren has only
two problems. One, he was born in New Town. Two, he's black.' Darren has
already 'done' a post office and was involved in the local riots and riots
elsewhere – although caught, a case could not conclusively be proven against
him. Darren in his final year at school went for an interview for a job in
London which involved taking an aptitude test. Darren is not a dull boy. He is
lively, verbally like a whip lash – but his written work is non-existent. He
failed the test. He said 'I was convinced I'd passed. When I heard I'd failed I
had tears in my eyes. That job would have changed my life.' Darren is well
liked by many of the staff and the pupils in the school although he can be very
troublesome with those teachers he does not like. I am inclined to consider the
job would have changed his life. Darren is determined to 'make it' – one way
or another. He continued to say that what he needed to do was 'do a nice little
bank' then he could travel the world – 'like Ronnie Biggs'. He had learnt from
the riots he said. Next time, they would do things properly. Under the cover
of the riots he could 'do his little bank'. Darren insists he does not want to go
on the dole or take a YOP place 'or any of that crap'. He will make his own
opportunities.

John F. Schostak

Confronting Crisis

One way to confront a crisis is to make it vanish in a cloud of words; that is, to present a definition of the state of the world which systematically avoids looking at the crisis. For example, the Solicitor-General, Sir Ian Percival, was reported (*The Sunday Times* 21 February 1982) as describing life in the UK as:

> "A land of people for the most part well fed and dressed and spending freely on comforts and pleasures. A land of people who enjoy the best free health and education systems in the world." Speaking at Sidmouth, Devon, he said that "despite all the problems, 88 out of every hundred of the total working population of all ages, are earning." Average wages were £121 a week for male manual workers over 21 and £163 for non-manual workers. As for the three million unemployed, Percival's view was also resolutely cheerful. "Almost everywhere there are lists of situations vacant," he said. His own Southport constituency, for example, had more than 100 work-opportunity places vacant.

By concentrating upon averages one can forget the unequal social distribution of the burden of unemployment, and of the unequal social distribution of income. Thus, for example, when in Southport, near Liverpool, it is to be forgotten that for Liverpool unemployment officially reached 18.2 per cent (the national average being about 12 per cent). On 30 January 1981 the local paper, *The Daily Post*, reported that: 'City Officials estimate Liverpool's real unemployment statistics at near 27 per cent'. And in *The Knowsley Reporter* (3 April 1981) it was reported that in May 1979: 'There were 21,771 vacancies in the North West and only 7,742 today. In Merseyside, the vacancies have slumped from 4,019 in May, 1979, to 2,139, while in Kirkby they have gone down from 110 to 47. *The Daily Post* (10 February 1981) ran a headline which said it all: 'Chances of an unskilled job: 4000–1'.

Unemployment is also, of course, racially distributed to the blacks' disadvantage. For example, Sargeant (1981) reports that:

> Historically, the economic prosperity of Birmingham has been based on the success of its industrial enterprises, in particular a flourishing motor industry. However, in the current climate of world wide recession, this has proved to be a liability, as is demonstrated by the almost daily collapse of manufacturing industries. Inevitably, black workers have been particularly hard hit – although constituting 11 per cent of the city's population, black workers accounted for 17 per cent of the total unemployed in February 1980. In Handsworth, where almost a third of the population is black, 45 per cent out of work.

The catalogue of woe could be extended to fill several books.

An alternative to averting the glance from the crisis and evoking an 'I'm alright Jack' response is to find a solution, or a partial solution, to the crisis which involves tackling the symptoms and not the causes; that is, to find a solution which does not place into doubt the basic social structures of society; ideally, to find a solution which acts as an agent of social control rather than as a force for change. It can be argued, and has, that the variety of schemes for training, work experience and so on, are little more than ways of socially controlling the working class unemployed youth – a more modern form of 'gentling the masses' (*eg*. Finn and Frith 1980). It would appear that the various schemes do not provide new opportunities but defer the realization of the lack of opportunities for young people. For example, the Principal Careers Officer for Knowsley, Liverpool, wrote[2]:

> Simply providing more YOP places, and particularly YOP schemes requiring entrants to be qualified or highly motivated, will only result in empty schemes without any reduction in unemployment. What is needed is a post-YOP provision which is *deemed by these young people to be a job*. (My italics)

Thus, for the borough as a whole only 10 per cent of all school leavers entered permanent work by 22 December 1981 *and the provision of places on YOP schemes has not reduced the number of long term unemployed*. In January 1979 the number unemployed was 1600 yet despite an increase by 1000 in the number of YOP places, in January 1982 the number of unemployed youth was 1600! In such areas as this, we are approaching the situation faced by the Croxteth area of Liverpool where 'Only 5.4 per cent of young people between the ages of 16 and 18 have full-time jobs' (*Guardian* 4 May 1982). Such schemes, of course, cannot provide jobs, they merely train youth, or provide them with experience of jobs, for which no jobs exist. Thus it is no surprise to learn in two studies by the Manpower Services Commission (1982) that in general the chances of young people getting a job after taking part in a government scheme are improved only marginally and blacks, the unqualified and those who have been unable to get jobs for a long period of time, do not do so well as others in obtaining work. In particular, Allinson (1980) reports:

> The ready and enthusiastic involvement of non-statutory agencies and community groups in the sponsorship of Youth Opportunities Programme schemes has been impressive. The initial appeal of the YOP to the voluntary sector was that Manpower Services Commission funds could be used to undertake long-cherished but previously impractical projects. In particular, many black community groups saw an opportunity to make real progress in provision for young people through flexible programmes of training, education, and, possibly, permanent community-managed jobs.
>
> Now, after two and a half years, this flexibility seems non-existent and the enthusiasm is beginning to wane. Some scheme sponsors making provision for young unemployed blacks are finding themselves impossibly constrained by MSC procedures on the one side and the demands of their trainees on the other.

Furthermore, 'increasingly, young black trainees are coming to resent what they feel to be a waste of time. They do not want to do what they perceive as the traditional shit jobs, either in a YOP project or in regular employment, and are refusing to believe that an MSC opportunity can be anything more than a device to keep them off the streets and out of the unemployment figures. The consequent difficulties of sponsors and staff in maintaining the attendance, motivation, and co-operation of trainees, have been strong contributory factors' in the failure of a number of schemes the author has earlier outlined in his paper. Sargeant (1981) also felt that 'black groups often favour responses which are not only at variance with MSC guidelines, but also go against the grain of official MSC thinking.' The schemes, in short, do not take into account the needs of the blacks. Sargeant goes on to say:

> Early impressions from a study of YOP provision and black youth in Handsworth on which I am currently engaged, points to the conclusion that YOP staff display a tendency to stereotype black trainees. They are regarded as either totally lacking in those social and cultural skills deemed essential for successful entry into the labour market as a consequence of their specific cultural background; or, alternatively, as having been socialized into a set of disreputable subcultural values and practices which are at variance with both the work and practices of the society more generally.

In interviews with staff and students I carried out at a college work experience course it is clear that such courses are not fulfilling the real needs of the students, that is, leading to *real* jobs. The students felt that such courses enabled them to learn something new occasionally, filled in the time and made a change from the dole queue which they felt to be a shaming experience – and of course, gave them money every 'Friday, sweet Friday'.

I asked four 17 year old girls – two black, two white:

> *JFS*: What are you going to do when you leave this course?
> *Cecile*: Well, I've got a clear idea what I'm going to do: back on the dole.

The other three girls agreed. A teacher estimated that usually two out of sixteen students will get a job when they leave the course. For the remainder it is back to the college for some other work experience course. At seventeen these girls are already old hands at WICs, WEEPs and so on: 'All I been on is YOPs courses, right?' And what are these courses for? 'It's supposed to teach us what we don't know and we've already learnt it anyway.' Or, 'It's supposed to be work experience but we're not getting any.' Or, 'The only reason I've come on this place is because I'm ashamed to go down the dole office every week.' The majority of the members of the course are blacks. For the forseeable future theirs is a life on the dole, a life where they create whatever excitement and self respect that they can, *by whatever means.*

A black girl said of her life 'All I've got is music, drugs and parties.' But with the police raids – 'If a black has a party it'll be raided' – even those pleasures are being denied. They talked of 'running away from unemployment' through parties, courses and rioting . . . a riot is at least exciting.

> "The reason why I'm trying to run away from unemployment is because I'm there, I mean I'm thinking 'fuckin' 'eck' – sorry to be rude you know – 'in another year's time I'll still be on the dole. Oh dear, what am I going to do?' You know? People are working, they must be getting some big lot of money an' enjoyin' themselves an' seein' life. Me, sittin' down there waitin', you know. It's ridiculous."

The confrontation is coming just like confrontations of years gone by, 'Only this time it'll be bigger and better organized, they'll be coming from all over – Liverpool, Bristol, all those places.'

And how is the college coping with the endemic problems of massive unemployment, black unemployment in particular, and confrontations between the police and the blacks? It has, of course, in common with other colleges taken upon itself the task of providing courses. This, in itself, has had repercussions on the staff and the organization of the college having now to cope with an influx of unemployed black youth:

"Well security has, I think, become a very big issue in most colleges. This college has a very strict security system whereby students who don't comply get sent home and so on. It's a very big issue amongst the staff and the students. These students feel, a lot of the students feel, quite harrassed by it and there's quite a few arguments on the door over security and it tends to be black students who get stopped. And the heaviest security is where most of the black students are. And they tend to get moved on in the passage and so on. It creates, I think, quite a bad, something of a fortress atmosphere. The reason it's there is not so much because of management but because the staff have asked for it. The majority of staff feel that the college is changing as a result of having a new student constituency which is the 16 to 19 unemployed kids who are mostly black."

The teacher goes on to say there have been three incidents involving theft. But in a college involving well over ten thousand students these are remarkably few incidents. Nevertheless there is a general desire for greater security.

The image of the college as a 'fortress' is unpleasant. Imported into the organization of the college itself is a continuation of the police surveillance procedures of the street, the 'sus' laws. It is a crisis of confrontation:

"I was the other day, I was walkin' down an' I was nicked for fuck-all. I didn't do anythin' an' it really hurt me 'cos I've never been in trouble before but because I'm black I have to stay back. And I'm tellin' yer I'm standin' firm, right, 'cos whatever they do I know I still got white friends if they still like to know me, you know, I'll call them, you know, it's a thing that, I don't like to be bugged at, bugged at all the time, you know. And they do. And that was what the Brixton riot was all about."

Being 'bugged at' is a common everyday experience. A black teacher, active in the black community, said:

"Amongst black people in Britain, there is a strong feeling of-um-of oppression. There is a feeling that we been put down. Whether or not it's imagined or true or what, the feeling does exist and especially among young people there is a feeling they want to get back at somebody or something and so it's very easy then for things like the riots to trigger off. We, we all hear stories about our friends or relations getting pulled by the police and getting treated very badly by the police."

The course at this college, and others like it at other colleges, are simply 'containing the problem' are simply 'getting the kids off the street for a while' because 'there are no real jobs'. Indeed, as a white teacher said 'The MSC programmes are based on a notion that the student is in some way inadequate – so when they find out they're on this course and it doesn't even offer any certification um that is in anyway nationally accepted um they think that this isn't a serious course.' New training initiatives being considered by the government extending training to one year in duration are seen simply as a 'super-YOP' or 'More of the same' only longer, since, at the end of the day, 'there are no jobs there for them to go to.' It is perhaps ironic therefore that the MSC Youth Task Group can report in April 1982:

> This report is about providing a permanent bridge between school and work. It is not about youth unemployment. What we propose will improve the prospects of young people to get and keep jobs but we have not been concerned with temporary measures.
>
> Our report is about greatly increasing opportunities, widening options and realizing the potential of our young people. It is not about eliminating choice or introducing compulsion.
>
> The scheme we propose will make a central contribution to economic survival, recovery and growth. Our aim is to provide for what the economy needs, and what employers want – a better equipped, better qualified, better educated and better motivated workforce. And it is to provide for young people what they them-selves actively seek – greater opportunities to equip themselves to make their way in the increasingly competitive and uncertain world of the 1980s.

We have an 'increasingly competitive and uncertain world of the 1980s' with only limited opportunity for work. Unemployment is expected to remain high – infact, climb higher than the three million at present. Young individuals are therefore merely running harder for the same number of jobs whether or not there is a 'super-YOP'. Unemployed youth is here to stay for a long period. Training schemes will do nothing but defer the problem, that is, raising hopes only to dash them with greater force than would otherwise have been the case, unless new jobs, *real jobs*, are created. Growth, economic growth, will only occur if there is a demand led industrial and commercial investment in the future, or if the government itself diverts some or all of the £1000 million it intends to spend on MSC programmes into creating real jobs. At present the job creation appears to benefit the employees of the MSC and the college teachers on MSC courses, and so on. The crisis confronting youth must be realistically confronted.

Concluding Remarks

As appears typical of educational initiatives, the young are being treated as materials to be shaped and moulded to fit preconceived ideas of their inadequacy (*cf.* Schostak 1982c). The needs, ambitions and creativity of the young are being disregarded in favour of the supposed needs of industry. Yet industry is incapable of creating jobs at the present time. There is a tension, therefore, between the advertised affluence of society and its inability to provide work opportunities. This tension has exploded in the past in terms of trade union struggles and race riots. In the recent rioting a comparison cannot be made either to the race riots of 1919 or those of 1958. The racial element was directed towards the police, with the phenomenon of white and black youth against restricitive authority being one feature of the rioting. But the police are merely a 'buffer' between the young-and-propertyless and the old-and-propertied, between the powerless and powerful, the governed and the governing – and so on. The 'invisible hand' of market forces has come between the young and their supposed right to have a job, and created an age of mass unemployment where the 'work ethic' may soon be replaced by a 'leisure ethic'. Racial discrimination certainly exists but unemployment, poor housing, insensitive policing foment the feeling of oppression and the desire to 'hit back'.

Instead of throwing money at the 'problem' of the inadequacy of school leavers to meet the needs of employers, it would be more sensible to throw money at the problem of the employers' inadequacy to generate real jobs. As Tebbit has said (Hansard 27 January 1982: col. 908): 'At present ... we need 200,000 new jobs a year merely to keep pace with demographic change.'

With unemployment costing about thirteen billion pounds per year (Varley, Hansard, col. 914–5) the government has much to gain by the generation of jobs. Instead, the government persist in throwing money upon the scrap heap of unemployment, financing its growth day by day. The new youth training schemes continue the policy of financing unemployment.

Youth are feeling powerless to effect changes in their lives. Many are growing cynical as to the government's intentions. Yet youth are not being consulted. As they are not being drawn into the democratic processes of bringing about change so they reject and resist what appears to them as authoritarianism. In particular, black youth are turning away from a society which report after report shows is discriminating against them.

The new training schemes, by extending childhood – or dependency upon adults – are merely increasing the sense of powerlessness. The black peoples appear to be more likely to be unemployed than white people. The opportunities to fail to satisfy white criteria in training schemes as opposed to school failure are now being offered to them. Yet again the blacks are being found 'deficient' in relation to the whites. The young and, in particular, the young black, are carrying the burden of unemployment. The MSC programmes will only massage unemployment figures for one year – as did Raising of the School Leaving Age – but the fundamental problems which have caused structural youth unemployment are still to be faced. The new jobs must be created, the work ethic must give way to a leisure ethic, and a more democratic involvement by youth in their future must be brought about. If these things do not happen, then goods and services will be redistributed through criminal activities, power will be found through rioting and the democratic dream will crumble under the repressive acts of frightened governments. We can either unleash the creative energy of youth or its destructive energy. The choice is ours. Our children – the black, the white – must have their say. And they will have their say, *one way or another*. And we must listen.

John F. Schostak

Notes

1 All names of all interviewees are fictional in order to avoid the chance of recognition.
2 From the *Report of the Principal Careers Officer for the Period 11 December 1981 to 11 February 1982*, Borough of Knowsley, Liverpool.

Bibliography

ALLINSON, C. (1980) 'A crisis of confidence', *Youth in Society* November.
BOLT, C. (1971) *Victorian Attitudes to Race* London, Routledge and Kegan Paul.
BROGDEN, A. (1981) '"Sus" is dead: but what about "Sas"'? *New Community* Vol. 9, No. 1.
CLUTTERBUCK, R. (1978) *Britain in Agony: The Growth of Political Violence* London and Boston, Faber and Faber.
DE MAUSE, L. (1974) *The History of Childhood* New York, The Psychohistory Press.
FINN, D. and FRITH, S. (1980) *Society, Education and the State* Milton Keynes, Open University Press.
FREUD, S. (1979) *Civilization and its Discontents* (Translated by Joan Riviere; revised and edited by James Strachey) London, The Hogarth Press.
HEER, F. (1974) *Challenge of Youth: Revolutions of Our Time* London, Weidenfeld and Nicholson.
JONES, C. (1940) *The Economic Status of Coloured Families in the Port of Liverpool* The University Press of Liverpool.
KAPO, R. (1981) *A Savage Culture: Racism – A Black British View* London, Quartet Books.
LANDAU, S.F. (1981) 'Juveniles and the police', *British Journal of Criminology*, January.
LAWRENCE, D. (1974) *Black Migrants: White Natives: A study of Race Relations in Nottingham* Cambridge, Cambridge University Press.
MANPOWER SERVICES COMMISSION (1982) *Employment Gazette*, Vol. 90, No. 1, HMSO.
MANPOWER SERVICES COMMISSION (1982) *Youth Task Group Report.* April 1982.
PEP (1967) *Racial Discrimination in Britain* London, PEP.
PEP (1976) *The Facts of Racial Disadvantage: A National Survey.* Vol. XLII. Broadsheet No. 560. London, PEP.
PHILLIPS, M. (1981) 'Rage that shattered Thatcher', *New Statesman*, 17 July.
RICHMOND, A.H. (1961) *The Colour Problem* Harmondsworth, Penguin Books.
SARGEANT, R. (1981) 'YOP Washes Whiter', *Youth in Society*, November.
SCARMAN, THE RT. HON. THE LORD, (1981) *The Brixton Disorders.* Cmnd. 8427, HMSO.
SCHOSTAK, J.F. (1982a) 'Cries for Help', *The Times Educational Supplement.* 2 April.
—— (1982b) 'Facing up to reality: a school and its community,' *Links.* Summer 1982. Wales, Links Association.
—— (1982c) 'The revelation of the work of pupils.' (Forthcoming) *Cambridge Journal of Education*, Vol. 12, No. 3.
THRASHER F.M. (1927) *The Gang: A Study of 1,313 Gangs in Chicago* Chicago, The University of Chicago Press.
TUTT, N. (1976) (Ed.) *Violence* Social Work Development Group. London, HMSO.
WALLER, P.J. (1981) 'The riots in Toxteth, Liverpool: a survey', *New Community*, Vol. IX, No. 3, 344–353.
WILENIUS, F. (1982) 'A focus of resentment' *Youth in Society*, No. 63, February.

4
Comparatives

Entrepreneurship Education and Job Creation in the United States

Robert Nelson and James A. Leach

Introduction

Regardless of whether the unemployment rate in the United States is comparatively high or low, the unemployment rate for youth is always higher than that for older workers. Competition for first jobs is especially keen in a labour market plagued with a high youth unemployment rate. The situation is compounded for youth who leave school early.

The traditional role of vocational education in the United States is to provide skill training to students (youth and adults) at all educational levels to prepare them for jobs. Approximately one-third of all high school students enrol in vocational subjects, and more than 50 per cent of the nation's community college enrolment is in occupational programmes. Total enrolments have more than doubled since 1968, from 7.3 million to over 15 million.

Evans (1981) described the three types of vocational education conducted in the United States as: (1) job-specific training, (2) occupationally specific vocational education, and (3) occupational area preparation. *Job-specific training* is designed to prepare people for a particular job with a particular employer. While most vocational training of this type is conducted by individual firms in the private sector, public school job-specific training has become more popular in some states as a counterpart to economic development programs designed to attract new industries and, in some cases, retain existing ones. *Occupationally specific vocational education* prepares people for employment in a certain occupational area but not necessarily for a particular employer. Examples include programmes to prepare welders, bookkeepers, and cosmetologists. *Occupational area preparation* is designed to prepare people for clusters of occupations that require similar knowledge, skills, tools, methods, and materials. Examples of vocational education for occupational area preparation include preparing workers for office occupations, medical careers, and building trades.

Vocational education for unemployed school leavers, although often combined with remedial general education geared toward earning the equivalent of a high school diploma, is generally similar to that provided to in-school students. For the most part, the unemployed school leaver has the responsibility for seeking and participating in vocational education programmes. Mechanisms to identify these individuals and actively encourage their participation in vocational education and training programmes have proved to be expensive and difficult to implement. For those unemployed school leavers who are identified and choose to participate, vocational programmes are usually conducted in community colleges which provide a different setting and environment than the high school. Vocational programmes for unemployed school leavers often utilize instructional methods which involve formal on-the-job training combined with classroom instruction.

Some critics of vocational education have accused vocational educators of conspiring with business and industry to 'condition' the work force, to produce employees who would: come to work on time, do what they're told, be complacent and respect authority. Vocational educators may be viewed as people who conditioned workers to conform. For both in-school students and unemployed early school leavers, it is time to look at ways that vocational educators can prepare more entrepreneurial workers; it is time to focus national attention on education for entrepreneurship and to restudy education and manpower programmes in terms of this concept.

Entrepreneurs are individuals who have chosen to assume risks, identify business and work opportunities, gather resources, establish organizations, and take action to meet some demand or opportunity. Entrepreneurship education can increase employment opportunities in two important ways. First, entrepreneurship education can provide individuals with the requisite characteristics and skills needed to create and expand work in any organizational setting. Entrepreneurship education can provide an important foundation upon which technical training can be based. To the extent that entrepreneurship education encourages youth to be adaptive, creative and farsighted, unemployment in later years is less likely. Second, and perhaps more directly, entrepreneurship education can create employment opportunities by providing individuals with the skills and attitudes necessary to establish small businesses and operate them successfully. Training youth to be entrepreneurs, whether for self employment or for working in large businesses, will prepare them to compete for first jobs and to maintain employment throughout their adult lives.

There is no shortage of work to be done in our society. The problem is translating work into jobs. Entrepreneurship education can help people discover work on their own and thus create employment opportunities for themselves and for others.

The Small Business Sector

The United States has a well developed and sophisticated small business sector, and it is one of the major factors which contributes to the economic strength of the nation. In the past, government intervention to support and develop this sector of the economy has been minimal. A distinguishing mark of small business owners is that they tend to be independent and self-sufficient, and they have some resistance to working with government or any other agency to meet common goals.

Many self employed persons in the United States want to be left alone to operate their business in a very individualistic manner, and this factor presents one of the major barriers to providing help to the small business sector. However, statistics concerning small business presented at the White House Conference on Small Business (1980) highlight the need for attention to this sector of the economy.

Of over fourteen million enterprises in the United States (including farms, franchises, and professional firms), two million are corporations, one million are partnerships, and approximately eleven million are sole proprietorships.

Of the fourteen million enterprises, 99.2 per cent employ fewer than 100 persons.

Eighty per cent of all small businesses fail within the first five years.

Nine out of ten small businesses fail because of poor management. Specific reasons include: lack of planning, inadequate controls, poor accounting methods, inability to read and understand financial statements, and inability to locate expert advice when needed.

Minorities form 17 per cent of the total population, but own only 4.3 per cent of all businesses and generate only 0.7 per cent of all business receipts.

Women make up 48 per cent of the work force, but own only 4.6 of all businesses and generate only 0.3 per cent of all business receipts.

Despite their high failure rates, small firms are of vital importance to the American economy. Small business in the United States accounts for 43 per cent of the Gross National Product (Quimby, 1980:23) and generates 60 per cent of all jobs (Birch, 1979:29). In slower growing areas and in rural areas, small firms may be the only significant providers of jobs, especially for young people. Most economic development programmes to stimulate new job opportunities have been aimed at a relatively few large corporations. However, it is the thousands of smaller firms that employ fewer than 20 employees that are the job providers in the older sections of our cities, as well as offering the major share of new jobs in expanding areas.

During the 1980s and beyond, the United States will face enormous challenges regarding employment productivity. One way to create new jobs and increase overall productivity in the economy is to promote the health and survival of existing small businesses and to develop an environment that will foster the growth and vitality of new firms.

Job Creation in Small Business

Job creation depends, in a large part, upon the births and expansion of small firms. Entrepreneurs have the ability to spark new ideas and develop new products and services that create businesses, which in turn create the need for new jobs. David Birch (1979) indicated in a recent study that between 1969 and 1976:

> On the average about 60 per cent of all jobs in the US are generated by firms with 20 or fewer employees, about 50 per cent of all jobs are created by independent small entrepreneurs. Large firms (those with over 500 employees) generate less than 15 per cent of all net new jobs.

This study was based on Dun and Bradstreet's data files of 5.6 million businesses. From the results of this study, it appears that the smaller firms are aggressively seeking out new business opportunities, while the large ones are primarily maintaining their current status.

The Birch report indicated that not all small firms are equally productive and it was the smaller, younger firms that generated most new jobs. Once these firms got much over four years in age, their job generation powers declined substantially. From the results of the Birch report, a profile of the job generating firm can be formulated; it is small, has been in operation less than four years, tends to be independent and is volatile. This profile does not appear to vary much across industries or across regions of the country.

Approximately 50 per cent of all new businesses fail during their first two years of existence. This serious problem is compounded by estimates which indicate that over 60 per cent of the money used to start new small businesses is generated through private sources such as personal family savings and borrowing from friends or relatives. The small business provides job opportunities for family members. The failure of a small business is a financial tragedy, but it is also a family tragedy, and the psychological problems of the people involved may be as great or greater than their financial losses.

During the past ten years, the literature has highlighted the importance of small businesses in achieving national economic goals. It is now time to focus attention on how specific problems relating to small businesses can be solved. Solving these problems will allow businesses to be more successful. Growth and expansion of small businesses will result and new job opportunities at the local level will increase. Consultants are especially helpful in solving specific business problems. However, there are very few small business experts or consultants in the United States. They may be considered first generation because they have received no specific training for dealing with the problems of small businesses. There is a lack of training programmes, extension services, and support organizations to prepare people as consultants to assist small businesses.

New types of assistance may be needed for the small business sector. The educational programmes and assistance given to farmers through the US Department of Agriculture and its network of cooperative extension services might be duplicated in the area of business. Although the principles and problems in business are in many ways unrelated to agriculture, the agricultural education model has many applications to small businesses.

A comparison might be made between the US. Small Business Administration (SBA) and the Department of Agriculture regarding their current ability to provide services to these two economic sectors. For every twenty farms in the United States there is one Department of Agriculture employee; however, for every 2,200 business firms there is one Small Business Administration employee. The total SBA staff of 4,500 is inadequate to satisfy the demands of over eleven million small businesses. Management assistance is currently being provided by the following groups:

470 SBA Management Assistance Officer (MAO)
9,500 SCORE (Senior Core of Retired Excutives)
2,500 ACE (Active Core of Executives)
20,000 College students enrolled in small business courses
2,000 Faculty involved with the Small Business Institute Programme

Only the 470 Management Assistance Officers are paid professionals. The remaining 34,000 persons may be considered volunteers who have varying degrees of commitment to providing assistance.

A major priority regarding the growth and expansion of small business is the development of integrated policies. In January 1980, the White House Conference on Small Business identified issues and made proposals concerning small business policies for the 1980s and beyond. Twelve policy issues that were addressed at the Conference and highlight the potential for future job creation activities include: (1) capital formation and retention, (2) federal procurement, (3) economic policy development in government programmes, (4) women in business, (5) government regulations and paperwork, (6) inflation, (7) international trade, (8) minority business development, (9) innovation and technology, (10) energy (11) veterans in business, and (12) education, training and assistance. Additional proof that the federal government is interested in the small business sector is reflected in the fact that more senators applied for membership on the Senate Select Committee on Small Business than any other Senate committee.

Contributions of Small Business

During the White House conference, it was noted that small businesses:

1 Strengthen the ability of local communities to withstand national economic turmoil.

2 Provide more than half of the major innovations and technological breakthroughs in business and industry that have contributed greatly toward raising the standards of American life.

3 Because of their greater flexibility and ability to relate more directly to workers, small businesses find it easier to motivate their employees to achieve increased productivity.

4 Provide the means by which deprived groups such as women, minorities, young people and the poor are brought into the economic mainstream.

5 Greatly enrich the lives of local citizens because of the diversity of their products and services and their emphasis upon courteous, individualized service to their customers.

Robert Nelson & James A. Leach

The issue paper on education, training and assistance indicated that:

> There is an urgent priority in the current national 'crisis of confidence' to encourage the expansion and vitality of small enterprises as a long-term factor in the American economy. It seems apparent that there is a need for re-establishing a strong base for small businesses and a reintroduction of the small business option to the American public. In other words, there is a need for a systematic nationally-directed programme of education for entrepreneurship.
>
> The White House Conference, 1980:377

Not only is there a need for continuing education and training in the form of management assistance and updating of specific technical skills, but there is also a need for educating young people who have potential of owning and operating small businesses in the future.

Involvement of Vocational Education

The results of the *Illinois: Today and Tomorrow* (1978) public opinion poll of 9,900 persons in the State of Illinois indicated that 'Job Opportunities' ranked second in the area of community problems. The ranking of the thirteen problem areas are listed below.

RANKING OF COMMUNITY PROBLEMS
1 Government-Citizen Relationship
2 Job Opportunities
3 Housing
4 Transportation
5 Pollution and Littering
6 Business and Industry
7 Law Enforcement
8 Recreation Services
9 Community Planning
10 Community Services
11 Education
12 Health Services
13 Public Safety

Increasing job opportunities is not only a concern of government, but appears to be a priority item for the general public in Illinois as well.

Vocational education has had a proud history of preparing people with the skills they need for employment. Since the early 1970s, vocational education has focussed on broader non-skill types of educational programmes and has played a leadership role in developing and implementing career education at all educational levels. Recently, there have been indications that vocational educators are becoming more involved in the area of attitude development. Occupational survival skills such as problem solving, human relations, decision-making, and effective communication are some of the new types of concepts which might be included in career preparation programs. Vocational education is open to new ideas concerning the preparation of people for work.

One type of new activity which has received attention at the national level is the idea that preparation for self-employment as a career option could be included in current vocational education programs. Vocational education prepares people for employment, but not much has been done to help people gain the knowledge and ability to become self-employed.

Developing New Approaches

Vocational education must define and develop new methods to link training to the small business sector. These methods need to be designed to meet the specific needs of potential and existing self-employed individuals. The following assumptions, which resulted from a survey conducted concerning entrepreneurial training efforts for the Illinois Advisory Council on Adult, Vocational, and Technical Education (University Consultants, Inc., 1980), might be helpful when initiating new approaches.

With the business and education communities, opinions vary sharply on the value of entrepreneurial training.

There has been a great deal of concern expressed about the availability of entrepreneurial training, especially for minority group members and, more recently, women.

Foundation support for entrepreneurial training does not exist on a significant scale.

Those training opportunities that do exist are very popular, which suggests that if more were offered, more people would participate.

A good deal of entrepreneurial training is being provided directly by the academic community, much of it in cooperation with the Management Assistance Division of the SBA.

Entrepreneurial training for prospective farmers is *not* available to the same extent as it is for other small business aspirants.

Entrepreneurial training opportunities are not equally accessible throughout the state of Illinois to all persons who might be interested.

Most of the available training activity is concerned more with the sustenance and expansion of existing businesses, rather than with the preparation of new entrepreneurs.

There seems to be a direct correlation between certain personality characteristics (which may not easily be developed through training) and entrepreneurial success.

In general, free forms of technical assistance are poorly publicized and regarded by most of the entrepreneurs who utilize them as being less useful than the instruction and orientation services for which they pay a fee.

The effects of entrepreneurial training are not carefully evaluated.

Robert Nelson & James A. Leach

These assumptions, coupled with the new enthusiasm to meet the challenges that entrepreneurship education offers, may provide the basis for a new dimension in vocational education. Vocational education can have a significant impact on increasing the opportunities for entrepreneurship in the United States through education and training efforts designed to prepare people for self-employment and to assist those individuals already self-employed to operate viable and growing enterprises.

A Role on the Demand Side

Vocational education has always been a primary factor in the supply side of the economic equation of supply and demand of skilled workers. However, there is no reason to believe that vocational education cannot also be involved on the demand side. Demand for trained workers comes with the inititation of new businesses and the expansion of existing businesses. When people become self-employed, they must hire workers who will also need training. It is the preparation of people with self-employment skills that will enable vocational education to approach the educational process from a totally different perspective.

The evidence suggests that vocational education has a role in training potential entrepreneurs. Of the approximately 15 million students enrolled in secondary and post-secondary vocational programmes (National Advisory Council on Vocational Education, 1979) a sizable portion prefer and/or become self-employed. Wenzel (1979) reported that a survey conducted in Middlesex County, New Jersey, indicated that of those persons graduating from vocational programmes 25 years ago, nearly nine per cent eventually owned their own businesses.

The American desire for independence was revealed in a study published in 1979 by The Survey Research Centre at the University of Michigan. For five successive years (1974–1979), the centre interviewed two million graduating high school seniors to determine what type of work setting they preferred. The results indicated that they strongly prefer an entrepreneurial setting: working for themselves, with a small group of partners or in a small enterprise, rather than in a large organization (SBA, 1980:1).

Vocational education can have a significant impact on the job creation process by helping to prepare those people who are interested in self-employment. It is the preparation of people with self-employment skills that will enable vocational education to approach the job creation process from a totally different perspective.

The Need for a National Programme

In recognizing the need for a systemic, national programme of education to encourage entrepreneurship, the White House Commission on Small Business specifically recommended that:

1 A National Policy should be established for the support of entrepreneurial education and training, continuing education and management assistance,

provided by the public and private sector, as an opportunity for every American who wishes to own his or her small business and should receive recognition as a priority from the highest levels of government.
2 Congress should enact legislation that would provide tax credits or other tax incentives for: expenses incurred to educate small business owners and operators regarding the management of business; and expenses incurred to conduct continuing education and training and to provide on-the-job entrepreneurship experience. (1980:91)

Responding to these training needs. Congress passed the Small Business Development Act of 1980, which includes a provision that authorizes $20 million in federal matching grants for Small Business Development Centres (SBDCs) to provide technical and management assistance to small entrepreneurs. These centres would be operated through state institutions.

Teaching Entrepreneurship

Entrepreneurs are usually thought of as self-employed persons who have the potential to spark and sustain economic growth. In a UNESCO publication (1968) *Readings in the Economics of Education*, Abraham Maslow, a psychologist known for his theories regarding human needs, indicated that the 'most valuable 100 people to bring into a deteriorating society would not be economists or politicans or engineers, but rather 100 entrepreneurs'. An entrepreneur may be defined as a person who can identify needs, gather resources and implement action to satisfy these needs. At a conference at the East-West Centre, Hawaii, the following entrepreneurial traits were identified from an extensive review of research studies:

A. *Self-confidence*
    1 Confidence
    2 Independence, individuality
    3 Optimism
    4 Leadership, dynamism
B. *Originality*
    5 Innovative, creative
    6 Resourceful
    7 Initiative
    8 Versatile, knowledgeable
C. *People-oriented*
    9 Gets along well with others
    10 Flexible
    11 Responsive to suggestions/criticisms
D. *Task-result-oriented*
    12 N ach (Need for achievement)
    13 Profit-oriented
    14 Persistence, perseverance, determination
    15 Hard work, drive, energy

E. *Future-oriented*
 16 Foresight
 17 Perceptive
F. *Risk taker*
 18 Risk-taking ability
 19 Likes challenges

There appears to be some agreement that people do possess entrepreneurial qualities to some extent and in some combination. If concepts regarding the above nineteen personal traits can be taught in vocational education programmes, potential entrepreneurs are more likely to initiate action and have a better chance for success in their business ventures.

Vocational education has been successful in fulfilling its traditional role of providing students with skills to prepare them for existing jobs in business. The primary focus of vocational education programmes has been on the preparation and development of job seekers (employees). A new area for vocational educators to explore is the preparation and training of job providers (small business employers). To be really effective, entrepreneurial concepts must eventually be integrated into vocational education programmes at all educational levels. If specific personal characteristics are essential to business success, then the education of potential entrepreneurs must not wait until they are adults, by which time they have acquired many non-entrepreneurial habits. Education for entrepreneurs should begin with basic entrepreneurial concepts during the student's formative years in primary and secondary school, and should be extended to activities in the home and in the community. Young men and women must be encouraged to develop their entrepreneurial talents. Only in this way can a society use its 'human resources' in an effective manner.

Vocational oriented programmes at the secondary school and post-secondary levels emphasize the training and skill development of students for occupations that are available in business and industry. These skills are taught, however, with the expectation that students will become employees working *for* some other person or business.

Vocational education materials are needed to teach concepts related to small business ownership as a career option. Awareness of self-employment opportunities could be included in existing vocational courses at the secondary level. At the post-secondary level, programmes could be developed consisting of two or three sequential courses relating to small business ownership and management. These post-secondary programmes would serve to expose students to the entrepreneurial skills, personal characteristics, and knowledge necessary for success in owning and operating a small business.

Curriculum materials have been developed in the area of entrepreneurship and small business management. These materials can usually be classified into two types: (a) the managerial or technical aspects of owning and operating a small business: and (b) the personal or human characteristics which entrepreneurs need to be successful in business.

Until recently, national educational agencies had little interest in implementing education and training programmes regarding entrepreneurship development. During a recent three year period, nine projects relating to education for self employment were funded by the Bureau of Occupational and Adult Education for a total of $674,327. This relatively small sum of money indicates that such programmes have had very low priority. In addition, the outcomes of these nine projects have had little impact on educational programmes to prepare new and emerging entrepreneurs because much of the content of these projects concentrated on techniques and materials for teaching finance, management, and marketing. There was little content relating to entrepreneurship education, possibly because the concept of entrepreneurship is relatively new and many educators really do not know what or how to teach this subject.

Entrepreneurship education is important because it is a primarily through the development of viable firms that job creation can take place in our economy. New businesses need to be initiated and weak businesses need to be strengthened. Stable businesses need to be assisted in developing plans for expansion and growth.

The small business sector is marked by instability and a high rate of failure. Instruction and training regarding entrepreneurship should be provided at the following levels:

1 *Career Awareness*: for young people in primary and secondary schools. Activities would focus on general information regarding self employment as a career possibility.
2 *Career Orientation*: for persons who are employed but are considering the possibility of becoming self employed in the near future. Courses regarding small business ownership and management are offered at community colleges and adult education centers. The Small Business Administration (SBA) also co-sponsor one-day workshops on starting a small business.
3 *Initiating a Business*: for persons who have made a commitment to become self employed and are in the process of starting a business. Intensive three-week workshops would focus on the procedures for starting a business. Major activities would include the development of a business plan and a review of the procedures for initiating a business.
4 *Small Business Maintenance*: for those persons who own a small business and are interested in improving the operations in areas such as marketing, finance, and management. Most post-secondary business administration programmes offer specific courses in the various functional areas of business.
5 *Business Expansion*: for those business owners who are operating a successful small business and are interested in becoming larger. As businesses become larger, different techniques and procedures may be needed in all phases of business activity. Business owners must be able to change their behaviours to grow and maintain their success. Because each business situation is unique, consultants might be best used at this stage of business development to provide expert assistance to growth-oriented businesses.

Separate educational programmes need to be designed to meet the of needs people in these five target areas. The primary objective of these programmes is to increase the chances of success of small business owners. Entrepreneurship education should begin at the elementary and secondary education levels and be continued at the adult level. People need to know the problems and prospects for self-employment, how to initiate action to become self-employed, the types of skills necessary to successfully operate a business, and the strategies and opportunities which can help businesses expand.

Innovative Programmes

The National Alliance of Business (1980) reported an innovative programme funded by the Comprehensive Employment Training Act (CETA) implemented by the Private Industry Council (PIC) of Berrien County, Michigan, to help CETA participants become involved in small business management. The PIC hopes to place twenty trainees in jobs which will teach them such management skills as supervising a small staff, meeting production schedules, and running an office. Approximately $52,000 in Title VII funds will support half their salaries during training periods lasting from four months to one year.

Although this programme is unique and innovative, the outcomes of the project are highly questionable. Can a small business manager be trained in one year or less? Is this project an efficient use of federal funds? Are there other methods which can be used to train future small business managers? Are there alternative educational programmes which can produce similar results? Is this type of training really necessary? Through evaluation, it will be possible to determine the effectiveness of this project and other projects which result in job creation.

On a broader scope, the Private Sector Initiative Programme has tried to create jobs through the private business sector. A report of this programme indicated that there is a lack of commitment by the business community to this programme and that private industry councils and the targeted jobs tax credit are inadequate methods for attracting meaningful business involvement. The report suggests that economically disadvantaged individuals would have better opportunities for securing jobs if firms receiving government contracts were required to set aside positions for them.

Actions by the public sector in the area of job creation have been relatively limited and ineffective, and new alternative programmes have been initiated with the cooperation of the private sector. However, in order for jobs to exist, there must be businesses willing to hire people for these jobs. Vocational education programmes for self-employed persons will make businesses more viable, and employment creation will become a natural outcome. Helping businesses, especially small businesses, will result in the creation of many new types of jobs.

A recent report by the Corporation for Enterprise Development (1979) indicated that job creation requires the successful combination of (a) unemployed people, (b) unsatisfied markets, and (c) under-utilized resources (capital and physical). This report suggests there must be a new relationship developed between the private and public sector which would encourage the growth of business and increased development of local, private-public enterprises which has unrealized potential for large-scale, targeted job creation.

The coalition of business, labour, community groups, and government agencies can combine their resources and capabilities in new ways. The resulting enterprises will bring together under-utilized resources and unemployed people to address unmet needs. The report suggests that these local private-public enterprises (LPPEs) are finding ways to fill gaps in the economy which neither the public sector nor the private sector has the capacity to fill alone. These needs include solar energy, waste recycling, industry revitalization, energy conservation, house rehabilitation, and inner-city food distribution.

It is envisioned that these local private-public enterprises can be successfully targeted to specific groups of employed such as minorities, youth, ex-offenders, ex-addicts, and displaced homemakers. Although the concept of these LPPEs is noteworthy, there is a need to determine the extent to which these types of enterprises can replace those businesses in the private sector. Is there really a gap between services provided by the public sector and services provided by the private sector wich can be meaningfully fulfilled through the LPPEs? It appears that once the LPPEs is initiated, these enterprises will still face similar problems to those in the private sector. Interventions to develop artificial business structures such as the LPPEs may not be a viable concept in the long term, and these initiatives may not be very effective.

The Full Employment and Balanced Growth Act of 1978 established full employment as the official long-term goal of the nation. The US Department of Labour is charged with the final responsibility for meeting these employment goals, particularly with respect to decreasing the rate of unemployment. The Full Employment Act reflects a changing perspective of the nature of the most productive means of job creation. The focus of job creation has shifted: whereas five years ago government was perceived as the growth sector, the evidence now suggests that small business development in the private sector will account for most of the new jobs in the future.

Various short-term programmes designed to train people for specific jobs have been funded with government money. Programmes like CETA, High Impact Training Service (HITS), and 'customized training and technical service programmes' have been initiated to prepare people for work in the private sector. The types of training received in these programmes tend to be for entry-level occupations. Many of these government funded training programmes are for occupations generally associated with large businesses. It appears that we have a corporate mentality when we think of job creation through employment programmes. However, the results of various employment surveys indicate that many of the participants in these training programmes may have difficulty in finding employment in large businesses.

It may be that vocational education must use a different approach to the job creation process. The creation of jobs does not necessarily depend on the quality of our vocational education programmes, but depends primarily on the ability of (a) existing businesses to expand and (b) new businesses to be initiated.

Many new small business owners start businesses which are similar to businesses where they worked as employees. Therefore, vocational education has the responsibility not only to prepare people with the skills necessary for employment, but should also teach skills which will enable employees to leave their employment situation and seek self-employment opportunities.

The Role of Technology

It is through change that economic growth is possible, and it is small businesses that precipitate change. Recently, a study conducted by the MIT Development Foundation compared job formation in 16 companies for the time period 1969–1974. Six of the companies were giant corporations having sales in the billions of dollars. Five were large companies with a history of innovation, and five were smaller new companies which had developed new technologies. The results of the study indicated the sales of the six giant companies such as Bethlehem Steel and General Electric grew 11.4 per cent a year, but their employment roles increased at the rate of only 0.6 of 1 per cent a year. These giant companies created 25,000 new jobs. The sales of the five large innovative companies such as 3M and Xerox increased 13.2 percent a year, and their employment roles increased at the rate of 4.3 per cent a year. These five companies created 106,000 new jobs. The sales of the five small high-technology companies such as Data General and Computer Graphics increased 42.5 per cent a year. Their employment roles increased at the rate of 41 per cent a year. Even though their total sales were less than 1/13 of those in the largest group, these five companies created 35,000 new jobs in five years (10,000 more jobs that the six giant corporations).

The National Science Foundation indicated that small firms produced four times as many new ideas per research dollar as medium-sized firms and twenty-four times as many new ideas as large firms. However, the formation of smaller companies which often create new ideas and create new employment opportunities has decreased in the last few years. In 1968, three hundred high technology small companies were created; however, as recently as 1979, the birth rate of such companies was practically 0 per cent. Last year, the federal government liberalized the tax treatment of capital gains. This new tax legislation has led to some improvement in the business birth rate, but the problem still exists.

Recommendations for Vocational Education

The following recommendations are designed to (a) initiate an expanded vocational education effort to emphasize the importance of job creation in the small business sector and (b) provide needed education and training.

Provide leadership for a national emphasis to include small business development and growth in the revitalization of the American economy. By utilizing the existing structure of the vocational education network throughout the nation, including the national and state advisory councils, a general public awareness of the problems and potential of the small business sector can be created. Vocational education should strive to encourage workforce policies that include and emphasize incentives for self-employment.

Emphasize education and training for self-employment at all levels of education. The concepts of owning and operating a small business should be introduced in career education programmes at the elementary level and explored further at the secondary level. Opportunities for education and training for self-employment should be made available to all students through vocational education programmes at the secondary and post-secondary level. Community colleges and universities should be encouraged to expand their efforts to provide education and training in small business management. How educational programmes can be modified to better prepare people for self-employment needs to be determined. Special efforts should be undertaken to prepare women and minorities for self-employment. The universities need to place emphasis in their teacher education programmes on the training of vocational educators to work with small business owners and managers and to become knowledgeable and competent in teaching skills necessary for teaching successful self-employment. The universities can also help to train needed small business consultants and conduct research to learn more about entrepreneurs and how to nourish entrepreneurial characteristics.

Define new approaches to link vocational education and training efforts to the small business sector. In order to provide education and training to meet the specific needs to self-employed individuals, new methods and concepts of delivering instruction will need to be explored. Small business owners and managers are extremely busy people who generally will not take time to travel to traditional classroom settings for theoretical instruction. No-nonsense practical approaches with flexible scheduling and instruction tailored to meet specific needs must be devised. Staffing of instructional programmes must utilize successful small business entrepreneurs. Methods to capitalize on the practical business experience of these individuals and on the pedagogic strengths of educators must be developed. Serious consideration must also be given to developing ways to work with other agencies, institutions and organizations (e.g., SBA, SBDCs, economic development corporations, CETA), which are attempting to provide training and assistance to small businesses.

Include Small Business Management Skills in Technical Education Curricula

Technical Education continues to attract increasing numbers of students who seek preparation for a variety of occupations. Opportunities exist in small business ownership and management for most technical fields including: industrial technologies, business-related technologies, civil technologies, electrical-electronic technologies, health-related technologies, medical technologies, consumer services, environmental control technologies, and public service technologies.

Technical education curricula need to become flexible enough to allow students the opportunity to acquire skills needed for ownership and management of a business. Prospective small business operators require adequate training in traditional small business management concepts such as record keeping, managerial planning, financial management, credit and collections, *etc.* Equally important is training in the development of personal characteristics necessary for successful operation of a business. Proficiency in human relations, communications, problem-solving and decision-making ability, the ability to cope with change and competition, and a strong desire to own and manage a business successfully will enhance an individual's changes of success.

Teaching small business ownership and management concepts to technical education students cannot guarantee success. However, educational training, coupled with some type of 'on-the-job-training' in a small business environment, can provide more informed students who have skills which will aid them in self-employment.

Emphasize job specific training programmes for employees of small businesses. Traditionally, public school vocational education programmes have provided education and training programmes which offer students an opportunity to learn skills necessary to work in a cluster of occupations. Vocational education can also provide training for employees of individual firms. Vocational education programmes in some states and communities already have made efforts to provide employer-specific training. In most cases, these efforts are part of an overall state or local economic development programme. However, these programmes are aimed primarily toward large businesses when it may be small businesses who need them more. In most cases, small businesses can not afford the costs of formal employee training programmes. Coordinated planning and delivery of employer-specific vocational training programmes can be useful to the small business sector. Programmes providing 'custom made' employees for small businesses can be based on individual requests or group requests for training. Employer-specific vocational training may be delivered in school classrooms, laboratories, or in the work place.

Provide education and training for home-based business. Toffler (1981) forecasts a new dimension of the probable continued growth and economic importance of the private small business sector by describing the 'electronic cottage.' This term refers to homes – rather than offices and factories – where work is being done primarily through the use of computer terminals. Toffler predicts the emergence of an infrastructure of small companies and organizations for organizing and coordinating such home-based operations. Businesses operated at home form a 'hidden' part of the economy. With the aid of increased technology and requisite education and training it is likely that the number and effectiveness of home enterprises of all types will increase, thereby creating relevant, new jobs.

Summary

Vocational education must define new approaches to link education and work. An economy maintains its vitality through change, and it is entrepreneurs who are willing to make changes by taking risks and being innovative. It is primarily small businesses that initiate change, and it is the large businesses which tend to perfect and refine those changes.

There is a need to develop strategies to create new employment opportunities. Public policies should be reviewed to find out how government may be discouraging the formation of small businesses. The concept of manpower policies needs to be enlarged to include and emphasize suitable incentives for self-employment. Business needs to be encouraged to redefine employment in more entrepreneurial terms, and there is a need to modify educational programmes to better prepare people for entrepreneurially-defined work. Although entrepreneurial skills may be just the opposite of technical skills, vocational educators may be in the best position to show the relevance of entrepreneurial skills to the development of technically skilled workers who want to be creative in their employment or become self-employed in the future.

References

BIRCH, D.L. (1979) *The Job Generation Process* Cambridge, Mass.: MIT Program on Neighborhood and Regional Change.

CORPORATION FOR ENTERPRISE DEVELOPMENT (1979) *Job Creation Through Enterprise Development* WASHINGTON, D.C..

EVANS, R.N. (1981) 'Reauthorization and redefinition of vocational education,' *VOCED*, 56, (January/February) 1:30.

NATIONAL ADVISORY COUNCIL ON VOCATIONAL EDUCATION (1979) *Preparation for self-employment: A new dimension in vocational education.* WASHINGTON, D.C.: Government Printing Office, January.

NATIONAL ALLIANCE OF BUSINESS (1980) 'Training new managers for small business' in *The Private Sector Initiative Program Clearing-house.* WASHINGTON, D.C.: Volume 1, No. 5.

QUIMBY, J.W. (1980) 'The small business administration and education', in SNIEGOSKI, S. (Ed.), *The Role of Education in the Re-industrialization of the United States* Washington, D.C.: Office of Occupational Planning, Bureau of Occupational and Adult Education, US Department of Education, March 30.

TOFFLER, A. (1981) Remarks before the Futuring Conference. Albany, NY, May.

UNIVERSITY CONSULTANTS, INC. (1980) *Education for Entrepreneurship and Entrepreneurial Development Activities in Illinois* Cambridge, Mass.

UNIVERSITY OF ILLINOIS (1978) *Today and Tomorrow* Urbana, US Small Business Administration, Office of Chief Counsel for Advocacy, Small Business and Economic Growth in the 1980s. (1980) *Current Topics.* Washington, D.C. Government Printing Office, September.

WENZEL, W. (1979) Comments at the job creation conference. Somerset, New Jersey, November.

WHITE HOUSE COMMISSION ON SMALL BUSINESS (1980) *America's Small Business Economy: Agenda for action* WASHINGTON, D.C.: Government Printing Office, April.

WHITE HOUSE CONFERENCE ON SMALL BUSINESS (1980) *Issue paper on Education, Training and Assistance* WASHINGTON, D.C.: Government Printing Office, January.

Boys off the Street and Girls in the Home: Youth Unemployment and State Intervention in Northern Ireland[1]

Teresa Rees

Introduction

The political unacceptability of large numbers of workless young people is evidenced by the universal response of European governments introducing packages of special measures of training, work experience and job creation. Even governments avowedly committed to the dismantling apparatus of state 'interference' in some spheres of activity – such as the current administration in the UK – are actually escalating intervention in the 'problem' of youth unemployment.

Equally, however, it is not politically expedient to acknowledge publicly that one of the consequences of industrial restructuring, new technology and the recession in the world economy is a permanent shortfall in the number of jobs. The British government is not alone in steadfastly demonstrating concern to engage the 'nation's rotting seedcorn' in some form of occupational therapy until the day when industry shall have need of them – even when over half the school-leavers are now thus engaged in some form of special measures and those special measures have to be made permanent.

A feature of the state's intervention in the problem of youth unemployment is its concern with the disadvantaged job seeker. In a 'free' labour market, some groups of young people systematically find it more difficult to secure employment than others. The European Commission, OECD and Manpower Services Commission have all identified girls, the handicapped and ethnic minorities as experiencing unemployment disproportionately. In some countries, attempts are made to compensate for this by ensuring, at very least, equal access to places on special measures. There are examples of pilot projects and even policies of 'affirmative action' or positive discrimination to enhance the competitive edge of certain groups of school leavers, given their disadvantaged position in a harsh and discriminatory labour market.

It could be argued of course, as it frequently is, that such measures are 'only cosmetic'. The efforts to provide positive discrimination in favour of the disadvantaged job seeker in ensuring access to a place on the special measures is, in the last resort, no more effective than providing one legged people with remedial hopping practise in a relentless game of musical chairs. In actual fact, as youth unemployment gets worse, the special measures become more significant in enhancing the life changes of trainees. Increasingly, they act as a screening device for employers. While not every school leaver who is given a place on one of the special measures will automatically gain employment – far from it – they certainly stands a better chance than someone who is not. In many European countries special measures are now an *alternative* to education or employment for the 16 to 19 year age group.

The growth in special measures is a response to a 'moral panic' about the effect of long periods of unemployment on school leavers not yet sufficiently imbued with the work ethic. Politicians and social commentators have frequently made links between rising youth unemployment and the likelihood of increased crime, vandalism, race riots and social disorder (see Atkinson *et al.* 1982). It was no coincidence that the timing of the announcement of the New Training Initiative, to supersede the Youth Opportunities Programme (YOP) in Britain, came hard on the heels of the summer riots in various English cities in 1981. The New Training Initiative, a veritable 'super-YOP' is to have an enhanced budget, a more permanent structure and better quality schemes.

Northern Ireland provides a particularly instructive example of youth unemployment and state intervention. The proportion of young people without work, two out of three in some areas, is higher than anywhere else in Europe; it represents the extreme example which clearly other states would seek to avoid. It is also unique: the long years of economic collapse, unemployment, poverty, hardship, civil and political unrest and the imposition of Direct Rule combine to create a society qualitatively different to live in from elsewhere. But this situation makes Northern Ireland more pertinent to examine: how is youth unemployment handled under the enhanced powers of Direct Rule and in the context of, rather than simply the *fear* of social and civil disorder? In addition, the state has an added dimension to consider in ensuring equality of opportunity to the special measures. Concern for the more traditionally identifiable groups of disadvantaged job seeker is over-shadowed by the political need to be seen to be carrying out effective policies geared towards the reform of sectarianism.

The focus of this paper is on the way in which one particular group of disadvantaged job seekers – young women – are, in effect, discriminated against in the special measures in Northern Ireland. They are offered fewer opportunities, proportionately, then young men. Those they are offered tend to be on the cheaper, poorer quality, placements which, while they may provide work experience, do not on the whole offer training or experience in non traditionally female work. In so doing the special measures serve only to reinforce the ghettoization of young women into traditionally female work in declining industries. In the final section I offer some speculative comments to explain the apparent lack of concern for female youth unemployment. These are couched in terms of the over-riding concern to be seen to be operating a fair allocation of opportunities to the two religious communities, and a moral panic about youth unemployment which is exclusively bound up with a fear of young men getting involved in the troubles.

In order to identify the role of the special measures in reinforcing the inequalities of the employment prospects of men and women in the Province, it is helpful to provide some background contextual description of the industrial structure of Northern Ireland, the employment and unemployment patterns of Catholics and Protestants, and those of men and women.

Industrial Structure

The economy of Northern Ireland has experienced a chronic decline since 1945. The major industries (ship-building and textiles) have suffered from the effects of the restructuring of world capital and have not been replaced by a firm economic base adapted to current world markets. The other important manufacturing sectors have also exhibited a slow fall in employment and output which is expected to continue. The reduction in full-time manufacturing jobs has only been partly offset by a growth in the number of part-time jobs.

In common with the rest of the UK, the only growth area has been in the service sector which now employs two out of every three of those in work. This is a result of the expansion in public services (particularly health and education) and the rapid growth in the numbers employed in public administration – particularly in defence and security – since the outbreak of civil unrest in 1969. Much of this expansion is in part-time work, and even this sector has declined in the recent past.

Women workers are clustered in a narrow range of occupations compared with men – to an even greater extent than is the case in Britain. One third work part-time (compared with 7 per cent of men) and these jobs are almost exclusively in low status, poorly paid work with no security and few training or promotion prospects. Unemployment has not dropped below 7 per cent in Northern Ireland in the whole of the post-war period and currently stands at 19 per cent (December 1981): some 60 per cent above the national average. It is the result of two marked mismatches: between the overall decline in the demand for labour and its increasing supply, and between the type of jobs needed by the labour force and those being created in the expanding parts of the economy. This latter mismatch is, it is claimed, the main factor in explaining the different unemployment rates of Catholics and Protestants.

Unemployment rates have always been significantly higher, among both men and women, for Roman Catholics than for Protestants. It is frequently argued that this is explained by the spatial distribution of the two communities: the Catholic population is concentrated in the non-industrial 'peripheral' regions of the Province (an explanation bordering on the tautological). While it is the case that unemployment is highest in the predominantly Catholic rural communities in the west and south, such as Strabane (36 per cent) and Dungannon (33 per cent), a more cogent explanation of the differential rates lies in the industrial and occupational distribution of the two communities. The Fair Employment Agency (FEA), set up by the government to counter sectarianism, draws attention to research work which shows:

> ... Protestants are disproportionately represented only in the non-
> manual and skilled manual occupations, while Roman Catholics are
> disproportionately represented only in the semi-skilled and unem-

ployed classes. It is particularly noteworthy that, while the median Protestant is a skilled manual worker, the median Catholic is a semi-skilled worker.

Aunger, 1975, quoted in FEA 1979:11

Higher unemployment is characteristic of low and semi-skilled occupations irrespective of the industry in which they are found.

While the registered unemployment rates for men and women have been increasing, that of women in particular is likely to be an underestimate, as Trewsdale and Trainor report:

> Married women exhibit a relatively low propensity to register as unemployed: when they lose their jobs they simply (as far as the statistics are concerned) disappear from the labour force.

Trewsdale & Trainor 1979:23

Unemployment among *young* people is arguably the Province's fastest growing industry and is higher than in any other region of the UK. While there are wide cyclical variations in line with school leaving dates, on average a third of the 16 to 19 year olds are unemployed, despite the Youth Opportunity Programme (YOP) and other measures. The population has grown from 104,787 16 to 19 year olds in 1975 to 117,183 in 1980, and is still growing. The traditional route to Britain in search of work has proved unfruitful since the recession of the mid-1970s hit the mainland; the blocking of this safety valve has had the effect of increasing an unneeded labour supply.

It is not simply the growth in the supply of labour which has been responsible for such high and escalating · rates of youth unemployment, however. Of a whole medley of factors on the demand side, cuts in recruitment is the most significant one. This means that young people are suffering disproportionately from the changes in industrial structure and decline in labour demand sketched earlier.

Between 1974 and 1981 youth unemployment increased by a staggering 320 per cent, from 3,521 in September 1974 to 14,840 in the same month in 1981. During that year, some 31,000 of 16 and 17 year olds (51 per cent) continued in full time education, about 12,500 (21 per cent) were estimated to be in employment, leaving 17,500 (28 per cent) who left school without jobs. This latter group subdivide into 7,000 YOP trainees, 9,500 unemployed and about 1,000 unregistered unemployed, sick or detained in young offenders' centres (Department of Manpower Services and Department of Education (N.I.) 1982: Appendix II). Unemployment has been growing much faster among young women than young men; they now account for 41 per cent of all unemployed 16 and 17 year olds. Equally, a far larger proportion of female unemployment is among the younger age group than is the case for men, although this may be partly due to underregistration on the part of older women.

A special feature of youth unemployment in Northern Ireland is its spatial pattern which closely resembles that of adult unemployment: this was brought out in a study by Harvey & Rea (1979). In the predominantly Catholic rural areas of the west and south of the Province, youth unemployment rates (including people on special measures) were found to be up to 80 per cent above the average. By contrast the Protestant enclaves of Ballymena, Bangor and Lisburn in the north and east were well below it. The most dramatic imbalances were in Belfast itself where both Catholic and Protestant areas of multiple deprivation had rates three times higher than the average.

The Special Measures

As youth unemployment levels have increased in the Province, so the activities of the state have accelerated through the expansion of the Youth Opportunities Programme. This section sketches the components of YOP in Northern Ireland. It draws on data supplied by the Department of Manpower Services (DMS) and fieldnotes from my study of some of the schemes.

YOP was established in 1977 (a year earlier than in Britain) as a direct response to rising levels of youth unemployment. Like YOP in Britain, it comprises a package of work experience, training and job creation measures, some of which predated YOP and were simply incorporated into the new structure. All young unemployed people are eligible for a place or places on the components of YOP and receive an allowance. YOP is funded by DMS which in turn receives monies from the European Social Fund. DMS describes the Programme as:

> designed to give young people ... who would otherwise be unemployed, a practical introduction to working life. It is not an alternative to conventional employment but provides training and experience which should enable young unemployed people to improve their employment potential. It is the intention that young people who join the Programme will move into conventional employment as soon as opportunities arise. Their experience on the Programme should enhance their attractiveness to prospective employers.
>
> DMS 1977:1

YOP is made up of a package of components, in 1981–82 the distribution of places was as follows: apprentice training (19 per cent) and the attachment training scheme (17 per cent); work experience (29 per cent) short training and work preparation courses (26 per cent); and job creation schemes (9 per cent). Compared with 1980–81 there has been a reduction in the proportion of places on apprenticeship training and a corresponding increase in all other schemes. There has also been a dramatic increase in the total number of places, from 9,975 in 1980–81 to 17,093 in 1981–82.

1 Apprentice Training and the Attachment Training Scheme

The DMS sponsors apprenticeship training in Government Training Centres (GTCs) for young people who would not otherwise have had the opportunity. The places are all in engineering, construction and motor vehicle trades. In addition employers are encouraged to take on extra apprentices through the provision of grants. Under the Attachment Training Scheme, DMS provides training for unemployed people, including young people, in occupations not covered by the GTCs: they attend Colleges of Further Education courses and use the training facilities of some employers.

2 Work Experience

There are two work experience schemes, the Work Preparation Units (WPUs) which offer community based work preparation and experience and provide 17 per cent of places on YOP, and the Work Experience Programme (WEP) which provides a further 12 per cent. The nearest British equivalent to the WPUs are Training Workshops while WEP is the same as Work Experience on Employers' Premises in Britain, but accounts for a much smaller proportion of places than WEEP. The WPUs are run by community groups fostered by the DMS. They undertake a wide variety of work; activities offered usually include metalwork, woodwork, car maintenance, construction, catering, upholstery, office practices and stitching, but the range varies from unit to unit. Some offer work experience in many other, more unusual, areas such as watch repairs, micro-computers, micro-electronics, musical instruments, radio and TV maintenance and jewellery.[2] Trainees spend up to twelve months in a unit and might be engaged in as many as six different activities, but they tend to specialize towards the end. Most units also carry out community service work such as painting and decorating old people's homes and land clearance and restoration work for the National Trust.

The day to day working aims of the WPUs are deliberately not spelt out by DMS in order to allow each unit to evolve naturally; some WPUs emphasize production and the instillation of work discipline, others emphasize personal development. The trainees are usually school leavers at the lower end of the ability spectrum: many are provided with social and life skills, literacy and numeracy training in or through local colleges. The number of places on WPUs has grown enormously. In 1980 there were 24 WPUs, there are now 40 already in existence or about to be opened, which will provide 2,800 places. Over a third are in Belfast; indeed, there has been a conscious attempt to locate them in working class urban areas of high unemployment, in both Catholic and Protestant areas. For example, DMS went to some lengths to obtain one particular building which was more expensive than they were usually prepared to pay because of its strategic position on the peaceline in East Belfast. The work force there is a mixed one.

While it is not a DMS objective to heal sectarian divisions in the community, the WPUs do in effect sometimes go some way towards that end. The staff are often youth workers in their spare time and take the trainees to reconciliation centres some weekends. They are probably more concerned with the trainees as individuals than one might expect, again, on WEP. In the words of one WPU manager 'if these kids are to avoid jail, danger and trouble, we have to teach them to survive'[3] – not simply give them work experience.

The Work Experience Programme has operated less successfully than the WPUs. Even in 1978, the first year of its operation, there were unfilled placements, and these problems persist (see Belfast Workers Research Unit 1980:58). The places available have increased from 400 in 1978 to 1000 in 1980–81. In Harvey & Rea's (1979) evaluation of WEP for DMS they account for this in terms of a mismatch between the spatial location of organizations taking part in the scheme and areas of high youth unemployment. In addition they noted an imbalance in industrial spread of employers taking part: 16 of the 19 sponsors studied belonged to the distributive and service industries and were thus offering a narrow range of work experience (largely shopwork).

3 Short Training and Work Preparation Courses

These account for a quarter of all places. They include special training courses at GTCs in engineering and construction for young people who may not be up to apprenticeship standard. The Youthways Course is aimed at the lower ability range of the young unemployed and includes residential elements. The aim is to instil the work ethic and thereby improve employability. The course includes work experience, industrial studies and social and life skills; it is run by the Department of Education. The Department also runs follow on work preparation courses based in Colleges of Further Education and provides day release facilities, largely for literacy, numeracy and social and life skills, for trainees on other components of YOP.

4 Job Creation Schemes

This component is for the older unemployed among the 16 to 19 year olds. The Community Service Volunteers organize a scheme called 'Young Help' which provides work experience and personal development in social and community service. It accounts for 3 per cent of places and is essentially a job creation scheme with placements of up to a year. Places on Enterprise Ulster (EU) and National Trust projects complete the job creation category: they tend to offer construction or environmental improvement work with a training component. EU and National Trust projects make up a further 6 per cent of trainees placed in 1980–81. Unlike the other components of YOP, workers on Young Help and EU are paid the rate for the job rather than a training allowance of £25 per week.

EU was originally set up as a job creation corporation in 1973 to act as a bridge for the long term out of work between unemployment and regular work, to guard against their becoming 'unemployable'. However, with the onset of rapid increases in youth unemployment, the corporation was asked to earmark 25 per cent of its places for under 25 year olds. Most of the labour force is employed on 78 sites. There are 19 Mobile Work Teams which maintain sites before the handover to sponsors, 33 Community Project Teams which undertake painting or decorating of old peoples' houses, and 3 workshops where light engineering and carpentry are taught and items for EU sites are produced such as park benches and children's playground equipment (EU 1981).

Attempts are made to match the provision of places to 'need' by allocating them on the basis of unemployment levels. However, the majority of sites are in the rural areas; the corporation has found it singularly difficult to establish them in Belfast, particularly West Belfast, for a number of reasons. The local authority and other public bodies have found it difficult to identify viable prospective schemes and there are land ownership problems. Supervisors and foremen are difficult to recruit in Belfast. In addition, more than in any other area, sites in West Belfast are plagued with problems emanating from civil unrest, such as burnings, hijacking, break-ins, theft, vandalism and so on. Hence, while some two thirds of EU schemes are in areas of 'greatest need', most of these are in the west of the Province rather than in Belfast.

In the early days of EU's existence, the Board was conscious that in order to survive it needed to get acceptance from all sides. It introduced a ruling that a guarantee of access to any amenity provided or improved must be given to guard against being seen to favour any one particular group. This was one of a series of overt attempts to avoid any accusations of sectarianism. In particular, strenuous efforts have been made to provide sites in both Catholic and Protestant areas of high unemployment in Belfast, despite the fact that these ghetto areas are also those most affected by the troubles, resulting in the operational problems referred to earlier. Account was taken of the travel-to-work patterns of the two communities: in the Belfast workshop (eventually closed down because of 'sectarian difficulties' (EU 1980:9) which was in a 'mixed' area, a back entrance was provided for Catholics so that they would not have to travel through a Protestant area. Minibuses have been used to transport Catholics past a Protestant area where men were being intimidated.

While it would clearly be difficult, if not impossible, to evaluate how successful EU has been in ensuring equal opportunities to the two communities, it is clearly an issue the corporation is conscious of and has gone some way to overcome.

Sex Stereotyping

YOP offers a range of courses, training and experience geared to the needs of the full gamut of the ability range of unemployed 16 to 19 year olds. Enterprise Ulster caters expecially for the long term unemployed. Both measures make efforts to overcome sectarianism. However, the design of both EU and YOP is geared, on the whole, towards the reproduction of labour in traditionally male spheres of employment, and young men do far better out of the schemes than young women.

Enterprise Ulster caters solely for men. No attempts are made by EU area personnel officers to encourage women to apply, nor do they suggest to employment office staff that they notify long term unemployed women of opportunities in EU. Apart from a few women in Enniskillen who were once offered places in the workshop during a period of recruitment difficulties, no EU places have ever been offered to women. The Board has discussed the employment of women occasionally, the last time being in 1977, but this did not result in any concrete proposals. Now that the corporation is operating under a restricted budget, it is unlikely to pursue the issue.

A partial explanation for the lack of recruitment of women to existing places offered by EU staff was couched in terms of sex stereotyping of other organizations. For example EU workshops in Derry recruit from people who fail the apprenticeship standard at the GTC. By definition they never have female recruits as women rarely present themselves to GTCs for engineering apprenticeships and 'we don't go out of our way to get women'.[4]

It could be argued that a policy of affirmative action would be necessary to ensure women are given places to undertake the traditionally male work of the workshop units, mobile work teams and sites. Women may well have as much difficulty in overcoming their own prejudices about doing 'men's work' as the staff of EU, given the very traditional patterns that pertain in the Province. The case is not as clear cut in painting and decorating however; in British schemes young women have been doing this work for years. In Northern Ireland, a Community Project Team supervisor argued that: 'While there is no reason why a woman should not be given a place on a Community Project Team, what painting contractor is going to take on a female apprentice?'[5] Clearly then, recruiting in GTCs, in Employment Service offices and by employers is all likely to be along sex stereotypical lines. But EU, as a government agency, does nothing to alter these patterns of gender reproduction in the labour market.

Women are not entirely invisible in EU; they are employed on the staff side, but almost exclusively to undertake clerical and catering work. And the corporation is not unappreciative of its women staff: reference is frequently made to them in *EU Forum*, a newspaper-style house journal. However, the remarks which accompany photographs of women staff together with congratulatory sentiments or fulsome praise, are frequently actually sexist in their undertones. For example:

> Pat Garret, Finance's friendly personality gives a welcome change in statistics...
> *EU Forum* Autumn 1979:1

> ... when Dora Robinson called in to visit the men at the Old Warren play area site in Lisburn there was no shortage of instructors to show her how the cement mixer works.
> *EU Forum* June 1977:1

> Personnel Pin-Up Pauline McGrath, our Page One Girl...
> *EU Forum* 1979:1

> Colett catches the eye: Pretty Colett Elliman, our Page One Girl, works in Personnel ... she enjoys going to discos.
> *EU Forum* Autumn 1980:1

Women are clearly viewed as attractive people to have about the office, but their long term unemployment is not an issue sufficiently serious to warrant attention.

In YOP less than a third of places were taken by young women in 1980–81, improving to just over a third in 1981–82. In Britain half the places on YOP are given to young women. In *Table 1* the distribution of the two genders on the YOP schemes is set out.

It can be seen that male entrants are concentrated disproportionately in the relatively high status, costly, apprenticeship training schemes – indeed, these accounted for nearly half of all males in 1980–81 and 27 per cent in 1981–82.

Table 1: Trainees entering YOP by scheme and gender, April 1981 – March 1982

	Male	Female	Total	%	% Females
Apprentice Training					
in Government Training Centres	1038	3	1041	6.1	0.2
in Employers' Premises	1891	323	2214	13.0	14.6
Attachment Training Scheme	871	1966	2837	16.6	69.2
Work Experience					
Work Preparation Units	1943	890	2833	16.6	31.4
Work Experience Programme	955	1147	2102	12.3	54.6
Courses					
Young Persons courses at GTCs	1725	162	1887	11.0	8.6
Youthways ⎫ Work Preparation Course ⎭	496	455	951	5.6	47.8
Job Creation					
Young Help	91	367	458	2.7	80.1
Enterprise Ulster	900	2	902	5.3	0.2
National Trust	105	6	111	0.6	5.4
Other					
ESF Pilot Projects/ERU	53	28	81	0.4	52.8
TOTAL	10901	6192	17093	100.0	36.2

Source: Calculated from information supplied by DMS

Most females are found in the Attachment Training Scheme (32 per cent), which includes Office and Business Training, and the Work Experience Programme (19 per cent). Women appear to predominate in schemes for the less able school leaver and the relatively cheap schemes such as the Work Experience Programme, while men are found in the high quality schemes that offer recognized training.

The Work Experience Programme is one of the components of YOP most open to criticism both in Northern Ireland and in Britain. In has the potential of merely providing employers with cheap labour and free screening of potential recruits. The training element is often scant and the further education element often not forthcoming. And as Harvey and Rea (1979) suggested, most WEP placements are in rural areas where *registered* female unemployment at least is not so marked – to the extent that there have been problems filling places.

Young Help, the community service scheme offering predominantly traditionally female work is a small component in YOP, but nearly 80 per cent of the participants are girls.

The majority of places on WPUs have always been held by males; the proportion held by girls is just nudging up to a third. The male domination was explained to me as a result of the fact that the first task was always to adapt the building, and this took 'male' strength.[6] The majority of skills offered are in traditionally masculine work, and very often the kind of work which it should be feasible for the boys to at least seek employment in locally afterwards. The more traditionally female work offered, such as textiles and sewing, do not enhance the girls' prospects given the rapid decline of the textile industry and its preference for part time, experienced, married women workers. Work in other traditionally female work, such as office administration and clerical work, is not likely to be offered to girls in WPUs, given their lack of qualifications.

This is not to suggest that girls are discouraged from doing 'male' jobs or vice versa. However, given it would take an unusual girl to opt for it, it would actually take staff encouragement to initiate the move. It is unlikely that such 'affirmative action' is part of everyday life in the units. In a visit to one WPU, I interviewed three girls who complained they had not been given an opportunity to work in the metalwork and woodwork shops (but they had not actually asked for it). In another, I discovered all the girls working in the canteen, making cloth toys or learning some typing and clerical skills while the boys were doing metalwork and woodwork. Before making a visit to a third WPU I was informed a girl was working in the woodwork shop there, but when I went in I found the boys gathered round the supervisor receiving instruction and the girl sweeping the floor.[7] These anecdotes are clearly far from conclusive evidence of blanket sex thereotyping in WPUs. However, it seems that they enhance boys' opportunities rather more than girls'.

It would be unfair to suggest that the schemes in Northern Ireland are exceptional in the way the places and work appear to be distributed along traditionally sex stereotypical lines. The Manpower Services Commission has drawn attention to such sex stereotyping in YOP in Britain (Bedeman and Harvey 1981:14). Nor is it fair to single out EU and YOP for reinforcing the sexual divisions of the labour market; they do not operate in a vacuum and some of the explanation for the pattern lies with careers officers, employers and of course the young people themselves. My concern is that whereas the MSC notices and draws attention to such patterns and at least initiates a special working party on girls and sponsors some pilot initiatives, in Northern Ireland such sex stereotyping goes apparently unremarked.

The schemes merely reinforce patterns begun in the schools. Byrne (1978) writes in her study of women and education:

> One message is clear. The education service has a good deal of homework to do, the first task of which is to raise the debate about sex roles in education to a serious intellectual level.... We should moreover begin to make socially unacceptable the common attitudes of triviality, and occasionally mockery, which has so far characterized public reaction to the ... questioning ... as to why the education of girls should be different to that of boys.

In 1977–78, 70 per cent of girl school leavers obtained either CSEs or GCEs compared with 60 per cent of boys. However, their examination successes were predominantly in arts subjects; they are 'under-represented in the physical scienes, while subjects such as technical drawing and woodwork are almost totally masculine' (EOC for N.Ireland 1981:1). Thirty nine per cent of girls continued their full time education in institutes for further and higher education compared with 33 per cent of boys. However, boys outnumber girls in both the University sector (by a factor of 2) and higher education in the polytechnic, whereas girls predominate in non advanced further education and teacher training (Department of Finance 1980:67). So despite being better qualified as school leavers they end up on lower level courses. As a result 'men are in the majority among those who are in receipt of a mandatory award while women are in a majority among those who are in receipt of a discretionary award' (EOC for N.Ireland 1981:8).

The development of Ulster Polytechnic helped *towards* the equalization of numbers of both sexes in higher education – overall some 44 per cent of these students are now women. But Reid and Goldie (1981) suggest that women are still studying in traditional sex stereotyped areas and 'within the "caring professions" such as welfare work, education and social and health studies. Engineering is as much a male preserve as ever'.

The pattern continues in the field of training. Trewsdale and Trainor (1981) illustrate the under-representation of women in *all* training programmes, using the 1979 Labour Force Survey. Only 13 per cent of young people released by their employers for part-time study and training were women in 1978–79 compared with 21 per cent in England and Wales as long ago as 1975 (EOC for N.Ireland 1981:10). Far more employed men are given the opportunities of day release and full-time courses, and a much higher percentage attend courses at their employers' suggestion and with their help.

Of those few women who do receive day release, the pattern tends, to a certain extent, to mirror their general employment distribution. Hence the majority are in clothing and footwear, textiles and the distributive trades. They are clearly likely to remain ghettoized in these declining sectors: their training will not necessarily lead to promotion or protection from redundancy. However, women are still grossly under-represented in day release courses in these industries where they actually predominate as the EOC for Northern Ireland has observed:

> ... women form 48 per cent of the workforce in electrical engineering but form only 2 per cent of day release students, 87 per cent of the clothing industry workforce but only 16 per cent of the students, 51 per cent of the distributive industry workforce but only 13 per cent of the students, and 69 per cent of workforce in professional and scientific services but only 17 per cent of the students.
>
> EOC for N.Ireland 1981:11

The prospects for the female school leaver then, are bleak, regardless of her abilities. The combined effects of education, training and special measures ensure gender reproduction in a secondary labour market. Traditionally female jobs in manufacturing are disappearing and public expenditure cuts are adversely affecting recruitment into the service sector. The advent of new technology is likely to lead to the loss of more female office jobs. Even were there to be a recovery in, say, the textile industry, there is evidence to suggest that, paradoxically, young women are adversely affected in competition for jobs by married women returners (Makeham 1980). While DMS and EU do identify some disadvantaged job seekers, such as the long term unemployed and the lower ability school leaver (on Youthways), girls are not so identified.

Conclusion

In September 1982, YOP is to be superseded by the Youth Training Programme (YTP), a new 'comprehensive package of training and education for young people in Northern Ireland'. It guarantees a year of education and training for all unemployed 16 year olds and other opportunities for 17 year olds who have completed the one year course. In addition, training and vocational preparation will be provided for young people in employment aged 16 and 17 for whom existing provision is inadequate and improved vocational preparation for young people remaining in full time education. For the unemployed, the YTP will comprise both the existing YOP and some new courses (see Department of Manpower Services and Department of Education (N.I.) 1982). The YTP is to be permanent and will have a vastly increased budget of £42m in 1982–83.

It seems quite possible that the YTP will, just as EU and YOP have, reinforce the pattern of gender reproduction in the labour market with the result that young women will be further confined to poor and declining job opportunities. In seeking to explain why, compared with Britain, female youth unemployment appears to be regarded as unimportant, the following quotations from Hansard provoke a number of speculations.

> *Mr. Kenneth Lewis*: I am sure that the Minister is aware that when young men cannot get jobs, especially in the circumstances existing in Northern Ireland, they become involved in violent mischief. When they obtain dead-end jobs, they become involved in moonlighting and violence. Is he aware that, according to my information, the opportunities in Northern Ireland for young men to be trained in skills are inadequate?
>
> *Hansard* 5 July 1979

> *Mr. James Prior*: Among the young unemployment is very high and that is an encouragement to men of violence to attract young people to their ranks.
>
> *Hansard* 28 April 1982

It would appear that a major rationale for state investment in training schemes and special measures for the young unemployed is a reaction to the particular brand of 'moral panic' about youth unemployment in Northern Ireland, that is a fear that unemployed young men become involved in 'violent mischief'. The underlying assumption appears to be that young men will both have their energies diverted through such training opportunities, and, presumably, by investing in such pursuits, will have more commitment to an ordered society. A second speculation drawn from one of these statements in the House is that only *skilled* employment will have the effect of grounding young men in 'acceptable behaviour'. As elsewhere, Northern Ireland has experienced 'deskilling' in the production process in what remains of her economy.

A final interpretation that can be drawn from these Hansard extracts is that female youth unemployment is not a problem. It is not suggested that there is full employment for young women in the Province, but rather, it is *assumed* that they do not get involved in the Troubles and *therefore* there is no special need for the provision of state funded opportunities for them. While it is not clear to what extent women are involved in the activities of para-military organizations, it is apparent from the references to the 'Men of Violence' that litter Hansard in debates on Northern Ireland that politicians amongst others, perceive of the perpetrators of violence as being exclusively male. EU both ignores female unemployment and complains:

> In common with many other organizations EU has paid a high price as a result of terrorist activities in the Province. Many people believe that the chronic unemployment situation is a big contributory factor in creating an atmosphere where hooliganism, vandalism and terror-ism will thrive. It is paradoxical that an organization totally dedicated to creating employment should itself be so badly hit.
>
> *EU Forum* 1981

A major concern in state intervention in youth unemployment in Northern Ireland, then, is not simply in ensuring that new recruits to the labour force are ready for when industry has need of them with appropriate skills and work orientation, but to divert young men from involvement in para-military organizations. On both counts girls are an irrelevance; the increased economic activity of married women during the expansion of the services sector is evidence of the reserve army of labour being well able to take up any slack in an expanding economy, and girls are not *perceived* at any rate as posing a threat to order by involvement in the Troubles.

The special measures in Northern Ireland, as those in Britain and elsewhere, are able to identify disadvantaged job seekers and provide special programmes for them. Youthways is such an example for less able, alienated young people. The main concern, however, is with the need to be demonstrably reforming sectarianism. O'Dowd *et al.* (1980) have illustrated how the British state, on the one hand, claims to be reforming sectarianism but, on the other, is actually engaging in reconstituting and managing sectarian class divisions. Abuses of the Unionist government in areas such as local government and housing are, then, seen to be tackled head on while at the same time state policy (on for example regional policy) illustrates a reliance on sectarian class relations. It is not possible to do justice to O'Dowd *et al*'s complex argument here, nor to discuss some of the criticisms that it has generated. My concern is to suggest that under direct rule there has been considerable attention paid to being seen, at least, to pursue policies of fairness to the two communities. Research published by the FEA illustrates that there are trends towards the equality of opportunity (Miller 1978) but that equality of opportunity is still far from a reality (see Cormack *et al.* 1980; Murray & Darby 1980).

The nature of state intervention in youth unemployment in Northern Ireland is then, I have argued, fashioned by a perception of the need to serve the needs of capital with a docile, trained male workforce and to divert young men from 'violent mischief'. Women, acting as a reserve army of labour, will present themselves for low level, poorly paid, part-time work when capital has need of them, and will 'disappear' again when it no longer requires them. Meanwhile, they too support the needs of industry in the role of domestic production. This situation is politically acceptable because in Northern Ireland women play a very traditional, differentiated role in society, a situation reinforced through the education and training systems, and by a whole range of social and political insitutions such as the churches and the trade unions. While the special measures must be seen to favour *some* types of disadvantaged job seeker, and must be seen to operate fairly along sectarian lines, there is no pressure from any quarter (except perhaps the Equal Opportunities Commission for Northern Ireland) to give a fair deal for girls.

The pattern of state intervention in youth unemployment is set firm. In the part of Europe where the problem has reached the very worst proportions, the state has an answer: 'boys off the streets and girls in the home'.

Notes

1   I am grateful to the European Commission for commissioning me to undertake a study of direct job creation schemes in Northern Ireland (Rees 1980) which I draw upon in this paper and to Paul Stokes who helped me in the original study. I am also grateful to all the staff and workers in Enterprise Ulster and the Department of Manpower Services who cooperated with the work. As usual I must thank Gareth Rees for his trenchant but constructive criticisms of an earlier draft. This paper represents the views of none of these kind people or institutions and any errors of fact or interpretation are my own.
2   From information supplied by DMS.
3–6 From fieldnotes

References

ATKINSON, P., REES, T.L., SHONE, D. and WILLIAMSON, H. (1982) 'Social and Life Skills: the latest case of compensatory education' in REES, T.L. and ATKINSON, P. (Eds.) *Youth Unemployment and State Intervention*, London, Routledge and Kegan Paul.
AUNGER, E.A. (1975) 'Religion and occupational class in Northern Ireland', *Economic and Social Review*, 7, 1–15.
BEDEMAN, T. and HARVEY, J. (1981) 'Young People on YOP: A National Survey of Entrants to the Youth Opportunities Programme', *Research and Development Series No. 3*, London, Manpower Services Commission.
BELFAST WORKERS RESEARCH UNIT (1980) 'Youth Opportunities Programme: Sweeping them under the Carpet', *Belfast Bulletin 8*, Belfast, Belfast Workers Research Unit.
BYRNE, E. (1978) *Women and Education*, London, Tavistock.
CORMACK, R.J., OSBORNE, R.D. and THOMPSON, W.T. (1980) 'Into work? Young school leavers and the structured opportunity in Belfast', *Research Paper 5*, Belfast, Fair Employment Agency.
DEPARTMENT OF FINANCE (1980) *Social and Economic Trends in Northern Ireland, No. 6*, Belfast, HMSO.
DEPARTMENT OF MANPOWER SERVICES (1977) 'Would you like to help? Youth Opportunities Programme in Northern Ireland', *YOPLI (NI)*, Belfast, DMS
DEPARTMENT OF MANPOWER SERVICES, DEPARTMENT OF EDUCATION (N.Ireland) (1982) *A Comprehensive Youth Training Programme for 16/17 year olds in Northern Ireland*, Belfast, DMS/DENI.
ENTERPRISE ULSTER (1980) *Seventh Annual Report and Statement of Accounts, 1 April 1979 to 31 March 1980*, Belfast, HMSO.

Teresa Rees

ENTERPRISE ULSTER (1981) *Eighth Annual Report and Statement of Accounts, 1 April 1980 to 31 March 1981*, Belfast, HMSO.

EQUAL OPPORTUNITIES COMMISSION FOR NORTHERN IRELAND (1981) *Girls and Education: A Northern Ireland Statistical Analysis*, Belfast, EOC for N.Ireland.

FAIR EMPLOYMENT AGENCY (1979) *Second Report of the Fair Employment Agency for Northern Ireland 1 April 1977–31 March 1978*, Belfast, HMSO.

HARVEY, S. and REA, D. (1979) *An Evaluation of the Employer Based Work Experience Programme, Report to the Department of Manpower Services of Northern Ireland*, Newtonabbey, Ulster Polytechnic.

MAKEHAM, P. (1980) 'Youth Unemployment: an Examination of Evidence on Youth Unemployment Using National Statistics', *Research Paper No. 10*, London, Department of Employment.

MILLER, R. (1978) 'Attitudes to Work in Northern Ireland', *Research Paper 2*, Belfast, Fair Employment Agency.

MURRAY, D. AND DARBY, J. (1980) 'The Vocational Aspirations and Expectations of School Leavers in Londonderry and Strabane', *Research Paper 6*, Belfast, Fair Employment Agency.

O'DOWD, L., ROLSTON, B. and TOMLINSON, M. (1980) *Northern Ireland Between Civil Rights and Civil War*, London, CSE Books.

REES, T.L. (1980) *Study of Schemes of Direct Job Creation in Northern Ireland, Main Report*, Study No. 790140, Brussels, Commission of the European Communities.

REID, N. and GOLDIE, R. (1981) *Northern Ireland Women in Higher Education*, Belfast, Equal Opportunities Commission for Northern Ireland.

TREWSDALE, J.M. and TRAINOR, M. (1979) 'A Statistical Survey of Women and Work in Northern Ireland', *Womanpower No. 1*, Belfast, Equal Opportunities Commission for Northern Ireland.

TREWSDALE, J.M. and TRAINOR, M. (1981) 'Recent Changes in the Female Labour Market in Northern Ireland', *Womanpower No. 2*, Belfast, Equal Opportunities Commission for Northern Ireland.

Notes on Contributors

Sue Bloxham studied Youth and Community Studies at Avery Hill College, London. She followed this with a BEd in Educational Sociology and in 1979 took up a post as Mobile Youth Worker for a rural area of North Lancashire. She is currently undertaking a PhD in the Education Department of Lancaster University on The Impact of Employment, Unemployment and Special Measures on School Leavers Friendship Patterns and Social Behaviour. She has published articles on Social Skills Courses for the Unemployed and Youth Work with Girls and is currently co-writing training materials for NAYC's Rural Youthwork Education Project.

Rob Fiddy taught in schools in London and Norfolk before lecturing in Sociology and General Studies and Courses under the YOP at Great Yarmouth College of Further Education. In 1980 he was seconded to the Centre for Applied Research in Education at the University of East Anglia to read for an MA in Applied Research in Education. He is currently undertaking doctoral research at CARE in the area of the transition from school to (un)employment.

Mary Hopkins' first introduction to youth work was as a student in Liverpool, working with a group of dockland kids at evenings and weekends. After university, a temporary job as a research assistant looking at the role of community groups in planning issues led her into full-time community work. She worked as a community worker in Lewisham for three and a half years, based in the Social Services Department, and then moved into the education field as a Community Tutor at one of the Leicestershire Community Colleges. In 1979 she joined Interskills, a YOP Community Project in Coventry, as Training Officer.

Derek Kirton gained a degree in Theology at the University of Kent, then work for three years as a local authority Social Worker. He is currently doing research at Durham University on the Transition from School to Work in the Durham Coalfield.

James A. Leach is an assistant professor in the Department of Vocational and Technical Education, University of Illinois at Urbana-Champaign. In addition to teaching small business management, Dr. Leach has conducted workshops and developed curriculum materials for the teaching of small business management, authored numerous articles on the topic and is an active small business consultant. His most recent work relates to the role of vocational education in reindustrialization.

Tom Logan taught at Countesthorpe, Leicestershire from 1973 to 1980 where he was Humanities Co-ordinator. In 1980 he was seconded to the Centre for Applied Research in Education at the University of East Anglia to read for an MA. He is currently undertaking a PhD at CARE in the area of the transition from school to work.

Martin Loney is lecturer in Social Policy at the Open University. In 1968 he was president of the Canadian Union of Students. In 1973 he was General Secretary of the National Council for Civil Liberties. He is the author of *Rhodesia: White Racism and Imperial Response*, Penguin, African Library 1975 and co-editor of *The Crisis of the Inner City*, MacMillan 1979; *Race and the Social Services*, Harper and Row 1981; *Radical Perspectives in Community Work*, Routledge & Kegan Paul 1982 (forthcoming). He has contributed to several books and is the author of numerous articles and papers.

Robert Nelson is Chairman of the Division of Business Education at the University of Illinois, Champaign-Urbana campus. Professor Nelson has written extensively in the area of entrepreneurship and small business development. He has directed several projects to develop curriculum materials for teaching entrepreneurship and small business management and has worked as a consultant with the International Labour Organization regarding various small enterprise projects in developing countries in Asia and Africa.

David Raffe Studied PPE (BA 1972) and then Sociology (B.Phil 1974) at Oxford University, before working for a year on the Nuffield Mobility Project. Since 1975 he has been working at the Centre for Educational Sociology at Edinburgh University. Since 1979 he has been Deputy Director of the Centre and lecturer in the Department of Education. He is co-author of *Reconstructions of Secondary Education* to be published by Routledge & Kegan Paul, Autumn 1982. He is the author of several papers and articles on the relation of education to employment and social mobility, the transition from school to work, youth employment and unemployment and Youth Opportunities Programme.

Teresa Rees is a Research Fellow in the Sociological Research Unit at University College, Cardiff. Her research interests include Youth Unemployment and State Intervention and Women and Work. She is co-review editor of *Sociology* and co-editor (with G. Rees) of *Poverty and Social Inequality in Wales*, Croom Helm 1980 and (with P. Atkinson) of *Youth Unemployment and State Intervention*, Routledge & Kegan Paul 1982.

John F. Schostak taught in a school in South London for three years before working in a London Tutorial College part-time whilst completing an MSc in Education. Since 1980 he has been a research student at the Centre for Applied Research in Education at the University of East Anglia. His research interests involve teacher/pupil relations in classroom and pastoral care settings-looking at lying, violence, truancy etc.

Howard Williamson graduated in Social Administration at University College, Cardiff in 1975 and subsequently obtained a PhD for research on Juvenile Justice. He is currently doing research on the Youth Opportunities Programme in the Department of Social and Administrative Studies, University of Oxford. A member of the National Youth Bureau's advisory committee for research services, he has published a number of articles on young offenders and youth unemployment and, with Pip Williamson, is the author of *Five Years*, NYB 1981.

Author Index

Subject Index

adults, 11, 12–18, 21, 27, 170
alternative work, 60–3
Attachment Training Scheme, 171–2
Australia, 122

Beckett, Sir Terrence, 34
black youth, 5, 87, 131–46
  see also ethnic minorities
boys, 86–7, 92–3, 111 n14, 167–82
  see also youth
British Nationality Act (1981), 138
Brixton, 138, 143

Callaghan, J., 11
Canada, 31
careers guidance, 4, 99–112
careers education, 99–112
Careers Office, 67–81
Careers Service, 55, 85–6, 90, 93, 94, 99–112
CEP, 11
Commonwealth Immigrants Act (1962), 134
Community Industry (CI), 19
Community Projects, 3, 4, 28, 30, 52 n2, 53–66, 125–6, 173, 175
Community Service Schemes, 3, 4, 28, 41–52, 125–6
  see also PBWE
Community Service Volunteers, 173
'competitive edge', 3, 12, 15–18
Comprehensive Employment Training Act (CETA), 160, 161, 163
Coventry, 4, 54–65, 125–6

Department of Agriculture, 152–3
Department of Industry, 6
Durham coalfield, 4, 99–112

employment, *passim*
Employment and Training Act (1973), 1
Employment Induction Course, 28

Employment Services Division (ESD, of MSC), 2
Enterprise Ulster (EU), 173–81
entrepreneurship education, 5, 149–65
Equal Opportunities Commission, 181
ethnic minorities, 5, 32, 83, 84, 86–7, 94, 131–46, 167
  see also racial discrimination
European Economic Community, (EEC) 32
European Economic Community Social Fund, 32, 35, 171
exploitation
  of youth labour, 83–95, 108

factories, 73–4, 101–2
factory training, 41–52
Ford (Motor Company), 34
France, 5
Full Employment and Balanced Growth Act (1978), 161
further education, 2, 4, 5, 68, 79

Germany (West), 119, 121
girls, 84, 86–7, 92–3, 111 n14, 167–82
  see also women; youth
Government Training Centres, 171–2, 173, 174–5

High Impact Training Service (HITS), 161
Holland, G., 2–3, 28, 29

Industrial Training Boards, 35
industry
  and education, 99–112
Illinois Advisory Council on Adult, Vocational and Technical Education, 155
Information Technology Centres (ITECs), 6
Interskills, 4, 54–65, 125–6

191